Note:- The cities of Decapolis,
according to Pliny (H.N.V.18) were:

Scythopolis
Hippos
Gadara
Pella
Philadelphia
Gerasa
Dion
Canatha
Damascus
Raphana

Fortresses are underlined.

Kingdom Boundaries ___
Region   "
City   "

5   0   5   10   15   20

NABATÆAN KI...

PHILADELPHIA

Philadelphia
(Amman)
Arak al Emir

Zia •
Gadara

PERAEA
Archelais
Phasaelis
Docus
Threx
Cyprus
Bethramtha
Herodium
Mt
Nebo

Heshbon •

• Madeba

Alexandrium
Isana •

COPHNA
JUDAEA
OR ORINE

Qumran •
Hyrcania

Callirrhoe
Machaerus •

Salt
Sea

• Rabbath Moab

• Charakmoba

THAMNA

GJERUSALEM

HÉRODIUM

Bethlehem

Bethsura

ENGEDI

Zoara

Thamara

KINGDOM

• Aphra • Aina

• Bosra

Lydda

EMMAUS
BETHOLETEPHENE
Pelle

Gezer

Marisa

Hebron •

Adoreos •

Jathira

Masada

Arad

Mampsis •

• Tophel

↓ To Petra
25 Miles

AN...
Joppa
(Jaffa)
Port

JAMNIA

AZOTUS
Port

En Rimmon

IDUMAEA

• Aroer

NABATÆAN

Orda

ASKALON
Port

GAZA
Port

• Beersheba

• Elousa
• Soubaita

• Eboda

Anthedon
Port

RAPHIA

• Auja

HEROD

The traditional view: Herod gives orders for the Massacre of the Innocents (p. 172). From a window in Chartres Cathedral, thirteenth century A.D.

THE LIFE AND TIMES OF HEROD THE GREAT

Stewart Perowne

ABINGDON PRESS
New York   Nashville

Printed in Great Britain by
The Camelot Press Ltd., London and Southampton

Herod I, the Great, king of Judea

ANTIQUAE DOMUS
MAGISTRO SOCIISQUE PRAECLARIS
POSTILIONI VIXDUM PERSOLVENDAE
HOCCE PIACULUM GRATO CORDE DICAVIT
S.H.P.
ANNO SALUTIS MCMLVI

The HASMONEANS

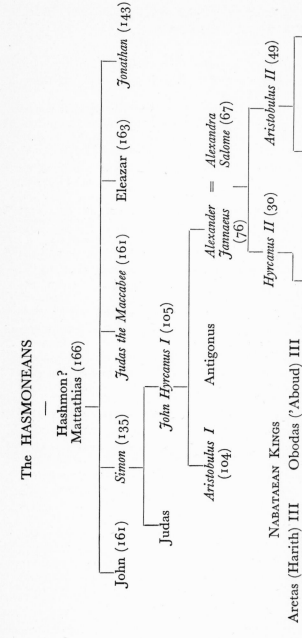

Hashmon?
Mattathias (166)

John (161)   Simon (135)   Judas the Maccabee (161)   Eleazar (163)   Jonathan (143)

Judas   John Hyrcanus I (105)

Aristobulus I (104)   Antigonus

Alexander Jannaeus (76) = Alexandra Salome (67)

Aristobulus II (49)

Hyrcanus II (30)

Alexandra (29) = Alexander (49)   Antigonus (37)

daughter = Antipater, s. of Herod

Aristobulus (38)   Mariamme (29) = Herod the Great

NABATAEAN KINGS

Aretas (Harith) III
87–62 B.C.

Obodas ('Aboud) III
30–9

Obodas ('Aboud) II
62–47

Aretas (Harith) IV
9 B.C.–40 A.D.

Malchos (Malik) I
47–30

High Priests and Rulers are in italics; dates of death are in parentheses.

SOURCES AND ACKNOWLEDGMENTS

THE ancient sources are mentioned in the Introduction. In addition, the following books and people have been of particular help to me in writing this work.

For a general picture of the world of Herod's day, the *Cambridge Ancient History* is invaluable. Being written by a committee it is sometimes dull; but it is always full and precise. On Alexander and Hellenism, the works of Dr W. W. Tarn and Dr Gilbert Murray are of the first importance. For a succinct, learned and luminous presentation of the whole story, Professor Louis Homo's *Alexandre le Grand* is specially commendable. On the clash of Judaism and Hellenism, Edwyn Bevan's books are still the best authority, particularly his *Jerusalem under the High Priests*. On many aspects of Judaism, articles in the *Jewish Encyclopaedia* are a valuable source. Joseph Klausner's *Jesus of Nazareth* and *From Jesus to Paul*, being the works of a Jewish scholar long resident in Palestine are indispensable for the understanding of the Jewish background of the preceding age. For its Greek setting, Professor A. H. M. Jones' *Cities of the Eastern Roman Provinces*, and for the story of Herod, his *Herods of Judaea* are paramount. To contemporary religion, other than Judaism, Franz Cumont's *Les réligions orientales dans le paganisme romain*, 4th Edition, is the best guide. Of Josephus and his work, *Josephus the Man and the Historian*, by H. St. John Thackeray is a scholarly and penetrating analysis. I am greatly indebted to his and Dr Marcus' translation of Josephus in the Loeb Edition; but I have generally preferred to quote from the famous translation made by William Whiston, the eccentric Professor of Mathematics at Cambridge, in 1737. The *Mishnah* I have consulted in Herbert Danby's English translation. For the topography of Jerusalem, the great *Survey* undertaken for the Palestine Exploration Fund in 1864 by Wilson and others, and *The Recovery of Jerusalem* by Wilson and Warren, 1871, are still the basic works. For the life of Augustus, I have relied chiefly on John Buchan's *Augustus*. Four other books must be named with special gratitude. Dean Millman's *History of the Jews* is a classic, which after more than a century can still be read with pleasure and profit. Emil Schurer's *History of the Jewish People in the time of Christ* is a work of such scope and depth that it is hard to see how it can

7

ever be superseded. It collates and analyses practically the whole of the ancient sources, and is accepted by Jewish no less than Gentile scholars as definitive. Finally and chiefly I must acknowledge my debt to the two great Dominican scholars, Abel and Vincent, whose association of more than sixty years in Palestine was broken only by Père Abel's death in 1953. During that period, they produced a series of works on the topography, archaeology and history of Palestine which must long endure as models of research, discipline, scholarship and interpretation. In the preparation of this book, I have consulted them continually, in particular the first volume of Père Vincent's *Jérusalem de l'Ancien Testament*, the proofs of the second volume and articles in the *Révue Biblique*, on the Antonia and the Temple, which appeared while I was writing, and, above all, Abel's *Histoire de la Palestine depuis la conquête d'Alexandre jusqu'à l'invasion arabe*. Without the continual support and enlightenment of Abel, I could not have written my book at all: only its faults are my own.

For personal help I have to thank my old friends Professor Leo Mayer and Professor Norman Bentwich, both of the Hebrew University; Professor A. H. M. Jones, of Cambridge, Professor A. W. Lawrence, of University College, Achimota, Père Roland de Vaux, O. P., Director of the École Biblique et Archéologique de St. Étienne, Jerusalem; the Director of the Royal Botanic Gardens, Kew. For help in the survey of the fortresses, I thank particularly Mr Richard Parker of the United States Foreign Service. For providing the illustrations, and for permission to publish them, I thank Mr John Allegro, Mr David Brewster, Sir Patrick Coghill, Elia Photo service, Sir Harry Luke, M. Henri Seyrig, Mr Robert Walmisley and the Directors of the Museums of Aleppo, Beirut, Damascus and Nicosia, the Boston Museum of Fine Arts, the British Museum, the British School in Rome, the Ny Carlesberg Glyptothek, Copenhagen, the Palestine Archaeological Museum, and Mr Denis Baly. For permission to reproduce a map and a plan from Abel's *Histoire*, I thank Messrs Gabalda.

In the preparation of the genealogical tables, I have relied largely on the *Cambridge Ancient History* and thank Mr Brooke Crutchley for permission to use these.

Chronology has been a problem, because Abel, the *Cambridge Ancient History*, Buchan and Paully-Wissowa do not in every case agree. I have done my best to effect harmony between them, and with Josephus and the other original sources as I have been able to understand them.

For the note on Herod's malady, I thank Mr Norman Manson and Dr Vicken Kalbian.

8

I have taken the value of the talent at £500. The modern equivalents of ancient values is a vexed and complicated question. It seems to me that £500 gives the best pictorial equivalent, even though not necessarily a statistical one.

To the Master and Fellows of Corpus Christi College, Cambridge, and to Mr Frederick Maxse of Kyrenia, I am deeply grateful for giving me comfort and seclusion in which to write the greater part of the book. Last, and very specially, I thank Mr Geoffrey Woodhead, Classical Praelector of Corpus Christi College, Cambridge, for reading the whole of the manuscript, and saving me from many errors of ignorance.

S. P.

CONTENTS

LIST OF ILLUSTRATIONS

13

INTRODUCTION

FOR the ordinary reader, the name Herod is little more than a shadowy synonym for Cruelty. Herod was the man who massacred the Innocents of Bethlehem. Herod was also the man (was he the same or another?) before whom Christ appeared for trial and who procured the death of St. John the Baptist, to satisfy the whim of an adulteress. Herod was also surely the name of the king before whom St. Paul appeared at Caesarea, and who was "eaten of worms", and died? Owing to the trying custom of the times whereby sons were constantly called by the same names as their fathers, it is easy to blur all the Herods into one confused picture of crime and punishment. Actually, these were four different men, of three different generations; but the stigma of cruelty attaches to them all. To distinguish them, posterity has grudgingly, and ironically, conceded the title "Great" to the founder of the line. Even so, very little is known of him.

Yet there is much to be known. Indeed, there are but few characters of antiquity about whom so much is recorded and so little remembered. For Herod, born as a younger son of an obscure Arab civil servant, on the very edge of the Levant, was to become one of the most glittering figures of one of the most glowing periods of human history. He was to be the friend or enemy of Antony, of Cleopatra, of Augustus' great minister, Vipsanius Agrippa, indeed of Augustus himself. He was a well-known personality in the Roman world. He was, too, the ruler into whose kingdom Jesus of Nazareth was born.

With the advent of Herod Palestine is no longer an unimportant and troublesome little country on the fringe of the desert: at one bound, the land and its king appear in a leading rôle right in the middle of the stage of world affairs. Nor is Herod himself a mere shadow. His life was full of action and incident, of peril and politics, of triumph and tragedy, his character an amazing psychological enigma. And the story of it has been recorded for us in detail by a great historian, Flavius Josephus.

Josephus was a Jew of Jerusalem, of a priestly family, with the royal blood of the Hasmoneans in his veins, who, as a young man in his early thirties took part in the terrible events which led up to the destruction of Jerusalem by the Romans in A.D. 70, and then retired to Rome, where for the next thirty years he lived as

15

the pensioner of the Caesars, and wrote the history of the War, a history of his People, an Autobiography and an Apologia for Judaism. Both the *War* and the *History* (or *Archaeology*, as he called it) give the story of Herod at considerable length. Josephus tells us that he never managed to master the Greek language, and so, to produce his books, all of which are in Greek, the literary language of the day, he employed assistants. The assistant who worked on the *War*, and on the first part of the *History* which relates to Herod, was a cultivated scholar, steeped in the Greek classics. The result is a tale well told, accurate and attractive. Only for the latter part of the *History* which deals with Herod are we in the hands of Josephus' second assistant, a rhetorical, ranting hack. The *War* is a much shorter work than the *History*—two octavo volumes in the Loeb edition as against five; it describes only the fighting and the events which Josephus considered had led up to it, a period of about two centuries. The *History* relates the story of the Jews from the Creation until the year A.D. 66. Yet in both books, so different in scope and intention, the proportion of space allotted to Herod is the same, namely one-sixth. Of such importance did Josephus, the historian and apologist, deem the life of this man.

The present book is an attempt to tell the story again for readers of to-day, for whose assistance a chronological table is provided on p. 181. Josephus is still the main and indispensable source. He is supplemented by other ancient writers, notably Dio Cassius, Plutarch and Strabo. There are references also to Herod or his times in Cicero, Virgil, Horace, Pliny, Tacitus and Suetonius. There are, too, the results of modern scientific archaeology, buildings, inscriptions and above all the study of ancient coins, for coins in antiquity were not only a means of exchange but an important, indeed, the one and only, method of popularizing political facts and claims. In the absence of newspapers, photographs and flags, it was the coin that took the image of the ruler into every man's home—as those who brought the tribute-money to Our Lord perfectly well understood. From coins, therefore, modern historians have learned much that we know from no written records. Modern scholars have interpreted these facts, and I give a short list of those who have helped me. Finally, acquaintance with Palestine, and with the many sites mentioned in the narrative, has helped to make the details of the story clear to a writer, and, it is hoped to a reader as well.

The Roman Empire and the Kingdom of Heaven: it was in the Palestine of Herod that they first met. Perhaps, therefore, an attempt to retell the tale will not come amiss.

16

Chapter I

ORIGINS

HEROD was born in southern Palestine in the year 73 B.C., in the reign of good Queen Alexandra. Alexandra ruled over the little Judaean principality which, for the last fifty years, had enjoyed the semblance of sovereignty. She was pious and capable, and she had lived through stirring times. She had survived two husbands, and now, at the age of sixty-four, as the Queen Mother, she had assumed the sceptre. No Jewess had ever done it before, and none would do it after her. But it was historically fitting that she should be the one queen to arise in the little Jewish state; for only under her rule, only for a brief nine years, did it ever know peace. It had been born of strife, and in strife it was soon to perish.

Alexandra was the last of the Hasmoneans or Maccabeans—the last that is to rule as a monarch. To understand her position, who she was and what she represented, we must go back a little, to the beginnings of the Maccabean Revolt.

When Alexander the Great died in Babylon, in 323 B.C., his empire, like some great diamond, was split up into fragments. After forty years of jealousy and strife, Alexander's family had ceased to exist, in either the male or the female line, and the vast conquests of Alexander had been reduced to three kingdoms: Macedonia, ruled by Antigonus Gonatas; Syria, ruled by Seleucus Nicator (Conqueror) and Egypt ruled by Ptolemy Soter (Saviour). All three were Greeks. The last two had been two of Alexander's marshals. They now became, and their children after them, bitter rivals. Palestine at first came under Antiochus, then Ptolemy conquered it. In the year 198 B.C., after a century of squabbles, it was captured by the northern kingdom of the Seleucids, as they were called after their founder. The Seleucids lacked the political sense of the Ptolemies, and in the year 168, Antiochus IV of Syria, who had assumed the modest cognomen of *Epiphanes* "God Manifest", in pursuance of a policy of Hellenization had goaded the Jews into revolt. The rebellion was led by a pious countryman called Mattathias of the family of Hashmon, and carried on by his son Judas known as the Maccabee. It was successful. The Seleucid power was by this time approaching its final eclipse. Hence it happened that the Hasmoneans were able not only to win their independence, but to enlarge the territory of Judaea until it was almost the size of the kingdom of Solomon.

Part of these conquests, the work of Hyrcanus, grandson of Mattathias, and Hyrcanus' sons, Aristobulus and Alexander, necessarily involved aggression against gentile neighbours. All three were successful, but in each of the three cases, the victories had results which, had they been foreseen, would have been greeted not with shouts of triumph but with tears of mourning by the Jews of Jerusalem. For Hyrcanus conquered Idumaea, in southern Palestine, and, by forcing the Idumaeans or Edomites to accept Judaism, made it possible for Herod the Edomite to become king of the Jews. Aristobulus reigned for one year only, but it was the most fateful reign in the whole of recorded history. He subdued Galilee, and forced Judaism on its inhabitants, thus ensuring that every child born of Galilean parents should henceforth be born into Jewry, including Jesus of Nazareth. Alexander had turned his arms against the Greek cities of the Palestine Coast, making certain thereby that sooner or later they would be avenged and restored by the new mistress of Greece and the Greek world, Rome.

Few foresaw this in the days of good queen Alexandra, who had been the wife both of Aristobulus, and then of his younger brother Alexander. When Alexander died in the year 76 B.C. he was only forty-nine; war and wine had brought him to an early grave. Alexandra was sixty-four, a great age for those days, but she was quite capable of directing the state. Had she not disposed with a sure touch, of all five sons of Hyrcanus, marrying two, arranging for two to be murdered, and for the fifth to retire into private life? She must now make similarly suitable arrangements for the next generation. For there was one drawback to Alexandra: being a woman, although she could become a temporal sovereign, she could not become a High Priest, and the rulers of the Judaean state had hitherto been both. Even Alexander, drunken sadist as he was, was nevertheless the High Priest of the Lord. To one of his sons, therefore, this august office must pass on his death.

Alexander and Alexandra had two sons, Hyrcanus and Aristobulus. Hyrcanus, being the elder, at once became High Priest as Hyrcanus II, with the reversion of the kingship when Alexandra should die. What was to become of Aristobulus? In those days to be a king's brother was a dangerous calling which nearly always brought death or insurrection. Indeed, Plutarch tells us that among the Seleucids (as afterwards with the Ottomans) it was regarded as a "mathematical axiom" that on attaining the throne, a king should murder all his brothers. Among the more humane Jews, the axiom did not hold; but the consequences had to be faced. His parents and his elder brother no doubt hoped that, like his youngest uncle Absalom, Aristobulus would be content to lead the life of a private citizen. As it turned out it was Hyrcanus who had inherited his uncle Absalom's temperament, and Aristobulus his father's. Hyrcanus was lethargic and weak-willed, Aristobulus bold and energetic. Hyrcanus sought only a quiet life, Aristobulus was eager to renew and enlarge the conquests of his father. Had the brothers been left to settle matters between themselves, there is little doubt that Aristobulus would have succeeded in ousting his brother, as he repeatedly attempted to do. It was not Hyrcanus that thwarted him. It was an Idumaean, a member of the race who were the hereditary enemies of the Jews, who had but lately been humbled by Hyrcanus' grandfather. This outsider was the grey eminence behind Hyrcanus. His name was Antipater, son of Antipater, and he was the father of Herod the Great.

The Edomites were Arabs, and they were the oldest surviving enemies of the Jews. They were in fact older than the Jews, as we learn from Genesis xxvi. Originally they had occupied the country to the south of Judah, below the Dead Sea, as far as 'Aqaba, the port at the head of the northern branch of the Red Sea. Their eastern neighbours were the Moabites, and the northern tribes of the Arabian desert. Sometimes Edom had been allied with the Jews, when there was some advantage to be gained by joint action; but more often they had been at enmity with them. Saul overcame Edom; and later kings of Judah, when they were strong enough to do so, chastened the traditional foe. But the chance of Edom came with the Exile: then, they moved up into southern Judaea, occupied Hebron, the city in which David himself had reigned for seven years before capturing Jerusalem, and seized the great frontier fortress of Bethsura. In Marisa and Adora they had two other flourishing towns, from the remains of which it is clear that the Edomites had by this time established relations with their wealthy maritime neighbours, the Phoenicians of Tyre and Sidon. In this migration to the north and west of their original home, the Edomites were probably encouraged by the Nabataeans, another Arab people who had established themselves in the mountain citadel of Petra. By the third century B.C., the Nabataeans were rich enough to attract the cupidity of the Seleucids, and strong enough to repel it.

The Nabataeans controlled the great trade routes from South Arabia, which brought to Petra and to 'Aqaba not only the spices of the Yemen (or Arabia Felix in its Latin translation), of the Hadhramaut and Somaliland, but also the rare gems, woods and beasts of India, the silks of China and the gold and ivory of Africa. With the growth of Greek commerce (stimulated by Alexander's putting into circulation the hoarded gold of Persia) and of Roman luxury, the demand increased. But the trade remained in Arab hands. Only they knew the secret of the monsoon. The Romans had not yet established themselves in Egypt. Incursions of Parthians and Armenians made the northern overland route unprofitably hazardous. The Nabataeans therefore reaped the ever-growing harvest of other men's desires and disputes. Petra became one of the greatest markets of the Levant; but to reach the Mediterranean, the hungry world of Greece and Rome, the caravans must plod on to Alexandria or to Gaza. In either case, it was through the land of the Edomites that they must pass. Even by the time of Alexander the warehouses of Gaza were re-plete with the opulence of the East: Alexander, after capturing the town, was able, Plutarch tells us, to send to his old tutor, Leonidas, rather more than 35 tons of spices. The demand for these spices, for frankincense, for cinnamon and for myrrh, indis-pensible for every smart feast or funeral, grew to such extravagant heights, that by the middle of the first century A.D., Pliny was complaining that at the funeral of the infamous Poppaea, Nero's wife, more than a whole year's produce of Arabia went up in smoke. It was of this rich and expanding market that the Naba-taeans and Edomites were the promoters and guardians.

When Judas the Maccabee led the Judaean revolt against the Seleucids, he was at first successful, and, in the deep valleys to the north-west of Jerusalem, inflicted humiliating defeats on the royal forces sent to quell him. Antiochus himself was busy in Parthia, where he soon afterwards died, but his relative Lysias, the viceroy of Syria, was bound to react. He would not risk another attack from the north, where the Maccabees had been the victors. He marched round Judaea, by the coast road on its western margin, and approached through Idumaea, occupying in his turn the fortress of Bethsura. The name survives to this day in the neigh-bouring Beit Sur. To the west Bethsura overlooks the road to Marisa, to the plain and the great coast road from Egypt. On the south, it guards the approach to Hebron, and, to the north it dominates the heights over which runs the road to Jerusalem, from which it is only 17 miles distant. Judas forestalled Lysias by a surprise attack; but the Edomites and their fortress were to give a good deal more trouble to the Judaean nationalists, and it became clear that only by the complete and final subjugation of

The first impact of the Aegean on the Levant is illustrated by these ivories of the ninth century B.C. in the Aleppo Museum. They are contemporary with each other; but note the contrast between the formal, inhuman Egyptian type above, and the gentle, natural Aegean type below.

The Lion frieze above the Greek cornice.

Tobiah's name, carved in Hebrew, at the entrance of one of the rock-cut chambers, as it appears to-day.

Edom could the security of an independent Judaea be assured.

Judas and his brothers had at their disposal only bands of zealous patriots. But thirty years later, Hyrcanus I commanded an army of Anatolian mercenaries, to find whose pay, it was reported, he had not scrupled to commit the patriotic sacrilege of robbing the tomb of King David. After a successful campaign against the Samaritans and a raid on Madeba, beyond Jordan, Hyrcanus occupied Marisa and Adora without difficulty. He decided to spare the inhabitants on condition that they embraced Judaeism, and to install as governor of the new provinces one of its most prominent and influential citizens. This politic clemency was to prove the undoing of his family, for it was Antipater the elder, Herod's grandfather, that he chose.

Of this man, whose progeny were to play a leading rôle in the political scene of the Levant for close on two centuries, we know almost nothing. Josephus tells us in the *History* that "King Alexander and"—a significant addition—"his wife appointed him governor of the whole of Idumaea, and they say he made friends of the neighbouring Arabs, and the people of Gaza and Ascalon, and completely won them over by many large gifts." The elder Antipater is not mentioned in the *Wars*. Josephus goes on to cite a story that Antipater was descended of one of the leading families of Jews who returned from the Babylonian exile, but only to dismiss it as the fiction of one of Herod's courtiers, who wanted him, as King of the Jews, to be equipped with a Jewish pedigree.

Of the younger Antipater, Josephus says in the *Wars*: "An Idumaean by race, his ancestry, wealth and other advantages put him in the front rank of his nation." In the *History*, he says that "he had a large fortune, and was by nature a man of action and a great party man".

Already, in these brief sentences, we can discern some of the outstanding characteristics of Antipater and his son Herod: the wealth, and, to put in bluntly and suitably to those times, the knowledge how to use it; next, the energy; and third, that flair for politics which in Herod was to amount to genius. A hundred years after Herod's death, Justin Martyr, one of the first Christian apologists, and himself a native of Nablus in Palestine, has a passing remark in his *Dialogue with Trypho*, (*LII*) "you say that Herod was from Ascalon" as though he himself thought so too. Eusebius, the great Church historian of the fourth century, also a Palestinian, quotes Julius Africanus, a Libyan who had lived in Emmaus at the end of the third century, and "no mean historian" as saying (Ch. VI and VII: he repeats the story) that "when Idumaean brigands attacked the city of Ascalon in Palestine, among other spoils they took away captive from the temple of Apollo which was built on the walls, Antipater, the child of a certain Herod, a *hierodoulos*, or temple servant" and that since he could not afford to pay the ransom, the boy was brought up by the brigands as an Idumaean; adding that "His child was the Herod of our Saviour's time". As it stands the story is clearly incorrect. Antipater the younger was beyond doubt the son of Antipater the elder, an Idumaean, and a man of wealth and power, not an obscure and indigent temple servant of Ascalon. Nevertheless, the story is so circumstantial, and attested so comparatively early, by Justin, himself a Palestinian, and then by so good an historian as Julius Africanus, who had lived in Palestine, and quoted with approval by Eusebius, another Palestinian, that it is hard to believe that we have not here the vestige of the truth, handed down by tradition, in a land where tradition is amazingly viable; but in antiquity, as now, the propensity of fathers for calling their sons by their own names led to confusion. Not Antipater the younger, but Antipater the elder, was probably the hero of the adventure. In the days before Hyrcanus' conquest, brigandage may well have been rife, though hardly after it; and the company and example of a band of highwaymen may well have instructed the youthful Antipater in the arts by which he was to acquire, and use, the considerable wealth he afterwards possessed.

It is, moreover, a fact that Herod cherished a particular affection for Ascalon. He embellished it with sumptuous buildings, including a palace for himself, and maintained its status as a free city, which it, alone of all the coastal towns of Palestine, preserved to the end of his days. Even at the height of his influence with Augustus, when new provinces were his for the asking, he never sought to incorporate Ascalon in his dominions. Piety towards his ancestor, Herod the hierodule, may beyond all reasonable doubt, be taken as the cause.

The elder Antipater had become a Jew by religion; but he was an Arab by race. His adherence to the Judaean state in as much as it had been imposed by force, was superficial only. He would use it for what he could get out of it. But his loyalty would remain with the Arabs. And so his son Antipater should marry an Arab. Besides, Antipater had no very high idea of the Judaean state, nor of its powers or chances of survival. On the contrary, he rated the prospects of his kindred and friends the Nabataeans a good deal higher. It was all-important to him that his connections with Petra should be maintained and strengthened. For the Nabataeans were going from strength to strength. Under their enterprising king, Harith III, or Aretas, by his Greek name, they had expanded northward with successful daring, and had actually occupied another great commercial city, the renowned Damascus itself. Young Antipater therefore should marry a Nabataean. Negotiations were opened, and since Antipater was rich and powerful, it was with the daughter of one of the leading families of Petra that the match was concluded. The girl's name was Kufra, which is the Arabic for the flower of the henna, (*Lawsonia inermis*) so highly prized for its scent. In Greek, the name became Cypros—the *chypre* of our day. In the Song of Songs (i. 14 and iv. 13) it is translated "camphire". It was a noble name for a noble woman. Antipater the younger and Cypros had five children, four sons, Phasael, Herod, Joseph and Pheroras, and one daughter, Salome —a name which her great-niece was to make notorious. All the children, strangely enough, were given Jewish names, except Herod, who was to be the King of the Jews: on him was bestowed the Greek name of Herod, *Heroides*, the Heroic. It was, no doubt, in honour of the romantic ancestor, Herod the hierodule, that the name was chosen; but it was a prophetic choice, for of all the children Herod was to be the least Judaic and the most Hellenic.

Chapter II

PATRIOTISM IS NOT ENOUGH

"THE Macedonian power had fallen into impotence, that of the Parthians was still immature, and the Romans were far away. So the Jews of their own accord inflicted kings on themselves. Expelled by the fickle mob, these princes regained power by force of arms, and proceeded to the banishment of freeborn men, the destruction of cities, the assassination of brothers, wives and parents, and the rest of the usual crimes of tyrants; while they exploited the dignity of the priesthood to buttress their political power, and so fostered the national fanaticism."

Thus does the Roman historian Tacitus, who was writing his history in Rome at the same time as Josephus was writing his, describe (*History*, V, 8) the situation as it was at Herod's birth. There was, in fact in the Levant, not for the last time, a "power vacuum". Alexandra the Queen Mother—she was very frail now —could hardly be expected to grasp the situation. For her, it was enough that from her palace in Jerusalem she could look out eastwards across the deep, narrow valley that separated the upper town from the Temple, and see, continually renewed, the smoke from the great altar of burnt sacrifice, whose flame never died. The worship of the One God was assured for all time! What a blessed change had been wrought by the patriots! A century ago, the very site of her palace had been defiled by the *Akra*, the citadel of the pagan Greeks, from which they had dominated the Holy Hill. Beneath its windows had arisen the abomination of the gymnasium, where young Jews, even the very priests, had competed naked or wearing the heathen hat in pagan sports and contests. The High Priest himself had encouraged these whoredoms. Small wonder if Antiochus had thought that Judaism was dead, and Hellenism triumphant. But the Holy One, Blessed be He!, had raised up the sons of Mattathias to drive out the heathen from His inheritance. Now all was restored, There was peace and plenty in the land, and God was praised in Zion.

Poor Alexandra! How little she understood either of the forces that were at work within her kingdom, or of those which were to batter it from without. Within ten years, Hellenism, the pagan Greek way of life and conduct, was to be predominant within the country, and a pagan Gentile was to stride unrebuked and un-chastened into the Temple—nay, into the very Holy of Holies itself.

For this double catastrophe there were two potent reasons. First, Jewish nationalism, which had started by uniting the Jewish people, ended by dividing it, hopelessly and irreparably. Secondly, by the time Queen Alexandra died and Herod was a boy of eight, the Romans were no longer "far away": they were in Jerusalem.

When Judas the Maccabee had started his campaigns, he had fought for the glory of the Lord. He had been able to count on the ardent support of the godly, the *Hasidim*, as they were called in Hebrew. The nation seemed to have returned to its true destiny, and to be once more a chosen, and victorious, people. But all too soon the glorious vision faded, to be replaced by a sordid and worldly ambition. Even in the first generation, when the leader-ship was held by three of the five brothers successively, it was only the first, Judas, who had been a wholly dedicated leader. Jonathan, the youngest of the five, who succeeded Judas, contrived to have himself recognized as High Priest. He was in no way entitled to the great and holy office, and only attained it through the support of the hated Greek, and a Greek usurper at that. Simon, the second of the original five, who succeeded Jonathan, not content with the High Priesthood, arrogated to himself the double title of "General" and "Ruler of the People", and struck his own copper coins, in emulation of secular sovereigns. He was murdered, while drunk, and replaced by his son, Hyrcanus, who as we have seen, was a worldly, if successful, soldier. Both he, and his son Aristo-bulus would have liked to call themselves king: Alexander Jannaeus did.

These proceedings outraged the pious. The Pharisees, or "Sepa-rate", the party which had grown out of the Hasidim, cham-pioned religion, and they, not the secular court, had the ears and hearts of the people. Alexander, High Priest of the Lord though he might be, was a hard-drinking brute. When, in the year 95, the populace at the feast of Tabernacles, had pelted him with citrons, he replied by a massacre. In the end, people called for his death and appealed to the very dynasty from whom Alexander's great-grandfather had freed them. Alexander defeated the royal troops, captured 800 of his countrymen who had sided with them, crucified them at a public banquet which he attended with his concubines, and had their wives and children murdered before their dying eyes. During the remaining nine years of his life he had no more trouble: but he ceased to call himself king, and on his death-bed advised Alexandra to make peace with the

Pharisees. She did so, but the rift had gone too deep. No wonder that in the writings of the Rabbis, the Maccabees find little place, that the books called "Of the Maccabees" never found their way into the sacred canon but have remained in the limbo of *Apocrypha*. The plain and sacred fact was that, as Josephus points out in his *Apology* (II, 165), the Jewish polity was completely different from any other. It "placed all sovereignty and authority in the hands of God". Josephus invented a special word for it: he called it *theokratia*, theocracy. The term is familiar enough nowadays: but it was Josephus who coined it to designate the constitution of the Jews. It was a hard saying but it made the Jew eternal.

The secular nationalism of the first Hasmoneans not only alienated the Pharisees, and the multitudes who listened to them: it was equally distasteful to the pro-western party, the Hellenizers.

The Macedonian power, as Tacitus says, "had fallen into impotence": but the Greek-speaking civilization on which it was founded had not. It was very much alive. It had come to the Levant long before Alexander himself. It was to continue until, in the seventh century after Christ, Islam vindicated the rights of the Semites to the primacy in that region which they have held ever since. Even then, the Levant would never be wholly eastern. In the heyday of Hellenism, it was in many ways predominantly western. Hellenism was not Hellas, any more than Spanish America is Spain. But the countries in which Hellenism principally flourished, that is to say Syria and Egypt, had adopted, in greater or less degree, the attributes, the accidents, if not the essentials, of Greek civilization.

Greece has given many gifts to mankind; those which were most highly prized in the Hellenistic world were two: the language and the city.

The vernacular of the Persian Empire, which Alexander's kingdoms had replaced, was Aramaic. It continued to be the vernacular of the masses. It, rather than Hebrew, was, as we know, the common language of Palestine in the days of Our Lord; even to-day it is not quite extinct, and may be heard on the lips of certain villagers near Damascus. But it was not a highly developed language. Greek was a far richer, far more flexible tongue. It easily became, as French and English were to become two thousand years later, the common currency of commerce, of the arts and sciences, of cultivated intercourse in general, above all of politics, of dealings with the government and its agents, great and small. Most people (as will already have appeared), adopted Greek names, either in substitution for, or as supplements to, their Semite names. And everyone who could, learned Greek. Even the sacred Hebrew scriptures were translated into Greek, at the instance of the second Ptolemy. Just as to-day, a Japanese and a Peruvian will find in English or French their common denominator, so in those days a Roman and a Jew or an Arab would find it in Greek. It did not follow that they loved the Greeks, any more than it does that all those who speak English love the English.

The second great Greek gift was the city, considered as a setting for happy living. Cities there had been before, great and splendid cities like Babylon or Persepolis or Nineveh. But they were rare and special, the capitals of great kings and gods. The idea that every man and woman was entitled to live in surroundings of beauty was absolutely novel. In Syria and Palestine, since the days when the first wall had been built around the first town, in Jericho, six thousand years before Alexander, the city had been a refuge against the enemy, a bulwark and a storehouse, a huddled citadel, to which men resorted in times of trouble, which meant pretty often. The Greeks designed their cities for use and convenience in peacetime. They sited them on plains, by pleasant rivers. Jerash, on the east side of the Jordan, in the hills of Gilead, is one of the best-preserved of Greek cities. There it lies before us to-day, the colonnaded street, the market-place, the temples, the theatres, the hippodrome—all the adjuncts of civilized life. As Aristotle put it in a famous sentence (*Politics*, I, 2, 8): "The city was invented to preserve life; it exists to preserve the good life."

As to-day, many of those who adopted western ways adopted them only that they might combat the west with its own weapons, but many also were convinced that only through adoption of western ways was there any hope of survival. Both these groups were to be found in Palestine when Herod was a boy.

There were thus two main political camps in the Judaea of Herod's youth: the Nationalists and the Hellenizers. Behind the Nationalists, for the time being, stood the Pharisees, won over by Alexandra's conciliation.

The Pharisees were not, however, the only representatives of organized religion. The great priestly families stood aloof from their movement. The "Sons of Zadok", or Sadducees, were quite content with the world as they knew it: they wanted no other, either here or hereafter. The "enthusiasm" of the Pharisees was odious to them, and they looked askance at these new-fangled notions about angels and spirits, and an invisible world, and resurrection. They were for the maintenance of decent and regular worship—after all, they lived by it—but as old-fashioned aristocrats, and men of property they could only deplore this playing up to the poor, and the exploitation of popular sentiment.

27

The Pharisees, in the eyes of the Sadducees, were a menace to the established order of things; and yet so powerful was their influence on the public that in matters of ritual the Sadducees were actually compelled by popular opinion to conform to Pharisaic rules.

This division in the ranks of the priesthood weakened the Nationalists. The Hellenizers saw their prospects brighten. Time, they said, was on their side, and (they added in a whisper) not only time, but Rome as well.

Rome had been getting nearer for some time. But Rome's eastern policy, like that of some of the great powers who were to follow her, was hesitant and lacking in continuity. The victory of Zama, in 202 B.C., had freed Rome from the menace of Carthage, which had beset her for two generations: she was now free to turn against Philip of Macedon. In 197 B.C. the Roman legion, at the battle of Cynoscephalae in Thessaly, had proved itself the master of the hitherto unbeatable Macedonian phalanx. Next it was the Seleucids' turn. Antiochus III had misguidedly given asylum to Hannibal, the famous but now fugitive general of Carthage. He was defeated in 190, at the battle of Magnesia, near Smyrna, which placed the whole of Asia Minor at the mercy of Rome. But Carthage itself still stood. Rome could claim an indefinite suzerainty over the Levant, and over Egypt too. When Antiochus Epiphanes made an expedition into Egypt, in an attempt to extinguish the Ptolemies, he was met outside Alexandria by a Roman Senator, Popilius Laenas. The two had been friends in the days when Antiochus had been a hostage in Rome after his father's defeat. But Laenas now curtly ordered him to get out of Egypt or to be regarded as the enemy of the Roman people. When the king said he would think about it, Laenas answered: "Think about it here", and drew a circle around him in the sand with his stick. The king's humiliation rang throughout his dominions.

But the preservation of the "balance of power" was enough for Rome at that period. As long as Carthage existed, Carthage was the enemy. Even when, in 146 B.C., Carthage ceased to exist, the Romans were very reluctant to become involved with another oriental enemy. In 133 B.C., Attalus, the last king of Pergamum, bequeathed his kingdom to Rome. This enlarged the Roman realm in Asia Minor. They still took no steps to occupy the Levant; yet across the Eastern Mediterranean the shadow of Rome now drew like an eclipse. The inhabitants of Palestine, always inclined to prefer the devil they don't know to the devil they do, thought that to offset the western dynasty of the Seleucids, they could invoke a still more western republic, in the shape of Rome. The

This fine head of a Ptolemy in the Cyprus Museum is believed to be that of Ptolemy II, 308-246 B.C. (p. 27). In Alexandria, his capital, he built the famous *Pharos*, or lighthouse (p. 118) and founded the Museum, or University, and the Library. He also opened a canal from the Nile to the Red Sea. In 276 B.C. following the custom of the Pharaohs, he married, as his second wife, his sister, Arsinoe II, he being her second husband. She thus acquired the additional name Philadelphus, which Ptolemy also bore (p. 67).

HELLENISM

Tombs in the Kedron Valley, below the south-east corner of the Temple. Note the mixture of styles. The right-hand tomb is a synthesis of Greek and Egyptian motifs, that on the left of Greek and Phoenician. The middle tomb is in almost pure Greek style. It bears a Hebrew inscription. Third century B.C. The surrounding tombstones are those of modern Jewish burials.

Maccabees sought their alliance. It was granted, and several times renewed—on paper: the Romans never stirred a finger to help the nationalists.

A Roman fleet operated against pirates in the Aegean, and Roman merchants appeared in the markets of Syria and Palestine, and even in Petra itself. But her land forces were still "far away". It began to look as though they never would reach the Levant. The wise Antipater knew better: he realized that Alexander Jannaeus' looting and destruction of Greek towns, and of their commerce, was bound to bring down, sooner or later, the heavy hand of Greece's overlord upon the wreckers.

It was an Armenian who precipitated the inevitable end. Dhikran, or Tigranes in his Latin garb, king of Armenia, had profited by the break-up of the Seleucid kingdom to occupy Syria, including the Seleucid capital, Antioch. That was in 84. All was calm for fourteen years, although technically Dhikran could be construed as an enemy of Rome, for having invaded the territories of a prince with whom they were in treaty relations. But in the year 70, the king of Armenia suddenly moved south, and invested the city of Ptolemais, or Acre. Alexandra could not fight so strong a foe; but she could pay. An embassy went north with a handsome bribe. Dhikran assured the ambassadors that he wished them well. Would he have made good his word? History suddenly interrupted herself. Rome struck. Dhikran was no sooner master of Acre, than he received a brusque message saying that an officer of the great Lucullus was waiting for him at Antioch. The Armenian had given asylum to Mithridates of Pontus, the enemy of Rome: he must surrender him. Dhikran refused. War followed. Dhikran was defeated: he lost his capital and his kingdom, including Syria.

The Seleucids had already ceased to be. Who, now, was to be lord of Syria? The answer was plain: Rome had arrived at last.

Chapter III

POMPEY

THE Armenian crisis killed the old queen. Aristobulus hastened her death. There was still a chance, he reckoned, that he might bring off a *coup d'état*, and so be the man in possession when the Romans reached Jerusalem. He hated his mother's policy, and her court, through which glided scheming Pharisees and the wily Idumaean. While she lived, they had at least been kept within bounds by her iron character. But once she was dead, Antipater would have it all his own way, using Hyrcanus and the Pharisees as a front. And that would be the end of Aristobulus and the nationalists. One night he slipped out of Jerusalem, with a single servant. Only his wife, a daughter of his Uncle Absalom, knew of his plans. She, poor woman, was left behind with their four children, two daughters and two sons, Alexander and Antigonus. From town to town he went, and within a fortnight, half the country was in arms under his banner. Alexandra tried not to believe it; but as messenger after messenger told of new defections, she gave in. Her ministers asked her what they should do. "Whatever you think fit," she replied. "The nation is sound, you have the army, and the treasury. I can no more; I am well nigh spent." She died soon after; in 67 B.C. Aristobulus struck at once. He defeated Hyrcanus near Jericho, and many of Hyrcanus' men went over to him.

Antipater knew that his life and that of his young children depended on his making a quick decision. Should he at once oppose Aristobulus, asserting the rightful claims of Hyrcanus? Or should he try to come to terms with the young usurper? His shrewd Arab sense told him that the latter step would be fatal. Aristobulus would never forgive him. Even if he did, of what use would so strong-willed a prince be to him? Far better use Hyrcanus. But Hyrcanus was too feeble, now, both in mind and in resources to withstand Aristobulus. Moreover the people, always avid of change, were clearly all in favour of Aristobulus— for the present. Antipater looked ahead. He knew that the coming of the Romans was only a matter of time. When they did arrive, they would have no use for nationalists, or for those who supported them. So he retired to Idumaea, where he was still paramount, and

30

waited. He thus had no part in the farce which took place in the Temple, where Hyrcanus, who had imprisoned Aristobulus' wife and children, solemnly agreed to change places with his brother. They swore oaths of fidelity, embraced, and then went off each to the other's home, Aristobulus to the palace, and Hyrcanus to his brother's private house.

Meanwhile, Antipater was busy. First of all, he ingratiated himself with Aristobulus' enemies among the Jews. These were many and powerful. Next he worked on Hyrcanus himself, and finally persuaded him that Aristobulus was out to kill him. Lastly, he started negotiations with his friend Harith, or Aretas in Greek, the Nabataean king. As a friend, and a kinsman by marriage, Harith was bound to come to Antipater's aid. As an Arab, he was bound to bargain. In the end it was settled that Harith would march against Aristobulus and restore Hyrcanus, who by this time had in his turn succeeded in leaving Jerusalem by night, and, together with Antipater, had reached Petra. The terms were stiff: a large subvention before the expedition started, and if it proved successful, the retrocession of the twelve cities which Hyrcanus' father, Alexander had occupied in Trans-Jordan and the Negeb. Antipater agreed. He was rich, and cities had been known to change hands more than once. Only let him set his protégé firmly in the saddle and all would be well. The campaign opened smoothly. With an army of 5,000 horse and foot, Harith and Hyrcanus approached Judaea. Back flocked the turncoats. Aristobulus' only refuge was with his old supporters, the Sadducees, who received him into the Temple, and shut the gates against the invaders. News of the civil war had of course reached Pompey's advance headquarters in Damascus, and his quaestor, Scaurus decided to intervene. His object was not so much to restore peace, as to make a handsome personal profit. Unfortunately, Hyrcanus had to act on his own. Antipater dared not show himself in a Judaea which was still full of Aristobulus' partisans. Hyrcanus was no gambler. He timidly offered exactly the same bribe as Aristobulus, 400 talents, or £200,000. Since Aristobulus could be dislodged from the Temple-fortress only by a siege, of which Pompey would hardly approve, and Hyrcanus could be pushed around at will, Scaurus came down on the side of Aristobulus. He ordered Harith to raise the siege and go home on pain of being declared the enemy of the Roman people—the usual ominous formula. Harith went. On his way he was attacked and beaten by Aristobulus, in a second battle near Jericho, in which Antipater's brother, Phallion, who was acting as his liaison officer, was killed. It was a terrible blow for Antipater. His brother had been sacrificed, and his plans had gone hopelessly awry. The Romans, on whom he had been counting, had backed his enemy. But he had learnt his lesson. Never again would he leave anything to Hyrcanus, or to any other intermediary. When it was a case of dealing with the Romans, he would deal with them face to face himself.

Aristobulus and the Sadducees were jubilant. But Antipater was confident that he would beat them in the end. His chance soon came. Pompey, after receiving Dhikran's capitulation, had turned his arms against Mithridates; but he was now on his way south from Pontus to Damascus, where he intended to settle the affairs of Syria once and for all. He came with the reputation of being almost a second Alexander. He had triumphed in Africa, he had triumphed in Spain, he had cleared the Mediterranean of pirates, and he was lord of Asia. Sulla had hailed him as *Magnus*, "the Great", a title he had proudly and justly accepted. He was only forty-three. Antipater hastened to meet him. So did a certain Nicodemus, as agent for Aristobulus. Antipater soon sized up Nicodemus. He decided to let him speak first. Not content with presenting a great vine of gold (worth 500 talents, £250,000), this time Nicodemus must needs go on to accuse Scaurus, and his associate, the tribune Gabinius, of having exacted bribes from Aristobulus to the tune of 1,000 talents, thereby, as Josephus drily comments, making two deadly enemies on Pompey's staff. Antipater said nothing. He waited for the durbar which Pompey had decided to hold the following spring at Damascus.

All three Jewish parties were there, the Pharisees, Aristobulus, and Hyrcanus, which meant of course, Antipater. To balance the Pharisees, Antipater had arranged for a deputation of respectable-looking Jewish notables to appear as supporters of Hyrcanus, the embodiment of outraged legitimacy. He accused Aristobulus of just those crimes which he knew would most irritate Pompey, piracy, and the sacking of Greek cities—and it was true that Aristobulus had ably seconded his father Alexander in his campaigns against the Gentiles, notably in the destruction of Samaria. Aristobulus was outmanœuvred, and made things worse by his entourage, which consisted of jewelled, over-dressed and scented young males. Pompey temporized: he rebuked Aristobulus; but he would settle Palestine, he said, when he had dealt with the Nabataeans.

The whole cavalcade set out together for the south. All went well until they reached the town of Dium, above the eastern shore of the Sea of Galilee, a town which Alexander Jannaeus had conquered. The memory was too much for Aristobulus. He

A characteristic Greek colony, one of the *Decapolis*, set amid the mountains of Gilead (p. 27). The Temple of Zeus is in the left foreground, the Forum in the middle. From it, runs the main street, flanked by shops, fountains and, later, churches. The Temple of Artemis appears at the back on the left. The city also contained a hippodrome, three theatres and two baths. The stones visible in the picture are nearly all of Roman date, but they replace earlier buildings, and conform to the original plan, which provided a spacious and beautiful setting for life, in stimulating contrast to the crowded squalor of the *tel* village or town.

HELLENISM

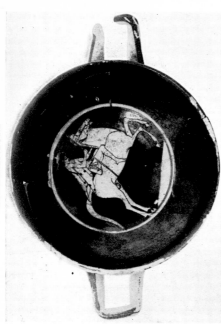

The Greek ideal of youth. This bowl in the Cyprus Museum shows a typical *ephebos* setting out for his javelin-practice, wearing the broad hat, or *petasos*, flowing cloak, short kilt and long leather boots which were the athletic uniform of his age and race. It was this garb that scandalized the Jewish priests and orthodox (p. 24), who saw in it a glorification of the human body, and as such a breach of the second Commandment.

THE NABATAEANS

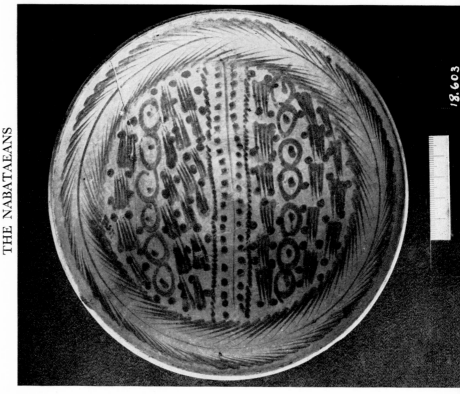

18.603

An example, now in the Palestine Archaeological Museum, of the rare and delicate Nabataean pottery. It bears a geranium-red design on a russet background.

abandoned the convoy, and hastened ahead to the great fortress of Alexandrium, or Sartaba as it was, and still is, called. It stands on a mountain top, 2000 feet above the Jordan valley, where the Wadi Far'a comes down from Nablus. From its summit, half Moab and much of Palestine, even distant Hermon, 80 miles away, is visible. It was crowned by a glaçis, 250 feet high, atop of which was a stone citadel, well-nigh impregnable.

Pompey altered his plans; instead of making for Petra, he marched down the Jordan.

Thus, at long last, Rome came to Palestine. Josephus has left us (*War*, III, 70 et seq.) a description of the imperial army, (written of course not for his western readers, who did not need it, but for what he calls his country cousins, the Jews of Babylon who had never seen a Roman soldier). It is so vivid that even to-day it evokes something of the sense of the might, the helpless terror and the fascination that these invincible fighters must have inspired. The camp, the march, the commissariat, the arms and armour, the eagles, the discipline and the ardour—all are assembled in one striking and awful picture. Palestine had seen many armies, and was to see many more. But never in its history can its inhabitants have been so overwhelmed as they were by this their first sight of the unconquerable legions of the west, moving slowly and irresistibly down that ancient river, glistening in the bright spring sun, thundering through the still morning air.

The terrible pageant, as it came to a halt at the foot of the Sartaba, sent a chill through Aristobulus. He tried to temporize. Pompey summoned him to come down. Down he came, several times, to parley and postpone. The Roman finally ordered him to surrender not only Alexandrium but all his other fortresses, and made him sign the necessary instructions. Aristobulus did so; but, determined on one last desperate throw, absconded to Jerusalem. Pompey followed, heard en route of the death of Mithridates, and greatly relieved, made for Jerusalem by way of Jericho, where he ordered the destruction of the fortresses of Threx and Taurus that stood above the town. Aristobulus, now contrite, offered him money, and the keys of the Holy City. Pompey relented and accepted them. But when Gabinius, his second-in-command, appeared before the gates, he was refused admittance. Pompey saw that there was nothing for it but to capture the city after the old Roman fashion. He established his camp on the site of what is now the Scots church, cut the Temple aqueduct, and formed a regular siege. It was the year 63 B.C., one of the most fateful in history, the year in which Cicero was consul, in which both Augustus and Agrippa were born.

The viaduct which joins the Temple to the upper city spanning the Tyropean valley, was demolished by the defenders, who thus isolated their fortress from the west. On the East and south, it was protected by deep ravines, surmounted by massive walls. Only on the north could it be approached, and on that side a great artificial ditch, the vestiges of which may still be seen beneath the convents on the north side of the Via Dolorosa, had first to be filled in. Slowly the difficulties were overcome, the fosse was levelled and battering rams got to work. After a siege of over two months, one of the towers was thrown down, a breach was made and Faustus Cornelius, Sulla's son, led a party into the sacred precinct. Hyrcanus' followers aided in the slaughter of their countrymen, and the priests mingled their own blood with that of the sacrifices, which to the last moment they had continued to offer. Twelve thousand Jews were killed. Pompey entered the holy ground with his staff. His behaviour was correct. He admired all, but took nothing. In Jewish eyes his forbearance was outweighed by his presumption in entering the Holy of Holies, where only the High Priest might enter, and he only on the Day of Atonement. Hyrcanus was rewarded by being once more proclaimed High Priest and President of the Nation. By not making him king, Pompey hoped to conciliate the Pharisees. Aristobulus, together with his two sons, Alexander and Antigonus, his two daughters, and their poor father-in-law, Uncle Absalom, were sent off to Rome to grace Pompey's triumph, the greatest spectacle that Rome had ever till then beheld. The walls of Jerusalem were razed, and thousands of captives were sent to the imperial capital to be sold as slaves.

Most of these men and women were devout Jews, loyal to their religion, and to its code of behaviour. The former quality made them unprofitable servants, for they refused to work on the Sabbath or to eat forbidden foods; the latter made them valuable associates, since their standards of conduct were far higher than those of the pagans among whom they were to live. For these two reasons the majority of them were soon freed, and became the nucleus of the Jewish community in Rome. Those who returned to Jerusalem established the Synagogue of the Freedmen, of which mention is made in Acts. Cicero was proud of Pompey: "Our Jerusalemite", he called him. Antipater was pleased, too. His candidate had won. It had been a costly victory, in one sense. The Jews would like him less than ever, now. But the Romans would like him a good deal more: he would see to that.

34

On young Herod, now a boy of ten, the whole crisis had a profound effect. As soon as the civil war broke out, Antipater had sent the children with their mother back to her country. They were confided, we are told, to the protection of King Harith himself. Herod was brought up to be more of an Arab than ever. But not only did he meet the Arabs of the desert, he came in contact also with the wealthy courtiers of the Nabataean capital, and with the merchants of all races and countries who flocked thither, Greeks, Persians, Indians, Africans, Romans. He learned their ways and the language of at least some of them. He was thus early habituated to the minds and methods of all sorts and conditions of men.

Chapter IV

FALSE DAWN

POMPEY's victory was complete; but it was not final. It had two abiding consequences. First, it produced a re-organization of Syria and Palestine politically and territorially. Secondly, it attached the Levant wholly and intimately to the fortunes and favours of Rome.

Generally speaking, Pompey's aim in his settlement was the restoration of the *status quo ante bellum*. He had no wish to innovate, only to restore. To this end, he first of all reduced the Jewish state to its rural districts—Judaea, Samaria, Galilee and Peraea or central Trans-Jordan. The Greek cities which Hyrcanus I and Alexander Jannaeus had forcibly annexed, both on the east and on the coast, he restored to freedom, adding some which were not Greek, such as Gaza and Joppa, and the Idumaean towns Adora and Marisa. All these cities were to form part of the new Roman province of Syria. Tyre, Sidon and Ascalon would remain free. The city of Samaria, not to be confused with the district of Samaria within which it lies, was restored as a Greek city, being made an enclave of the province of Syria. With one exception, Pompey did not rebuild or re-people these wasted cities—that was to come later. The exception was Gadara, which Pompey restored to please his favourite freedman, Demetrius.

The coastal cities would always be easy to protect; but those beyond Jordan needed some joint organization for mutual defence. Thus was founded the celebrated *Decapolis*, or *Ten Cities*, of which Damascus was the most northerly, Philadelphia (Amman) the most southerly. Scythopolis (Beisan) although on the west bank of the Jordan, was included because it provided a link with Samaria and the sea. The Decapolis was one of Pompey's most lasting creations. The ten cities eventually became fourteen, and the confederation was to endure for centuries. It was a pleasant, easy sort of life they lived. How complete was the synthesis of east and west they had already achieved, under the garb of their Greek language and polity, may be judged from an epitaph which the poet Meleager, born in Gadara of a Greek father in the middle of the second century B.C., composed for himself: "Art thou a Syrian? *Salam* (peace) to thee; Art thou Phoenician? *Audoni* (Long live my Lord); art thou Greek? *Khaire* (Greeting). And do thou the same to me."

Only three kingdoms were allowed to survive, the Itureans, in what is now the southern region of Syria and the Lebanon, namely the Lebanon range, the Anti-Lebanon and the region of Baalbek; the Jewish, now reduced almost to its ethnic limits, and the Nabataeans. The two former were little more than Protectorates. The Nabataeans were to outlast them both. For 168 years after Pompey's settlement they preserved their independence and their riches from the greedy Romans. Ironically enough, it was the insubordination of Aristobulus which had deflected Pompey from his intended swoop on the Nabataeans, and had thus saved them from almost certain spoliation. Scaurus, his venal quaestor, thought he would carry out Pompey's plan, to his own profit. With his army he set out for Petra. This placed Antipater in an awkward predicament. He had no desire to alienate either Scaurus or Harith. He solved the problem in a characteristic way. He induced Hyrcanus to furnish the Roman forces with corn and other provisions, well knowing that they would find Petra impregnable. When they did, Antipater intervened to suggest that they might, without loss of face, abandon the campaign for a suitable consideration. Scaurus settled for 300 talents, £150,000, which Antipater guaranteed, thus putting both Scaurus and Harith in his debt. The lesson was not lost on young Herod, who was to remember it many years later.

Gradually, the *Pax Romana* was diffused. Scaurus' successors had to wage punitive war against marauding Bedouin, and undertook the reconstruction and re-peopling of the ruined cities. But the *Pax Romana* could be radiated only from a Rome herself at peace, and that Rome was not. Nor would she be for another thirty years. The civil strife in Italy was bound to affect the fortunes of the Levant, and uncertainty as to policy was to bring, as it always does in that region, insecurity.

Gabinius, who as Consul in 58 had procured the banishment of Cicero and had shared in the loot of his country house, returned to Palestine as Propraetor in 57. He was Pompey's man; but Pompey was by no means master of Rome. It was therefore not difficult for Alexander, Aristobulus' son, to escape, make his way back to Judaea, and there once more to start a guerrilla war against Hyrcanus. He even tried to rebuild the walls of Jerusalem, which argues that he, and not Hyrcanus, was in command of them, but the Romans who were encamped there stopped him. Clearly Gabinius must act.

Once again, after a defeat in the field, the Hasmonean retired to the Alexandrium. Once again, after a long siege, it was taken, and once again the other fortresses, Hyrcania, the Bastille in the wilderness to the south-east of Jerusalem, and Machairus, above the eastern shore of the Dead Sea, were surrendered, this time at the instance of Alexander's mother, whose husband and other children were still prisoners at Rome, and who had inherited the pacific nature of her father Absalom. She prevailed upon Gabinius to demolish the fortifications of these citadels, so as to forestall another war.

In this little campaign, a certain young Roman greatly distinguished himself. He, too, was an enemy of Cicero, and had welcomed the opportunity of winning his spurs—he insisted on being Master of the Horse—under Gabinius. His name was Marcus Antonius, or Mark Antony. He was twenty-six, Herod was sixteen. The two became firm friends, and remained so. Not even Cleopatra, at the height of her sway, was able to extinguish Antony's affection for Herod. It remained undimmed to the end, and was to be a ruling factor in the fates of all three lives.

Meanwhile, the reported success of Alexander had led Pompey's enemies to connive at the escape of his father Aristobulus and his brother Antigonus. The besotted insistence of this family on raising hopeless revolts is a fitter subject for the psychologist than the historian. For the third time in ten years, the peak of the Alexandrium was the rallying-point of the rebels. It was a hopeless struggle. With his largely unarmed followers, Aristobulus withdrew across the Jordan to Machairus. There, on the ruins of the fortress which was later to become the last prison and place of execution of John the Baptist, Aristobulus capitulated. For the second time he was sent to Rome. On this occasion he was put in irons and imprisoned. The Senate freed his sons, because that was a condition which their mother had exacted from Gabinius, when the fortresses were handed over.

Gabinius found time, amid these martial alarms, to reorganize the internal administration of Palestine. It would be wise, he decided, to break down the centralized government of a people so given to revolt. He therefore divided the country into five provinces, or districts. Judaea accounted for three, Jerusalem, Jericho and Gezer, the ancient fortress which commands the approaches to Jaffa from the east and the main road from Egypt to the north. Peraea was administered from Amathonta, in the Jordan valley, a little north of the Alexandrium on the eastern bank. Sepphoris, to-day Saffouriyeh, north-west of Nazareth, became the capital of Galilee. There is no mention of Idumaea. Technically it came within the jurisdiction of Jerusalem. Actually, the omission of Hebron as a provincial capital was no doubt due to Antipater, who preferred to govern the territory as a personal fief.

This system of district administration suits the country. Despite all the upheavals of history it has survived in essence to this day.

The fortunes of Antipater were now steadily advancing. He proved himself a valuable go-between in a campaign which Gabinius conducted in Egypt, for the restoration of Ptolemy XI, *Auletes* or *the Piper* (for a consideration of several million sterling). Once again, Mark Antony commanded the cavalry, and he never forgot that it was due to Antipater that the army was supplied with food and water during their passage through the desert, and that it was Antipater who induced the Jewish garrison at the Egyptian limit of the wilderness to desert the usurper Archelaus and come over to that of Ptolemy. It was to reinforce his consideration for Antipater's son, Herod.

No sooner was this campaign concluded in 54 B.C., than Antipater once more had to intervene to help quell yet another Hasmonean rising, led this time by Alexander. Antipater did manage to persuade a good number of the folly of their ways, but Alexander persisted, and besieged some thousands of his adversaries who had taken refuge on the summit of Mount Gerizim, to the south of Nablus, which was, and still is, the holy hill of the Samaritans. Gabinius chased him away to the north and utterly defeated him beneath Mount Tabor. In gratitude to Antipater, Gabinius enhanced his authority in the Capital. Poor Gabinius: he went back to Rome expecting a triumph. Instead, he was condemned, despite Cicero's defence of him, for peculation, sentenced to restore the millions he had received from Auletes, and being unable to pay, was forced into exile.

The Roman world was now overshadowed by the uneasy alliance known as the First Triumvirate, which consisted of Pompey, Julius Caesar and Licinius Crassus. The last of these is one of those characters of antiquity, who, more than those of any intervening period until the eighteenth century, seem to be of our own familiar day and generation. He was a common racketeer, who had grown rich, says Plutarch, "by fires, wars and public calamities". He was now old, vain and greedy. He was also jealous of his two martial partners, and decided that he, too, at the age of sixty, must be hailed as a great general. He set out for the Orient, intent on defeating the Parthians, the barbaric power which had established themselves on the débris of the Seleucid dominions to the east of the Euphrates.

On reaching Syria, instead of pressing his attack against the Parthians, Crassus indulged in temple-robbing, or *hierosylia*, for it

39

was such a common occurrence that the Greeks had a word for it. First, he looted the shrine of the Mother Goddess at Bambice (Membidj) in Northern Syria. Then he came down to Jerusalem, and carried off the immense riches which Pompey had respected— something over 3 millions sterling. A terrible retribution awaited him. At Carrhae, the ancient Harran, in the far north-west corner of Mesopotamia, Crassus met the now confident Parthians and was utterly defeated with all his host. The Romans lost 20,000 dead, 10,000 prisoners, and the eagles of no less than seven legions. Crassus saw the head of his son paraded on a pike, before he himself was beheaded. Molten gold, so one story has it, was then poured down his miser's throat. His head was carried off to the Parthian king, who was entertaining his friend the king of Armenia at a banquet. A celebrated tragic actor, Jason of Tralles, was reciting excerpts from the *Bacchae* of Euripides. When Crassus' head was brought in, Jason seized it, and broke into the final scene of the play, in which Agave, the frenzied Bacchante, displays the severed head of Pentheus. Nemesis indeed: the actor and his two august auditors had all suffered at Roman hands.

The disaster rang through the whole East. It might well have brought the Parthians back to the Mediterranean, from which Alexander had expelled their ancestors nearly three centuries before. Fortunately for the west, the Parthian king murdered his best general, and on the Roman side the leadership of the remains of the Roman forces fell to a thoroughly competent commander, Cassius, best known for the part he later played in the murder of Caesar. The Jewish nationalists naturally exploited this humiliating Roman defeat. But Antipater did not waver. He was of the greatest help to Cassius in quelling the inevitable revolt, which showed itself once again in Galilee. On the shores of the sea of Galilee, 30,000 rebels were rounded up and sold into slavery, and on Antipater's advice the ringleader, Peitholaus (Aristobulus was still detained in Rome) was executed. Young Alexander was overawed into signing an undertaking to be of good conduct. Yet another threat to peace, and to Antipater and his children, had been overcome. But it had been a bad set-back to their plans. Rome was not invincible, after all. Was it really worth while to back these Western intruders against the resurgent East? Antipater, in the face of all the evidence, decided that it was.

Chapter V

JULIUS CAESAR AND THE JEWS

THE death of Crassus in 53 B.C. brought into the open the harsh facts of Roman political life. It was now a straight fight between Caesar and Pompey for the supreme power. Caesar won. On the 10th January in the year 49 he moved south from Ravenna and crossed the Rubicon, the little river which was the limit of his legal jurisdiction, thereby challenging the Senate and the constitution. When he reached Rome, Caesar found that among the measures taken by the Senate in favour of Pompey (i.e. against himself) was the appointment of Pompey's brother-in-law, Metellus Scipio, as governor of Syria. Aristobulus, who had suffered so much at the hands of the Pompeians, and had now been a prisoner in Rome for fourteen years, was Caesar's natural ally. Caesar gave him two legions, and bade him return to Judaea. But before Aristobulus could leave Rome, the Pompeian underground succeeded in poisoning him. At the same time, Pompey sent orders to his brother-in-law to put an end to Alexander, Aristobulus' son. Metellus arraigned him for his past insubordination and executed him. His poor wife, with his surviving son, Antigonus, and the two daughters, was living at Ascalon, where she was safe from Antipater and Hyrcanus, but not from misfortune. One of her daughters, called Alexandra, captivated the son of a princeling of Chalcis at the foot of Mount Lebanon. He married her. His father, being jealous of the boy, murdered him and married Alexandra himself, and also appointed himself protector of her sister and brother. They would be useful pawns in his dealings with his southern neighbour.

To such miserable humiliations were the Hasmoneans reduced.

On the 9th August, in the year 48 B.C., the immediate future of Rome and the Roman world was decided at Pharsalus, in Thessaly. Caesar's star was now lord of the ascendant, Pompey a fugitive. The next month, Pompey lay dead on the shores of Egypt, where he had been treacherously butchered as he landed. A few days later, Julius Caesar arrived, only to find that the Egyptians, even if they had murdered one Roman benefactor, had no wish to adopt another.

At this point, yet one more famous and familiar character enters the scene, namely Cleopatra. She was the seventh of the name, the daughter and heiress of Ptolemy the Piper. She was to succeed him jointly with her brother, whom in accordance with Egyptian custom, she would marry. A rival general, Achillas, backed by troops who had formerly fought under Pompey, disputed Cleopatra's claim. Caesar was infatuated with Cleopatra, then aged twenty, and was determined to restore her. The ensuing war, which lasted from October 48 till March 47, naturally drew in Palestine.

Antipater had supported Pompey. But Pompey was dead now. Caesar was therefore his man. It was the easier, because Caesar was known to be favourable to the Jews, and prodigies had hailed him after Pharsalus as the avenger of Jerusalem, profaned by his defeated rival. Besides, he was a newcomer, and he was successful, always a passport to acceptance in the Levant.

Caesar badly needed troops. Achillas had 22,000, Caesar only 4,000. He summoned his friend Mithridates of Pergamum to raise levies in Cilicia and Syria. But Mithridates found himself too weak to attack Egypt from the north. Antipater now was everywhere. From Emesa (Homs), from Ituraea, his friends sent detachments. Malik, the new king of the Nabataeans, sent cavalry. Antipater himself brought 3,000 Jews, and Hyrcanus as well.

Antipater, who knew his ground from the campaign of Gabinius nine years earlier, led the army through the desert, and by a stratagem took Pelusium, the northern gateway of Egypt. He then set Hyrcanus to work on the two chief Jewish colonies of Egypt, outside Alexandria. It was a clever move, for Hyrcanus was the High Priest of the Lord, and he was the first ever to visit these remote but powerful Jewish communities. They had been inclined to oppose Caesar at first, taking their line from their brethren in Alexandria which was in the hands of Achillas. But moved by Hyrcanus' and Antipater's arguments, they came over to Caesar. In the encounter with the main Egyptian army, the Pergamene troops gave way, but the resolution and personal bravery of Antipater turned the scale. Caesar, now master of Egypt, and of Cleopatra, highly commended Antipater. The young queen was restored. Her intended husband had been drowned in action, so she was married to his, and her, younger brother aged fifteen. She soon poisoned him: Caesar was the man she loved, for the moment.

After two months of dalliance, spent with Cleopatra on a trip up the Nile, Caesar had to bestir himself to extinguish a revolt in Pontus, in northern Anatolia, on the shores of the Black Sea. He left Alexandria on the 25th June, reached Antioch on the 13th July, entered Cilicia on the 18th, smashed the king of Pontus in a single battle on the 2nd August, forcing him to flee to the Crimea where he was murdered. It was this campaign that Caesar described in the three famous words: *"Veni, vidi, vici"*, "I came, I saw, I conquered".

Antipater had been right. Rome's prestige, in the person of Caesar, was now at its zenith.

During his short stay in Antioch, Caesar made various new dispositions. He rewarded the cities which had helped him, who in gratitude adopted a new Caesarian era for their coinage. He readily forgot Antipater's former attachment to Pompey, and generously rewarded him for his services in the Egyptian campaign. He made him a Roman Citizen—then a rare and coveted honour for an alien—and exempted him from taxation. Hyrcanus he confirmed as High Priest.

The wretched Antigonus tried to queer the pitch. He accused Antipater of being a dissembler, who served Caesar for his own ends only, and recalled his father Aristobulus and his brother Alexander, done to death by Pompey's minions. Antipater had little difficulty in answering this inept harangue, and clinched his argument by displaying the wounds he had received in Egypt. To make it quite clear to all that he favoured Antipater and Hyrcanus, and not Antigonus, and to put an end to all dangerous doubts, Caesar declared the High Priesthood hereditary in Hyrcanus' line, and told Antipater that he could rule Judaea in any guise he chose. Antipater, of course, left the choice to Caesar, who then appointed him Procurator.

At last the supreme power was his. He had worked for it long and patiently. Roman citizen, exempt from taxes, Procurator of Judaea. It was a golden reward. He hastened back to Judaea, to inaugurate the new régime. Copies of the decree which constituted it were sent to Rome, where it was to be set up in the Capitol, and to Sidon, Tyre and Ascalon, where it was to be inscribed in the temples in Latin and Greek on plates of bronze. In addition, Caesar granted Antipater a major concession, which was a signal sign of confidence: he allowed him to rebuild the walls of Jerusalem, which had been in ruins since Pompey's capture of the city, sixteen years before.

All these measures were taken and approved by Caesar at Antioch between the 13th and 18th July, 47 B.C., just before he hurried away for the Pontic campaign, leaving his relation and friend Sextus Caesar in charge of Syria. The other side of the coin was to appear later in the year, when a decree was promulgated defining the Jewish tribute. Except in the Sabbatical years (i.e. every seventh year, when, in accordance with Leviticus xxv. 1-7, no crops were sown or reaped and the land lay fallow) the state was to pay into the Roman treasury one quarter of the total corn sown, delivery being made at Sidon. Joppa was excepted from the tax. In addition, the traditional tithe was to be paid to Hyrcanus and his descendants. On the other hand no one was to be allowed to levy auxiliary troops on Jewish territory, nor to exact contributions for winter quarters (when armies did not normally fight or move) or on any other pretext.

Antipater toured the country to explain the new constitution, the folly of opposing it and the advantages to be gained by quietly accepting it. It was at this time that the city of Athens voted a golden crown to Hyrcanus, and a bronze statue of him to be erected in the temple of the People and the Graces, near the Market.

Antipater at once set about rebuilding the walls. Three years later Julius Caesar issued another decree, of which Josephus gives the text, authorizing "these men", (meaning Hyrcanus and his sons mentioned in the immediately preceding decree confirming Hyrcanus as High Priest), to have and to build walls for the city of Jerusalem. In the second year of the rent-term, a reduction of 11 bushels was to be made in the rate of tax.

This document has puzzled scholars. Some have regarded it as a belated "covering authority" for the rebuilding orally authorized three years before, others have made it fit in by the simple method of altering the date. Neither of these expedients is necessary. Antipater remembered not only Pompey, but Crassus. The old, First Wall, as it is known, left the whole of the north side, and half of the west side of the Temple exposed, to attack. At some period, an outer wall running from the western bastion of the upper town to the north-west corner of the Temple, where it joined the fortress which stood there, was added. When, or by whom, it was built, Josephus does not tell us. At the time of Pompey's siege, there is no mention of a second wall which made the Temple less vulnerable. Twenty-seven years later (see page 66, below), it was in existence. It is wholly in keeping with Antipater's character, and the circumstances in which he now found himself, that it was he who erected this new wall, known as the Second Wall, and that we have here the decree empowering him to build it. Indeed, it is hard to see who else could have constructed it.

Having thus pacified Judaea, and fortified Jerusalem, Antipater had to ensure that the state of which he was Procurator was properly governed. Hyrcanus was now senile, and less capable than ever of taking any active part in the direction of affairs. He was quite happy therefore, when Antipater suggested appointing his eldest son, Phasael, prefect of Jerusalem, and his second son, Herod, governor of Galilee.

Chapter VI

HEROD'S DÉBUT

HEROD was now twenty-six. He was well-equipped to be a leader. He was tall and handsome, with a charm of address that over and over again was to enable him to ingratiate himself in the most unpromising circumstances. He was athletic and had great endurance. He was a fine horseman, an expert wrestler and a first-class shot. Of his features we have no direct record, because he never dared to put his head on his coinage: it would have outraged the Jews, to whom it was a breach of the Second Commandment. For the same reason, no statues of him were erected in Judaea. Outside its bounds they were, but none of them has survived to our day.

Both his parents were of Arab stock. That he had dark hair we know. It is not hard, therefore, to imagine him as he was, with the fine features of the Arab, the golden complexion, the thin, sensitive lips, the delicately-moulded nose, the small, crisp ears, the large, liquid, oval eye, shaded by fernlike lashes, beneath sable eye-brows. From his father he had inherited the flair for politics, the quickness of perception, the instinctive knowledge of other men's minds and motives. He lacked Antipater's calm, almost northern temperament. Instead he had the sanguine, impetuous character of his mother. At times, it was to enable him to surmount awful crises and perils, at others to reduce him to a condition of nervous excitement not far removed from madness.

He had been educated in a hard and practical school. As he grew up, he had been more and more with his father. As the patriarchal custom of the Arabs is, he accompanied him in courts and camps. He met men and women of many races—Jews, Arabs, Greeks, Romans, Egyptians and Persians. And he noted how his father dealt with them, he studied the different minds of Crassus and of Antony, of Hyrcanus and Antigonus. He learnt many useful lessons. Unfortunately he learnt some vicious ones as well. It was a brutal and violent age. From his boyhood Herod had been habituated to treachery, to sedition, conspiracy and rebellion, to battle, murder and sudden death. Family affection was born strong in him. He could be quixotically faithful and loyal to a relation or a friend. And yet he could murder his own kith and

45

kin. It was a strange and frightening mixture, a psychological tangle which became more involved as he grew older. It had its origin in his early youth, when the traditional family piety of the Arabs—it is one of their strongest traits—came into conflict with the stark competition for power and survival which alone governed the Roman world during his boyhood, and for some years after it.

At the very outset of his career, Herod was given an opportunity of proving his superiority both in the field and in the council-chamber. A certain Ezekias had organized a band of guerrillas, with which he was terrorizing the frontier region between Palestine and Syria in the hills of Upper Galilee. Josephus calls him a brigand, but as he regularly uses the word for political rebels, Ezekias no doubt regarded himself and was regarded by others as a struggling patriot. Herod rounded him up, and killed him with many of his gang. The Syrians were delighted and hailed the Idumaean as their liberator. Sextus Caesar, too, was grateful to him.

The sudden rise of young Herod to popularity, combined with his brother Phasael's conspicuous success as governor of Jerusalem, was too much for Antipater's enemies. They went to the feeble-minded Hyrcanus, and expostulated with him for being so blind to his own interests, and to the inevitable fate which awaited him unless he curbed the ambition of this upstart family, who were really not his servants at all, but his masters and openly acknow-ledged as such. And did not Antipater use Hyrcanus' money to ingratiate himself with the Romans? Hyrcanus said he did not really mind if he did: all he wanted was peace and quiet. The accusers then tried a different attack. Herod had executed Ezekias and his men without trial by the Sanhedrin, thereby violating the Law. The Sanhedrin, which had been reconstituted by Alexandra the Queen Mother was modelled on the *Synedrion*, the Assembly, of the Greeks. It now contained three orders, the heads of the leading families, or Notables, certain Priests related to the High Priest, or distinguished by merit or favour, and—Alexandra's innovation—the Scribes, or jurisconsults. These were Pharisees, and soon gained a preponderant influence in the Sanhedrin. The Sanhedrin therefore, was the supreme legislative and judicial tribunal of the state. Not even Antipater could flout it. Herod would have to appear to answer the charge. Besides, the widows of the dead gangsters kept on demonstrating in the Temple, and demanding justice. Hyrcanus was forced into action.

Antipater and Herod were equal to the occasion. Antipater advised his son to come to Jerusalem, accompanied by a body-guard large enough to protect him en route, but not large enough to justify the suspicion that he was trying to put pressure on Hyrcanus. Herod meanwhile had obtained from his friend Sextus, who looked on him as a son, a letter telling Hyrcanus that he was to acquit him. When Herod entered the court, which met within the precincts of the Temple, beautifully dressed and accompanied by his soldiers, the lawyers trembled. No one dared open the case. Only Shemaiah, a venerable and upright man, calmly told the court that it was they who were to blame for allowing such irregularities, warned them that one day Herod would punish them and the king as well, and demanded the death penalty. Hyrcanus, seeing that the court was determined to put Herod to death, even though they dare not say so, adjourned the case, and secretly advised him to flee the city. Herod fled. He went straight to Sextus Caesar, told him how his orders had been disregarded, and obtained from him, in return for a handsome present, the governorship of Coele-Syria and Samaria. This immensely increased Herod's authority and resources. He started to march on Jerusalem at the head of an army. Antipater and his brother Phasael hurried northwards, and succeeded in convincing him how fatal such a course would be to all his hopes. Herod retired to Galilee, content with having at least shown the people that he was capable of overcoming the opposition even of the Sanhedrin itself. The incident proved to Herod something else: that he could rely on no section or party of the Jews, and that he must depend like his father on the Romans. It made it all the more necessary for him to know how to back the winner in the second round of the Roman civil war which was about to begin.

Chapter VII

WAR AND MARRIAGE

THE first victim of the new struggle for the mastery of the
Roman world was Herod's friend, Sextus Caesar. He was
murdered by a Pompeian called Caecilius Bassus, who took over
his command and his army. So blind was his hatred of Caesar,
that he allied himself not only with an Arab prince called Al-
Khaidaun, but also with Rome's most dangerous enemy, the
Parthian Pacorus. The Caesarian troops under Antistius Vetus
besieged Bassus in Apamea, a strong city on the river Orontes in
northern Syria. Antipater naturally stood by the Caesarians, and
sent a contingent commanded by his sons to help in the siege.
Julius Caesar himself, also, sent reinforcements, because no one
realized more clearly than he the menace of Parthia.

That was in the autumn of 45. On the 15th March 44 Caesar
was murdered. Around his funeral pyre, Suetonius tells us in his
life of Caesar, of all the foreign communities in Rome, the Jews
distinguished themselves by the assiduity and depth of their grief.
Not only in Palestine, but throughout the Roman world, Caesar
had shown himself their friend. He had confirmed them in the
free exercise of their religion, including the right, often contested,
to send contributions in bullion to the Temple in Jerusalem, he had
restored to them the vital port of Joppa, he had abolished—it was
one of his very last acts—the hated system of tax-farming, which
enriched the contractors, or "publicans", at the expense of both
taxpayer and treasury. Moreover, the Jews were exempted from
military service. In Rome, Hyrcanus' ambassadors were to be
treated as being of senatorial rank. Well might the Jews be grateful
to the dead dictator. It would be many a long day before they
would again have so good and powerful a Gentile friend.

Cassius did all he could to reverse Caesar's generous policy.
What he was out for was cash, and plenty of it. He therefore came
to an arrangement with Bassus, raised the siege of Apamea, and
started collecting funds. Palestine was assessed at 700 talents,
£350,000. There was nothing for it: the money must be collected.
Antipater told his sons to set about it. There was also at Hyrcanus'
court a sinister figure called Malichus—no connection with the
King of the Nabataeans. He hated Antipater, and was well-liked

A view in Petra, the Nabataean fortress-capital. The Nabataeans carved their tombs from the very rock of their stronghold, the early ones, such as these, being modelled on traditional Assyrian designs, with "step" crenellation. Later, the Nabataeans, like their neighbours, adopted Greek and Roman styles, in which the more familiar façades of Petra are worked. On the extreme right, a whole tomb has been overthrown by an earthquake.

This portrait bust of Gnaeus Pompeius, 106-48 B.C., now in the Ny Carlesberg Glyptothek, Copenhagen, displays in every line a Roman who fully deserved the *agnomen* of *Magnus* (p. 32). Although Pompey was defeated by Julius Caesar, he was regarded by many in after generations as a great patriot. In the second century A.D. the Emperor Hadrian restored his tomb as an act of piety.

in consequence by a section of the Jews. The doting Hyrcanus, thinking that it might be a good idea to have a counterweight to the all-powerful Idumaeans, patronized Malichus. He, also, was charged with the collection of a portion of the tribute.

Herod, brisk as usual, had his quota of 100 talents ready in no time: the Galileans knew his methods too well to attempt resistance. Not so the others. Malichus tried passive resistance, whereupon Cassius sold four whole towns into slavery, Gophna (Jifna) between Jerusalem and Nablus, Emmaus, Lydda and Thamna, north-west of Gophna. Cassius wanted to execute Malichus. It was Antipater who, providing 100 talents, £50,000, from his own treasure, induced Hyrcanus to beg him off.

This leniency was fatal. Malichus, far from being grateful, was emboldened by what he thought was Hyrcanus' favour and Antipater's weakness. So dangerous did his conspiracy become, that Antipater had to retire East of the Jordan, to raise an army of Arabs. Phasael and Herod of course hastened to their father's side, whereupon Malichus tried to laugh the whole affair off as a misunderstanding. He succeeded, too. Marcus, Cassius' praetor, would willingly have executed Malichus, but once again Antipater and his sons intervened to save him. Why were they so lenient to this enigmatic enemy? Was he a relation of Cypros, Herod's mother? Josephus does not tell us. Whoever he was, Antipater was to meet his death at his hands. In the summer of 43, Malichus persuaded Hyrcanus' butler to poison Antipater, while both he and Malichus were dining at Hyrcanus' table. As he was leaving the banquet chamber, Antipater fell dead. It was a foul stroke. No doubt Malichus hoped that Herod and Phasael would think that it was Hyrcanus, the man who more than any other owed his life and position, his office of High Priest and Ethnarch, to Antipater, who had plotted his death, that Herod and Hyrcanus would thus be set at odds, and that Malichus himself would be the gainer. He miscalculated.

Antipater's death naturally caused disorder in Jerusalem, which Malichus suppressed. Herod, impetuous as usual, was all for opposing force with force. Phasael once again counselled patience: at all costs they must avoid giving ground for the charge that they were starting a civil war, which would put them wrong with the Jews and with the Romans, from whom Herod had recently received not only an army, both horse and foot, but a fleet as well, and to top it all, a promise from Cassius, that when they had beaten Antony and Caesar's great-nephew and adopted son, Octavian, he would make him King of Judaea. It would be fatal to throw all that away. So Herod pretended to accept Malichus' protestations of innocence, and retired to his new province of Samaria, where he set about restoring law and order.

In October Herod decided to go up to Jerusalem for the Feast of Tabernacles. He went accompanied, as usual, by a bodyguard, not all of whom were Jews, by any means. Malichus was alarmed. He persuaded Hyrcanus to forbid Herod to enter the Temple on the pretext that it was not right to admit a crowd of foreigners when the people were in a state of ritual purity. Herod took no notice of the ban, and entered the city by night. Malichus was terrified. He was more ostentatious than ever in his mourning for his dear friend Antipater; but he, too, secretly provided himself with a bodyguard. Herod in his turn, savouring the irony, treated Malichus with smiling deference. He knew he would get his man.

Cassius, to whom Herod had reported the whole affair, determined to suppress Malichus, who was clearly a danger to the state, and sent word to his Tribunes at Tyre to help Herod avenge his father. Cassius, who had just defeated the Caesarians at Lattakia, was holding his court at Tyre, and both Herod and Malichus, among others, were bound thither with congratulations and gifts. Herod expected that Malichus would be killed on arrival. But Malichus suspected that something was amiss. He stopped short of Tyre, intending to come into the city later to recover his son, who was held as a hostage by Cassius, and, then, when Cassius was busy fighting the Caesarians again, make himself ruler of Judaea. Herod was too clever for him. He went out to meet him, invited him to dinner, him and Hyrcanus, and sent a servant on ahead, ostensibly to prepare the banquet. As they strolled along the beach in the glow of the autumn afternoon, Herod was in his most charming mood; the three men on whom the fate of Judaea depended were now such good friends: it was delightful. And there ahead, coming out to meet them, were the Roman Tribunes. What a flattering attention! As soon as the two parties met, the Tribunes whipped out their daggers, and killed Malichus there on the beach. Hyrcanus was struck dumb. When he recovered, he asked why Malichus had been killed and by whom. When he learned that the deed had been done on Cassius' orders, he applauded it, and said that Malichus was a wicked man and a traitor to his country. Herod had avenged his father; but he never forgave Hyrcanus for having harboured and favoured his murderer.

Even now, Hyrcanus had not learned his lesson: he still imagined that possibly some other power than Rome might somehow come to control the Levant, and that therefore a little "insurance" would not be unwise. Why not continue to flirt with the Nationalists? He was unable to see, as Herod so clearly saw, that though Rome might have many masters, Rome herself would always be mistress.

The so-called Second Triumvirate had now been formed, (November, 43), consisting of Antony, Octavian and Lepidus. Lepidus was a nobody: the two men who counted were Antony and Octavian. As soon as Cassius left Syria to rejoin Brutus, a certain Helix, who had been left in charge of Hyrcanus' troops while he was absent at Tyre, tried to unseat Phasael as governor. Herod was ill, and could not help his brother; but Phasael succeeded in cornering Helix, and then let him go free under a truce. But Hyrcanus' folly did not stop with appointing Helix: he had actually committed the fortresses of the state to the care of Malichus' brother, including the strongest of all, Masada, where a century before Jonathan had built a citadel which was said to be impregnable.

Herod, as soon as he was well again, recovered them all, and captured Malichus' brother. But he too, was released under a truce. Phasael had to be content with reproaching Hyrcanus for encouraging his declared and proved enemies. He could obtain no substantial redress.

This weakness encouraged others. Antigonus, the one surviving son of Aristobulus, was now, it will be remembered, at the court of the ruler of Chalcis in the Lebanon, Ptolemy by name, who had married his sister. Ptolemy allied himself with the prince of Tyre, Marion, with the object of putting Antigonus on the throne of Judaea. Herod met the threat with his usual vigour. He defeated Marion before he could join Antigonus, taking care to send the Tyrians back to their city not only unscathed, but with gifts in their hands: he needed good friends on his northern frontier. He then turned on Antigonus and defeated him on the borders of Palestine. On his return to Jerusalem, Herod was greeted as a hero by Hyrcanus and the populace alike.

Herod now took stock of his prospects. Within Judaea, he could not pretend that he was loved. The people had repeatedly shown their attachment for the Hasmoneans. But he was feared, and he was in control. Over in Macedonia, the fate of the world was soon to be decided, when Cassius and Brutus met Antony and Octavian. For thousands, in three continents, the issue was critical; it would bring prosperity or ruin according as one side or the other prevailed. Herod was in the unique position of being equally secure either way. This Arab prince of thirty-one was the personal friend both of Cassius, who had promised him a crown, and of Antony, who was most unlikely to refuse it to him.

51

With hope of a kingdom running so high, the time had come, he decided, to end the domestic feuds. In antiquity, and indeed into quite recent times, there were two recognized methods of settling quarrels between states or factions: war and marriage. Marriage was preferred, because it caused misery to fewer people. Herod had tried war successfully, he would now try marriage. He already had one wife, a common girl called Doris, who had taken his youthful fancy. His religion did not restrict him to one, or to any prescribed number of wives. It happened that there was now an opportunity of a match with a woman who not only united in herself both branches of the Hasmoneans, but was also of surpassing beauty. This was Mariamme. She was the daughter of Alexander, Aristobulus' son, who had been executed by Pompey at Antioch, and of yet another Alexandra, who was herself the daughter of Hyrcanus. By becoming betrothed to her, Herod hoped that the old rift between Hyrcanus and Aristobulus would be healed, and that he himself would now be regarded not as a foreigner, but as a member of the old royal family. Never were brighter hopes doomed to more tragic disappointment.

CLEOPATRA

From a *tetradrachm*, now in the British Museum, struck at Ascalon in 30 B.C. (p. 68), the last year of her life. She was thirty-nine. This is generally regarded as the most authentic likeness of Cleopatra extant. It shows a woman of commanding and subtle intelligence. The blob on the end of the nose is a blemish of the coin, not of Cleopatra.

MARK ANTONY

From a gold coin, now in the British Museum, struck at Ephesus in 41 B.C. when Antony, with Octavian and Lepidus, was a member of the Second Triumvirate (p. 51). It was in this year that he met Cleopatra. He was forty-two, she twenty-eight. The face is that of a jolly, but ravaged, roué.

AGRIPPA

OCTAVIAN

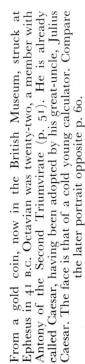

Marcus Vipsanius Agrippa, 63-12 B.C., from a coin in the British Museum, "The supreme example in history of a man of the first order whom loyalty constrained to take the second place", *Buchan* (p. 82 and Chapter XXII). This coin was struck fifty years after Agrippa's death—an impressive posthumous tribute to Augustus' great minister. It shows the face of a firm, far-sighted Roman.

From a gold coin, now in the British Museum, struck at Ephesus in 41 B.C. Octavian was twenty-two, a member with Antony of the Second Triumvirate (p. 51). He is already called Caesar, having been adopted by his great-uncle, Julius Caesar. The face is that of a cold young calculator. Compare the later portrait opposite p. 60.

Chapter VIII

FLIGHT AND TRIUMPH

THE victory of Philippi in October 42 brought Antony back to Asia as its overlord. As soon as he reached Bithynia, delegations came from all directions with protestations of their own loyalty and denunciations of their enemies. The scene recalled the arrival of Pompey in Damascus twenty-one years before. Among the deputations were two from Judaea, Herod's and a group of Jewish notables who came to denounce him and Phasael for having usurped the power of the Ethnarch. Naturally, Antony refused to hear a word against his old friend, who had besides brought him a very nice present.

Of more avail to the Jews was a deputation sent by Hyrcanus when Antony had come south to Ephesus. They brought a golden crown, and asked Antony to free those whom Cassius had enslaved over the tax-collection, and to restore their property and goods which had then been sold. Antony granted all these requests. The necessary orders were sent to Tyre, Sidon, Antioch and Aradus (Ruadh), the island market off the coast of Tripoli. Emmaus, Lydda, Gophna and Thamna were thus freed and re-peopled.

Finally, Antony reached Antioch, and took up his quarters in the neighbouring park of Daphne. Again, Herod's enemies returned to the charge, and again they were discomfited. Hyrcanus was present, and when Antony asked him point blank who were the better leaders of the nation, Hyrcanus naturally answered "Herod and his party". Antony thereupon appointed Herod and Phasael Tetrarchs, arrested fifteen of their adversaries and would have executed them, but for Herod's intercession. Even then, the notables were not satisfied—they pursued Antony to Tyre, 1,000 strong. Herod and Hyrcanus went out to them, where they had assembled on the shore, and urged them to go away. They might have remembered what had happened to Malichus on that very beach, but they would take no advice. The Roman soldiers fell on them and killed or wounded a considerable number. Hyrcanus provided doctors for the wounded and burial for the dead. The survivors still murmured, so that in the end Antony lost all patience and executed those whom he had taken prisoner.

The title *Tetrarch*, which, as applied to Herod's sons is so familiar from the New Testament, is here used for the first time

53

by Josephus. It meant originally "ruler of a fourth part, or quarter"; and was so used of federations in Thessaly and Galatia; but just as the English word quarter has ceased to mean only a fourth part and has come to denote any region, so the word tetrarch could be used to describe the ruler of any region. It could be applied to the ruler of a portion of a federation, even though the number of portions into which it was divided was greater or less than four. And it could also be used of a princeling, who had neither power, nor suzerainty. Hyrcanus still remained *Ethnarch —Ruler of the Nation*—and High Priest. He was still, that is to say, the figurehead. But the new tetrarchs were to exercise military and financial authority, and had practically unrestrained access to their Roman masters.

Antony realized, as Caesar had realized, that the greatest threat to Rome was the Parthians. He decided to mount a grand expedition against them. Meanwhile, on his way from Ephesus to Antioch, he had sent his legate Dellius to summon Cleopatra to give an account of her attitude during the late war. She was now twenty-eight, and had by no means lost the charm which had captivated Antony when, as master of the horse to Gabinius, he had first beheld her fourteen years before in Egypt.

It was on this occasion that she sailed up the river Cydnus, to Tarsus where Antony awaited her, in the silver-oared barge which Shakespeare has made immortal. Antony was enslaved. He followed her to Egypt, for, as Père Abel puts it in his *Histoire de La Palestine* "What consideration would be strong enough to prevent the departure of a man who had been invited by Cleopatra to pass the winter at Alexandria?" But while Antony was frolicking with his "Egyptian dish", the Parthians were moving. Orodes II had been king of Parthia for fifteen years. It was before him that the head of Crassus had been displayed. He had followed the Roman civil war with relish, and now harboured at his court an ardent Pompeian, who, like himself, had no reason to love the new masters of the Roman world. This was Quintus Labienus, a son of Caesar's famous lieutenant. He had been sent by Brutus and Cassius to make a treaty of alliance with Orodes, and, when those who had despatched him were defeated at Philippi, he felt it would be imprudent to return within Roman territory. He went further, and formed the plan of launching the Parthian army into the realm so ill-guarded by Antony. He was to command the expedition jointly with Pacorus, the Parthian Crown Prince. He struck his own coins, calling himself *Imperator Parthicus*.

Ptolemy of Chalcis, the little Lebanese principality, had been succeeded by his son Lysanias, who readily lent himself to the

Parthian scheme. His ward, Antigonus, the Hasmonean pretender, was easily seduced into sharing in the enterprise. In return for the throne of Judaea, he promised Pacorus 1,000 talents, half a million sterling, and 500 women, who were to be of good family. The first onslaught of the Parthians brought them to Ptolemais (Acre), where at last they stood once more on the shores of the Mediterranean Sea from which Alexander had expelled their predecessors three centuries earlier. Their army was commanded by a general of the same name as the king, Pacorus, who easily defeated, on the plain below Mt. Carmel, the forces which Hyrcanus sent to oppose him, and pressed on to Jerusalem.

Once again, the Holy City was to be rent by civil war, for the Parthian plan was to let Antigonus and Herod fight it out, and to intervene only if it was necessary to assure Antigonus' victory. Herod and Phasael held the palace and the wall, and after a skirmish in the market-place, confined the invaders in the Temple. The feast of Pentecost approached, and Antigonus reckoned on support from those who flocked into the town from all sides. Many of them were armed; but Herod broke them up.

Antigonus' plans had gone awry. It was not so easy as he thought to oust Hyrcanus and Herod. He now turned to his Parthian allies. Pacorus proposed negotiations, and suggested that Hyrcanus, Herod and Phasael should visit the satrap Barzaphanes, who was in Galilee. Herod, who had all his father's political flair, saw through the scheme at once. He refused to budge. His brother and Hyrcanus were less wise. Despite Herod's warnings they set off for the north. When they reached the little village of Zeeb, north of Acre, they were loaded with chains, told that Antigonus was now king in place of Hyrcanus, and treated as felons. Phasael could have escaped, through the good offices of a rich Syrian friend, but he resolved to stand by Hyrcanus, and to take no step that might endanger Herod, should he also have fallen into the hands of the Parthians. Hyrcanus and Phasael were both later handed over to Antigonus.

Hyrcanus had been High Priest for thirty-six years, ever since the death of his father, Alexander Jannaeus. But Antigonus was determined that he should be High Priest no longer. He therefore cut off (or as one account says, bit off) the old man's ears, a mutilation which would, in accordance with Leviticus xxi. 17, disqualify him for the supreme pontificate. He was then led off to captivity in Babylon. Phasael could no longer bear the terrible reversal of fortune. Rather than live a captive, he decided to kill himself. Being bound hand and foot, he leaped headlong on to the rocks below his prison, and so perished. Before he died he had heard from a certain poor woman, no doubt a member of the Herodian underground, that Herod had escaped, and so was confident that he would be avenged.

Herod's fortunes had reached their nadir. But recently a Tetrarch, a Prince and a General, he was now a fugitive.

As soon as he heard of the treacherous imprisonment of Hyrcanus and his brother, he knew that this instinct had been right: he, too, was condemned in advance. This was no question of differences between Pompeians and Caesarians. Once Palestine became a Parthian province, it would be all up with men like Hyrcanus and Herod, who had derived their powers from the enemies of the Great King.

Already, Herod had sent into Idumaea much of his treasure, and he had advised his friends to do the same. He had also had the great fortress of Masada prepared to receive a number of fugitives. Jerusalem was becoming too dangerous. Although he refused to stir from the palace, from its windows he could see the ring of hostile sentries gradually closing in.

One dark night, Herod slipped down into the Tyropean valley, and out by the Dung Gate. With him were his mother, Cyrpos, his sister, Salome, his youngest brother, Pheroras, his little nephew, Phasael's son, Alexandra, daughter of Hyrcanus, and her daughter, Mariamme, Herod's betrothed. The party also perforce included the 500 ladies whom Antigonus had promised to Orodes in part-payment for his throne. Partisans and hangers-on raised the total to some 9,000. It was a miserable cavalcade that straggled south through the night across the gaunt hills and precipitous valleys of the wilderness. Even Herod's resilience seemed to be quelled. One of the overladen wagons, in which his mother was travelling, over-turned. He thought she had been killed, and was on the point of committing suicide. Fortunately, she soon recovered. Herod pulled himself together, and the long train of despondent men and howling women went on its way.

The next morning, when the flight was discovered, both the Parthians and the Jews gave chase. Herod was now again master of the situation. Just beyond Bethlehem he turned on his enemies and routed them. This was the most critical engagement of his career. Had he lost it, he would certainly have been killed, and his family enslaved. He was later to mark the site with a great fortress, which remains to this day as his most conspicuous memorial.

Herod dismissed the partisans, telling them to disperse through-out Idumaea. He placed in Masada only his own family and the 500 ladies. Their disappearance was a great blow to Antigonus, who feared that he might have to replace their value in cash. It also exasperated the Parthians, who gave themselves up to looting

Jerusalem and plundering the countryside of Judaea. They even penetrated to Marisa and sacked it. Once again nationalism was proving costly to the nation.

Herod's plan was to make his way to Malik, the king of the Nabataeans, and seek his help.

Antipater had advanced considerable sums of money to Harith, Malik's predecessor; and what Herod most needed now was cash, because, not knowing of Phasael's death, he was prepared to offer up to 300 talents, £150,000 in coin, to ransom him. He took along with him Phasael's seven-year-old-son as security. But Malik, thinking that Herod would be an embarrassing guest, and possibly a demanding one as well, sent a message to the effect that the Parthians had forbidden him to receive their enemy.

Herod was now utterly alone. No one would rally to him. He had no friends left, except in Rome, and Rome was a very long way off. But Herod decided to go there. He was confident that Antony would stand by him. It was a fantastic dream, that this discredited Arab, evicted by the Parthians, harassed by the Jews, and spurned by his own kin, could succeed in achieving anything in the imperial capital, even if he got so far. But Herod was confident.

He set off for Egypt. At El Arish, the last town in Palestine, he heard of his brother's death, which greatly shocked him. Malik, meanwhile, had thought better of his churlishness, and tried to overtake Herod, but Herod was already 80 miles away in Egypt. The shipmasters in the harbour of Pelusium refused to give him passage; he overcame their opposition, and was sent off with every mark of respect to Alexandria. Cleopatra received him. It was the winter of 40 B.C. It was no time for navigation, Italy was disturbed by civil strife, Antony was away. Why not seduce this handsome Idumaean, use him to command the expedition she was planning against Ethiopia, then poison him and so obtain his kingdom? After all, it had originally belonged to her ancestors: it was hers, by right, really. The plan was attractive; but Herod was no Antony, he was not to be fooled. Winter though it was, he would press on to Rome, or perish. So he said No to Cleopatra. Both as a queen and a woman she never forgave him.

With much difficulty Herod took passage in a ship bound for Rhodes. They ran into a storm, were nearly wrecked, and had to jettison the cargo. When he arrived at Rhodes, destitute as he was, he decided that he must make the right impression on his Roman patrons, and that it was essential that he should arrive on board his own ship. He induced the Rhodians to build him a splendid trireme. He showed his gratitude by raising enough money from his friends in Rhodes to repair the war damage which Rhodes had suffered when withstanding Cassius two years before. In later years, he gave the Rhodians further tokens of his gratitude. Herod remembered his friends, as well as his enemies. He landed safely at Brundisium, and set straight off to Rome.

He called on Antony, and poured out the whole story to him. Antony, says Josephus (*War*, I, 282) "was moved with compassion at his reverse of fortune; and influenced by the recollections of Antipater's hospitality, but above all by the heroic qualities of the man before him, determined there and then to make him King of the Jews, whom he had previously appointed Tetrarch". Besides admiration for Herod, he had as strong an incentive in his aversion for Antigonus, whom he regarded as a promoter of sedition and an enemy of Rome.

"Caesar (i.e. Octavian—it was their first meeting) proved a yet more ready champion than Antony," (continues Josephus) "as his memory recalled the part Antipater had borne his own father (i.e. adoptive father, really great-uncle, Julius Caesar) in the Egyptian campaigns, his hospitality and invariable loyalty, while his eyes rested on Herod and read his enterprising character. So he convened the Senate, to which Messala, seconded by Atratinus, presented Herod and dwelt on the services rendered by his father and his own goodwill towards the Roman people; demonstrating at the same time that Antigonus was their enemy, not only from the earlier quarrel which they had had with him, but because he had also just been guilty of contempt of Rome in accepting his crown from Parthian hands.

"These words stirred the Senate, and when Antony came forward and said that with a view to the war with Parthia it was expedient that Herod should be king, the proposal was carried unanimously. The meeting was dissolved and Antony and Caesar left the Senate house with Herod between them, preceded by the consuls and other magistrates, as they went to offer sacrifice and to lay up the decree in the Capitol.

"On this, the first day of his reign, Herod was given a banquet by Antony."

It was a personal triumph. Herod had not intended to seek the kingdom for himself (so Josephus, presumably quoting Herod's own memoirs, tells us) but for Aristobulus, Mariamme's brother, whom he afterwards murdered. But he had so impressed himself both on his old friend Antony, and on Octavian, whom he had never seen before, that they decided, unasked, to place the diadem on his brow. The whole affair has taken just a week.

Herod had conquered Rome: King Herod had still to conquer Jerusalem.

Chapter IX

HEROD THE KING

ANTIGONUS had rid himself of Herod for ever, he thought. Nothing now remained but with the help of his Parthian friends to occupy and pacify the country, and to that end, the first thing to do was to reduce Masada. The rains were late that year, and the great cisterns of the fortress were running low. Herod's brother Joseph, who was in command, decided to escape with 200 of his men to Petra, where he could now rely on a welcome; but a sudden and plentiful shower of rain, such as often marks the end of the Palestine summer, saved the situation. The besieged decided to await deliverance, possibly from Herod, more likely from the Roman general Ventidius, Antony's legate, who was now on the track of Labienus. Ventidius was a brave soldier, but, like practically all of his class in the Rome of that age, utterly and blatantly venal. (It was seventy years, now, since an African prince had called Rome "a city for sale".) Having prevented the junction of Labienus and Pacorus, Ventidius came down into Palestine, giving out that he would soon relieve Masada. He contented himself with "fining" Antigonus, and also Malik and Antiochus of Commagene (in the extreme north-east of Syria) for helping the Parthians, and then leaving the country in charge of an inert lieutenant, called Silo, whom Antigonus bribed without difficulty to keep quiet.

Such was the situation when at the beginning of 39, like one returned from the dead, Herod suddenly landed at Acre. He soon saw that he would get little help from Ventidius and Silo, and that he himself would have to conquer the country. The campaign called forth all his best qualities, his energy, his confidence, his personal ascendancy and his tenacity. First, he set out for Galilee, where he had made his début nine years before, and where many of his old friends joined him. Thus reinforced, he swooped on Jaffa, and then round through his native Idumaea to Masada. Despite Antigonus' attempted ambushes, he raised the siege of Masada, ejected the nationalists from their last Idumaean stronghold, and moved on Jerusalem.

In this lightning campaign, Herod had three parts encircled Judaea, cutting off Jerusalem from the west (which meant the sea), the south and the east. On the north lay Samaria, which had already returned to Herod's allegiance—it had an important Greek population. The Holy City was isolated. Not wanting to subject it to the horrors of yet a third siege in less than twenty-five years, Herod tried the effect of propaganda. He sent his loudest speakers to proclaim to those within the city that he came for the good of the people, the safety of the city and without any desire for vengeance even against his worst enemies. Antigonus made it a crime to listen to Herod's broadcasts, and impressed on the Romans that he was the legitimate king, and that Herod was a mere upstart, and not really a Jew at that. Silo, thinking to exploit the situation, induced his troops to complain to Herod that they had no provisions, that they could not be expected to winter in the neighbourhood of Jerusalem, so recently devastated by the Parthians, and that they must disperse to more comfortable quarters. Herod was quite capable of dealing with this move. In no time, he had abundant supplies sent down from Samaria to Jericho which was to be his winter supply depot. Antigonus tried to intercept the convoys, but Herod descended on him with a mixed force of Romans and Jews, cleared the heights above Jericho and garrisoned it. He then arranged winter-quarters for the Romans in Idumaea, Samaria and Galilee where they would be under his supervision. Once again, Herod had out-manœuvred the Hasmoneans. All Antigonus could do was to bribe Silo to let him have a small detachment to winter at Lydda, which was just within his jurisdiction.

The Romans might now rest, living on the fat of the land; but Herod was as active as ever. First, he sent Joseph down to Idumaea, with 2,000 infantry and 400 cavalry, to make sure that there would be no trouble there. After settling his mother and his relations, including his betrothed, Mariamme, in Samaria, he set out for Galilee, and arrived at Sepphoris in the middle of a snow-storm. The defenders had fled, thus leaving Herod in possession of the capital of Lower Galilee and all its abundant stores. As usual, the mountains of Galilee harboured brigands, who have always found it easy to dodge back and forth between Palestine and the fastnesses of the Lebanon. Herod fought a preliminary action with them, and pursued them as far as the Jordan, but he left their eradication till the spring, meanwhile resting and rewarding his chilled and tired troops.

As head of his commissariat, Herod appointed his youngest brother Pheroras. His recent experience at Jericho had shown him that the Samaria-Jericho supply route, via the Wadi Far'a and the Jordan valley, could best be supervised from Alexandrium.

Caius Julius Caesar Octavianus Augustus, 63 B.C.-A.D. 14, an idealized marble head now in the Museum of Fine Arts, Boston, Massachusetts. Compare the earlier portrait opposite p. 53.

Marcus Vipsanius Agrippa, 63-12 B.C., as shewn in what is known as the "Butrinto Head".

This fortress had been in ruins since Gabinius had had it demolished nineteen years before. Herod now rebuilt it.

It was the spring of 38. Ventidius recalled his troops, which he needed to meet the threat of a heavy Parthian mobilization in Mesopotamia. Herod was not sorry to see the last of Silo; and set himself once more to the tough task of mastering his kingdom.

He started with the Galilee brigands. They had retired to what they imagined to be the unscaleable heights of the Wadi Hammam, to the west of the north end of the Sea of Galilee. The southern side of the valley is honeycombed with caves. Once the ladders by which they were reached had been drawn up by the defenders within, it seemed impossible that any adversary should climb the sheer cliff face. It was. Herod overcame the difficulty by having cages made, and lowering them from above. No one had ever done this before. It was completely successful. With their grappling hooks, the soldiers in the cages grabbed the inmates of the caves and dragged them to the brink, or else smoked them out. Many surrendered. Others, despite Herod's personal appeals, preferred death.

Herod expected that this example would cow the last of the fanatics, and set out for Samaria. He had to return almost immediately, the departure of the Roman troops having given new hope to the extremists, who murdered Herod's commander in Galilee. Herod turned on them. This time there was no quarter, and the rebellious towns were fined 100 talents, £50,000.

Ventidius had repulsed the Parthians, and on Antony's orders, now sent a force of two legions and 1,000 cavalry to assist Herod, in charge of a general called Macheras. Herod was then at Amwas, planning an assault on Jerusalem. Macheras was as venal as Silo: he thought he would go up to Jerusalem and do a deal with Antigonus. But Antigonus, still trusting in the Parthians, refused to admit him, and repulsed his men by force. Macheras was furious, and returned to Amwas, slaughtering every Jew he saw, including the Herodians.

This sort of thing could not go on. Herod, unlike Antigonus, was a realist. He understood only too well, that with Hyrcanus II out of the way, Antigonus, foolish and impractical as he was, nevertheless focussed in himself the aspirations of nearly all the people. How could a mere Idumaean hope to compete with the great-grandson of Hyrcanus I? Even the Pharisees, who had no love for him, were bound, now that it was a choice between Antigonus and Herod, to make common cause with their rivals the Sadducees, and back the nationalist. There was only one thing for it. Rome had appointed him king, and Rome must be made to make her word good.

Antony was in Syria again, and so, in the autumn of 38, Herod went once more to see him there. He left his brother Joseph in command in Palestine, with strict orders not to risk a battle, or to quarrel with Macheras, and travelled north. Ventidius was besieging Antiochus of Commagene in Samosata, a town on the Euphrates 200 miles north-east of Antioch, ostensibly because he was helping his son-in-law Orodes, in reality because he was reputed to be enormously rich, and might be expected to pay a handsome *douceur* to have Ventidius raise the siege. Antony was disgusted at this method of conducting a war, and took over the siege himself. There were numbers of people in Antioch who wanted to join Antony, but were afraid to make the journey through the countryside overrun by Parthian marauders. Herod at once offered to conduct them, trounced the Parthian ambush he encountered en route, and brought the convoy together with much recovered property to Samosata two days later. Antony sent a guard of honour to welcome his old friend, greeted him as a king, and promised to send him two legions as soon as ever the siege was concluded. Sosius, the new Governor of Syria, was to be in command. Antiochus capitulated shortly afterwards, and Antony departed to Greece, to spend the winter there with Octavia, Octavian's sister, whom Antony had recently married, his second wife. Fulvia, having died. The match served to defer for another six years the inevitable and final clash between the two imperators.

Herod and Sosius went south together. While they were at Daphne, near Antioch, Herod had a terrible dream distinctly warning him of his brother's death. He sprang from his bed in horror, to be met by messengers from Palestine: Joseph, they reported, had disregarded Herod's counsel, had risked a battle, had been beaten and killed. Antigonus had cut off his head as a trophy, despite Pheroras' offer to redeem it. At once revolt had flared up again both in Galilee, where a number of prominent Herodians were seized and drowned in the Sea of Galilee, and in Idumaea, where Macheras had been constrained to re-fortify the ancient Gath. Herod's resolution was fixed. He pushed on by forced marches to Lebanon, where he recruited a force from the hardy mountaineers, and was joined by one of the two Roman legions he had been promised. At Acre, he turned eastwards into Galilee, defeated the enemy by a night attack, and, despite the winter rains which had now set in, the second legion having come up with him, marched on to Jericho.

One evening, he entertained at Jericho the chief notables of the district. No sooner had the banquet ended and the guests departed, than the house collapsed. This omen of deliverance cheered Herod and his troops; the next day they attacked at dawn. In the face of great odds they cleared the heights above Jericho, which lies 800 feet below sea level, Jerusalem being 2,500 feet above. Herod was wounded in the side, but succeeded in forcing his way into the uplands, and finally cut the road between Jerusalem and the north which is the main artery of Palestine. This compelled Pappus, Antigonus' general who was besieging Macheras in Samaria, to fall back towards Jerusalem. Herod fixed his head-quarters in a village perched above a precipitate *wadi* 10 miles south-west of Samaria called Qana, and in a series of brilliant but savage raids captured five towns and put 2,000 captives to the sword. He was determined to avenge his brother. Herod was now joined by numbers of adherents, some (to quote Josephus, *War*, I, 325) "drawn by hatred of Antigonus, others by his own successes, the majority by a blind love of change". Herod was once again showing his superiority in mountain warfare. He now moved south against Pappus who had pitched his camp at a spot called Isana.

The road from Jerusalem to Nablus runs through the olive-clad, limestone hills a distance of some 40 miles. Most of the way it follows the contours of the peaks, or traverses the slopes and plains that unite them. There is one short stretch, and only one, begin-ning 20 miles north of Jerusalem, where the road is confined in a narrow, deep and precipitous wadi, in which there is barely room for the track above the torrent bed. It is called to-day the "Valley of Thieves", and within living memory it has been the scene of highway robbery and murder. At the very narrowest point, now marked by a police post, was Isana. Here was fought the battle which was to prove decisive for the possession of the country. It ended in a complete and overwhelming victory for Herod. Pappus was killed. The nationalist forces were not only routed but annihilated. Those who took refuge in an unnamed village further down the valley were butchered where they lay. It was the bloodiest battle of the whole war. It would have ended all resistance but for the onset of a blizzard, which turned the tracks to quagmires and prevented Herod's immediate advance on Jerusalem, which Antigonus was on the point of abandoning. Once again Herod had what was regarded as a providential escape. Being tired out he went into his quarters in the captured village to have a bath. He was naked, and only one attendant with him. A soldier of the beaten army ran out through the room where he was, and then a second and a third, all with swords in their hands. Fortunately, not one of them recognised him in their hurry to escape. The next day he cut off Pappus' head and sent it to Pheroras, for it was Pappus who had killed their brother Joseph.

When the storm subsided, Herod moved on Jerusalem. It was two and a half years since he had seen it. Then he had left it by night as a fugitive heading south. Now he came back as a conqueror, from the north. He decided to besiege the city on the same plan as Pompey had done, i.e. by attacking it from the north, the only side on which it was unprotected by ravines. It was a terrible siege, which lasted five months. Once more all the trees in the suburbs were cut down to make siege engines and fascines; mine was met with counter-mine. From three different quarters Herod's battering-rams assaulted the very walls, both the first and the second, which his father had raised.

He knew he would win, this time. To show his contempt for Antigonus, he decided to get married to Mariamme, Antigonus' own niece, to whom he had been engaged for five years. After the disappearance of Hyrcanus, Herod's patron, and the liaison between him and the Hasmoneans in general, the family had naturally demurred to a match which would in any event be harshly criticized, and might prove their ruin. Herod, on his side, was not loath to put off as long as he could, the inevitable screech which would go up from Doris and her common relations, as soon as they found that she was being superseded by a princely rival.

Now the time had come. Mariamme was still at Samaria, so in Samaria the fatal nuptials were solemnized. In Antioch, that same year, Herod's friend Antony was also celebrating a wedding. He married Cleopatra. Both unions, so full of happy omens, proved disastrous.

Herod was joined by Sosius, and the two together pressed the siege. Finally the day came, in June, when a picked storming party of Herod's army scaled the crumbling walls, followed by Sosius' men. In the *War* Josephus says the siege had lasted five months until this final assault. In the *History* he says the second, or outer, wall fell after forty days, the first after another fifteen, but that the Temple and the Upper City still held out. Those in the Temple asked that they might be permitted to have animals sent in for sacrifice (which meant also, of course, for food). Herod allowed this, thinking that his foes would yield to so clement a conqueror. On the contrary, their opposition became more bitter. In the end —Josephus gives no period—Herod was forced to assault the Temple and the Upper City, including the fort on whose site he was later to build his Upper Palace. Perhaps, therefore, the discrepancy in the total period of the siege is not so great as it appears.

ALEXANDRIUM

The view from the summit of the Alexandrium (pp. 33, 105), looking east across the Jordan to Gilead or *Peraea*. In the foreground are the ruins of the Herodian citadel.

MACHAERUS

The great fortress which guarded the frontier with the Nabataeans (p. 106), seen from the east. Below can be seen the Dead Sea, 1,296 feet below sea-level, with the hills of Judaea beyond. Machaerus was later to be the scene of the beheading of John the Baptist

The day of the final attack was the very same, men said, as that on which Pompey had taken the city. Romans and Jews alike were determined to show no quarter. In the houses, in the narrow streets, in the Temple itself the butchery went on. Antigonus, in despair, rushed down from the Baris, the castle at the north-west corner of the Temple, and threw himself at Sosius' feet. Sosius laughed at him. He called him "Antigone", and sent him off in chains.

Herod had mastered his enemies: he now had to control his allies. The Romans claimed that the city was theirs to sack by the custom of war. Herod said they would leave him king of a desert if they did. By the use of main force, and liberal payment, in lieu of loot, he stayed the devastation. Sosius offered a crown of gold to the God of Israel, and departed.

Herod rewarded his supporters, and hunted down those of his enemy.

Antigonus, the last of the Hasmoneans, was beheaded.

It was the summer of 37 B.C. Herod was thirty-six years of age. He was nearly bankrupt, he even had to melt down his plate to find the money to provide a present for Antony. He was hated by the majority of his subjects, who laid at his door this new spoliation of Jerusalem, the fourth in less than twenty-five years. But he was King of Judaea, and Mariamme was his wife.

Chapter X

WOMEN AT WAR

B Y the age of thirty-six, Herod had raised himself from obscurity to a throne. He had attained this eminence by his matchless gift of triumphing over men, sometimes by arms, sometimes by policy, sometimes by charm. So far he had not met his superior. Nor would he. But from this very moment of his triumph as a king, his decline as a man set in. As the years passed, the gulf between the king and the man was to widen, so that to his contemporaries Herod seemed to have in himself two contrary natures.

Outwardly, Herod was the enterprising monarch, the fascinating Arab, the friend of Caesar, the most distinguished non-Roman in the whole world, known throughout the empire for his wealth, his splendour and his munificence. Inwardly, his soul seemed to shrink in proportion as his reputation and influence expanded. He became mean, murderous and finally mad. The origins of this decay must be sought in Herod's own character and physical condition: but the instruments of it were women, and the women of his own household and family.

That he could be a match for a woman, Herod had already shown in the case of Cleopatra; and no sooner had he entered his capital as king than he was called upon to try conclusions with her again. It is perhaps wiser not to attempt any new estimate of Cleopatra's character and personality. A woman who could captivate Julius Caesar must have been a great woman: one who could hold Antony must have been a clever woman. Shakespeare has given her immortality as a "lass unparalleled". Nevertheless to many of her own age and time, Cleopatra appeared in a very different guise. In Rome, where she had lived for some time as Caesar's mistress, her enslavement of Antony made her first hated and then feared. To her neighbours, and especially to the Jews, she appeared as rapacious and lewd. Josephus sums up a catalogue of her crimes with the words: "Yet did not all this suffice so extravagant a woman, who was a slave to her lusts, but she still imagined that she wanted everything she could think of, and did her utmost to gain it." As it happened, her greatest dream was not personal at all: it was dynastic. She wanted to restore the glories of the Ptolemies. Had not the first Ptolemy, the bravest and wisest of

Alexander's marshals, had not he founded the city of Alexandria? Had not his son and successor established the Library, the greatest and most famous in the world, and the University, which now outshone Athens and Corinth? Had he not, too, engrafted himself and his dynasty on the old Egyptian tree, by marrying his sister, who, like him, was thereafter called Philadelphus, *brother-lover*, and were not a score of Philadelphias up and down the Levant memorials of that union? Cleopatra felt herself destined to revive the glories of her illustrious house. Caesar had given her an heir, little Caesarion, but he could hardly be acclaimed as legitimate. Nor could the twins, Alexander and Cleopatra, whom she had borne to Antony. But just after Herod had imposed himself effectively on his subjects as their king, the whole situation of the Orient was transformed. Antony finally broke with the West. He abandoned his wife, the saintly Octavia, (thereby of course declaring implacable hostility to her brother, Octavian, who, in marrying her to Antony had, as was his callous custom, sacrificed her to advance his own ends), and openly announced his marriage to Cleopatra, in accordance with Egyptian rites. Rome was outraged. Octavian did not scruple to violate the archives of the Vestal Virgins to extract Antony's will. By this testament, not only did Antony leave enormous donations of Roman treasure and territory to his children by Cleopatra, including little Ptolemy Philadelphus born soon after the "marriage", but he actually declared, formally and solemnly, that Caesarion was the legitimate and undoubted son, heir and successor of the great Julius, his father, which meant, quite simply, that Octavian was an imposter. Only war could settle so stark a quarrel.

Cleopatra was delighted. Antony was irrevocably hers now, not only as a lover, but for his very life. He could not abandon her, and survive. At once, he must be put to work on the great plan. First, remembering the measures which the first Ptolemy had taken to secure his independence, she insisted that she, too, must be able to draw on her own supplies of timber to build her ships. Since Egypt lacks forests, that still meant, as it had done in Ptolemy's day, that she must possess Cyprus, and, if possible, some at least of the Lebanon as well. Cyprus was handed over by the willing Antony. So was the little kingdom of Chalcis, in the Lebanon: Lysanias was executed, on the ground that four years before he had "collaborated" with the Parthians and with Antigonus. Cilicia Trachea was thrown in. Cleopatra had her forests. How easy it was! Damascus was a fine city: she would have that, too, and why not Hippos, and Gadara, the Athens of the East? She had them all. And the coastal cities, except of course Tyre and

Sidon, could she not have them too? They were hers, from the river Eleutheros north of Tripoli, the river which had once been the northern frontier of the Ptolemies, right dov. n to the Egyptian frontier. Even Ascalon seems to have been given to Cleopatra, to judge from the city's coins, one of which struck in the last year of Cleopatra's life bears the fine effigy of her which appears in this book.

Herod's kingdom was almost isolated. Having appropriated the lands immediately or almost adjacent to it on the west and north, and part of that on the east, Cleopatra thought the time had come to round off her booty by annexing Judaea, and at the same time punishing that upstart Herod, who when a miserable fugitive had dared to repulse and humiliate her. And of course, Trans-Jordan was hers by right: was not its capital called Philadelphia? Cleopatra had trained Antony so thoroughly in the disposal of others' property, that she was taken aback when he refused to sacrifice Herod. He could not hear of it, he said. Cleopatra reproached him with preferring this Arab friend to her, and she hated Herod more than ever. Under the lash of her upbraiding, Antony hit on a compromise. Cleopatra should have Trans-Jordan and part of the Hauran, which belonged to Malik, and she should have the exclusive right of exploiting the bitumen of the Dead Sea. Bitumen was the plastic of antiquity, and was much used for embalming corpses. Certain quantities of it rise to the surface of the Dead Sea from time to time, and their collection was a much-prized and lucrative concession. Cleopatra should also have just one little piece of Herod's kingdom—Jericho. Jericho was already a favourite winter retreat, which was to be greatly enlarged and embellished by Herod himself. But besides being a winter resort, it was a valuable economic asset. For it nourished two products of great rarity—date-palms and balsam. In the Bible, Jericho is sometimes called "the city of palm trees". The ancients counted forty-nine varieties of date-palm. That which flourished in Jericho was the finest to be grown on a commercial scale. It was called *Palma Caryota*, or "hangover-palm" from the strength of the wine its dates produced. Herod was to make the groves famous once more—so much so that Horace would dignify them by a mention in one of his Epistles, as a byword for opulence. The balsam gardens, too, were a source of wealth, for balsam was believed to grow only in Jericho. The Jericho balsam was probably *Commiphora opobalsamum* (*Balsamodendron opobatsamum, B. gileadense*) known as balm-of-Gilead, which despite its name is not a native of Gilead, but is indigenous to Arabia, and the East Coast of Africa opposite to Arabia. There was a great demand for balsam. It was prized for its scent above all other aromatics, and was used also for medicinal purposes: it cured headaches and relieved cataracts.

There were two separate balsam-groves in the neighbourhood of Jericho, one of twenty acres, one rather smaller, and so greatly had the cultivation of the plant been improved, that it was said, with some exaggeration no doubt, that in the days of Herod one plant produced as much as the whole plantation had done in the days of Alexander, when balsam was worth twice its weight in silver. The palm-groves covered twenty square miles. Thus, by giving Cleopatra Jericho, Antony hoped to slake her greed at the minimum cost of actual territory to his old friend.

But Cleopatra was soon to have another opportunity of harassing Herod.

Following the evil precedent recently established by his Roman friends, Herod decided to "purge" the Sanhedrin. He had not forgotten those who, ten years before, had done their utmost to have him condemned to death. It was Herod's turn now: he condemned them to death, and had the sentence carried out. There were forty-five of them, all of course adherents of Antigonus. Their goods were confiscated, and even their funeral biers were scrutinized, to ensure that no gold or valuables escaped seizure. But Herod spared old Shemayah, because he alone, when Herod had appeared before the Sanhedrin, had had the courage to speak openly against him, and to warn the court that one day Herod would be their master. So convinced of this had he been, that during the recent siege of Jerusalem, he and another Pharisee, called Abtalyon, had done all they could to persuade their fellow-citizens to open the gates to Herod. Once again, Herod remembered his friends, who were rewarded from the estates of the proscribed. The total strength of the Sanhedrin being seventy-one, there were now only twenty-six survivors, who could do nothing against the forty-five new nominees of the king. Thus, the supreme legislative and judicial body of the kingdom, the Senate of Israel, was at one blow reduced to negligible impotence. There remained a far thornier problem. The Jews were a theocracy. They were not like all the nations: they were different, and always would be, because their destiny was not of this world, but of another. The embodiment of this difference and of this destiny could never be any secular monarch. It must, so long as the dispensation of God lasted, be God's High Priest. But Herod could never be God's High Priest. Not by gold nor by steel could he ever win the right to enter the Holy of Holies of the Temple of the Lord. This dilemma—the necessity for recognizing as necessary and august an authority which could never be his—was one of the chief trials of Herod's whole reign. Unfortunately, at the very outset, it was aggravated by another—Mariamme.

Herod's marriage to Mariamme was the one political mistake of his whole career. It may have been convenient as a passport to the throne, but (as Lagrange, quoted by Abel, points out) "it was fatal for his reign, because he would have found it far easier to struggle against the old factions if they had not been installed in his household". He would also, adds Abel, have spared himself the cruel rigours which have blackened his private life. It was a mistake to have married Mariamme; but Herod committed an even more disastrous error: he fell in love with her. Mariamme did not return the passion, but she saw no reason why she should not exploit it. Nor did her mother, Alexandra, old Hyrcanus' daughter, and a woman of the vilest stamp.

Herod had hit on a typically ingenious solution of the High Priesthood difficulty. Hyrcanus, having been mutilated, could not resume his pontificate. Herod therefore sent a special embassy to Babylon, begging the old gentleman to return to Jerusalem, where he would be treated with royal honours by his grateful grandson-in-law, while an old friend of Herod's, a quite obscure priest from Mesopotamia, called Ananel, who had no connection with any of the Jerusalem parties, was nominated as High Priest. Many of Hyrcanus' friends advised him to stay "beyond the river", where he was treated as a prince; but Herod's offer was too tempting, and as the king of Parthia, Phraates IV, offered no objection, back he went to Jerusalem. Here, Herod made it clear that he was regarded as High Priest in all but name. He was treated with the greatest deference, and granted precedence immediately after the king. Once again, Hyrcanus was showing himself the servant of his Idumaean master. Ananel was Herod's lackey in any case. As usual, Herod had arranged things beautifully. The arrangement might have lasted, but for the intrigues of Alexandra and Mariamme. They were determined to have the High Priesthood in their family, and to make it a reality. Mariamme had a brother, Aristobulus, who like his sister, was renowned for his beauty. He was in the first flower of boyhood; and since youth is not among the disqualifications for the office mentioned in Leviticus, once elected, he should be able to look forward to a long pontificate. Mariamme therefore asked Herod to make Aristobulus High Priest. Herod refused.

Alexandra then got to work. She wrote a letter to Cleopatra, and sent it to her by the hand of a musician. Cleopatra put pressure on Antony, who, as usual, refused to go against the wishes of his old friend Herod. He temporized. While the women in

Jerusalem were wondering what was happening in Egypt, one of
Antony's staff, the fop Dellius, who was later suspected of being
Cleopatra's paramour, came to Jerusalem. He was overcome by
the beauty both of Mariamme and of Aristobulus, and made the
disgusting suggestion to their mother that she should send their
pictures to Antony, who would certainly fall in love with them
both, and do anything that Alexandra wanted. The unnatural
mother did as he advised, and Dellius, when he got back to
Alexandra added his own encomiums of the brother and sister,
whom he described as "really divine". Antony dared not ask for
Mariamme: after all, she was Herod's wife, and besides Cleopatra
would never forgive him. But "he sent in the most decent manner
he could for the young man". Herod was horrified. Aristobulus
was just sixteen, the same age as Herod had been when he first
met Antony. Knowing Antony and his tastes Herod was afraid
that if he once saw Aristobulus, he might forget his former friendship, and that as the recompense for his shame the handsome boy
might return as king of Judea. It was a risk that he could not
afford to run. He therefore wrote to Antony that the lad was so
popular that if he left the country, there would be riots.

Mariamme and Alexandra persisted. If the boy must be kept in
the country, the best way to ensure that he should never leave it
would be to make him High Priest. Herod yielded. Ananel was
put aside and Aristobulus invested with the sacred office. At the
same time, he placed Alexandra under close surveillance, well
knowing that it was she who had started the whole intrigue. Once
again Alexandra wrote to Cleopatra, who wrote back urging her
to escape from Herod's harshness and come to Egypt, bringing
Aristobulus with her. Alexandra decided that the only way of
eluding the king's detectives was to leave the palace in a coffin.
News of the preparations came to the ears of one of her staff who
had been suspected of complicity in the poisoning of Antipater,
and now saw a means of ingratiating himself by turning informer.
Herod said nothing: it would be more humiliating, he thought, to
catch his mother-in-law in the act: she would look foolish, being
ejected from a coffin. Having caught her and Aristobulus as they
were leaving the palace in this unusual conveyance, he pretended
to forgive them; but he realized that by the brutal rules of the
game then in vogue, Aristobulus must go.

When the Feast of Tabernacles, the great festival of harvest,
came round, and Aristobulus passed through the Temple courts
in his rich and glittering robes, the crowd went mad with enthusiasm. Here was a real Hasmonean, and the darling of the people
as well. Herod heard the cheers, and made up his mind.

When the festival was over, the court went down to Jericho, to stay in Alexandra's palace. In the gardens, just to the east of the palace, there was a swimming-pool—it is still there. In the heat of the day, Herod took Aristobulus aside. He showed him marked affection, so that the lad was flattered and charmed. As they came to the pool, they found a number of Herod's staff and servants swimming in it. Herod suggested that Aristobulus join them. The handsome boy was shy; it was not seemly that one of his rank, and the High Priest too, should expose himself naked before such a company. He preferred to wait until it was dusk. As darkness fell, he stripped and plunged in. The waiting servants welcomed him with smiles, and started to play with him. They "ducked" him, as is usual on such occasions. But they went on ducking him until he was dead.

The funeral was magnificent, Herod was loud in his lamentations. But no one was deceived. Alexandra wrote a third time to Cleopatra, who gave Antony no peace until he had agreed to investigate the affair in person. So he sent for Herod to see him at Lattaqia. Jerusalem waited breathlessly for the outcome. To Antony, who in the Roman proscriptions had sent his own nephew to death, the removal of a tiresome brother-in-law, even one so beautiful as Aristobulus, was a mere trifle. Herod returned white as snow.

Nevertheless, during his absence, he had left nothing to chance. As lieutenant of the realm he had appointed his paternal uncle, Joseph, who was also the husband of his sister, Salome. He gave him orders, moreover, that if anything happened to Herod, he, Joseph, was to kill Mariamme, because he loved her so much that he could not bear the thought of her being another man's wife after his death. By a blunder of indiscretion, Joseph told Mariamme of this injunction. Mariamme did not take it as a mark of affection by any means. Confident that her appeals to Cleopatra must result in Herod's death, she tried to escape to the lines of the Roman legion which was encamped near Jerusalem, until a letter from Herod reassured her. When Herod returned, she was colder than ever to him, and finally taunted him with the fatal order. Herod was overcome with jealousy and anger. He was convinced that Joseph must have had guilty relations with Mariamme, a suspicion which had already been sown by Salome, who was tired of her ageing husband, and would be happy to see him disappear, specially if at the same time she could injure the hated Hasmoneans. Herod thought of killing Mariamme but his passion for her saved her. Joseph he ordered to be executed out of hand; and had Alexandra kept under stricter guard and in chains.

Thus did Herod take the first steps on the fatal path of family discord and bloodshed. It is almost unbelievable that so shrewd a man could have been so worked upon by women of the stamp of Alexandra and Salome, that he could have been overcome by such jealousy as made him distrust Mariamme and murder Joseph. It is hard, sometimes, for a spectator to credit the reaction of Shakespeare's Othello to Iago's poison; yet Herod, as the story is told in the minutely detailed pages of Josephus, acted on far flimsier grounds. There is no reason to believe that Shakespeare had ever read Josephus: "he needed not the spectacles of books to read nature; he looked inwards and found her there"; but his analysis of jealousy and the madness it induces is psychologically vouched for by the history of Herod.

Chapter XI

ACTIUM AND AFTER

FOR Cleopatra, at least, the sands were running low. She made one triumphant tour of her new dominions, and paid a state visit to Judaea. Herod was in two minds whether to kill her or not. He would gladly have her out of the way, and he was convinced that only her death could save Antony, whom she would destroy when it suited her. On that point he was right, but his friends argued that Antony would hardly see it in the same light. So he abandoned the idea. Instead he received Cleopatra with simulated delight. He showed neither hatred to his despoiler, nor yet weakness to his would-be seducer, for Cleopatra still had personal designs on her fascinating host. Herod took the opportunity to make one of his celebrated "arrangements" with Cleopatra about the Ceded Territories. He would farm Jericho from her for an annual rent of 200 talents, £100,000, and go surety for the King of Arabia's rent as well. Herod would rather risk being bilked by Malik, than having Cleopatra's agents so near to him. He loaded the queen with presents and escorted her back to Egypt. Once again, Herod had won. It was their last meeting.

Antony still had friends at Rome; but opinion was turning against him, and in favour of his pale young rival, Octavian. Antony's Parthian campaign had been a costly failure; his annexation of Armenia an empty flourish; his execution of Sextus Pompeius a blunder which had antagonized the strong Pompeian faction. But it was his complaisance to Cleopatra, and his support of her grandiose dynastic ambitions that doomed him. When his will was published, with its clear implication that a new monarchy was to rule the East from an Egyptian capital, the anger of the Roman people forced the Senate to decisive action. Antony was stripped of his *imperium*, and his election to the consulship for the coming year, 31 B.C., was cancelled. Before the temple of Bellona, Octavian, as officiating priest, formally declared war, in the presence of the Conscript Fathers. War against Cleopatra only. In Buchan's words: "The issue was not between Octavian and Antony, but between Rome and the queen of Egypt, between the West and the East."

The two consuls, one of whom was the Sosius who had helped

Herod to capture Jerusalem, and a number of sympathizers left Italy, and joined Antony at Ephesus, where he was assembling his forces for the campaign which was to end at Actium, on the 2nd September, 31 B.C., in the utter ruin of Antony's forces. Many of his supporters had already ratted, including Dellius, who was to live to be the unworthy recipient of one of Horace's noblest odes. Cleopatra, in the middle of the sea battle, suddenly hoisted her sails and made off to Egypt. Antony followed, and went on board Cleopatra's flagship, where he sat, a ruined and silent slave, during the awful voyage back to Alexandria. Cleopatra was threatened by Roman troops at Mersa Matruh: her plan to escape to the Far East by way of the Red Sea was thwarted by the Arabs, who burnt her ships. She was at bay. There was only one hope—Octavian. Would he yield to her? It was worth trying, indeed, essential to try. Antony was now obviously redundant. But she could hardly kill him openly. She devised his death in a manner wholly in keeping with her character: she ordered her agents to bring to Antony's ears a false rumour of her own death, judging that he would then have no more wish to live. She was right. Antony at once attempted to kill himself, had himself conveyed to the tomb-tower in which Cleopatra was confined, and died in her arms. She was now ready for Octavian.

In these momentous events, which were to settle the shape of the world for centuries to come, Herod had no direct share. He had wished to accompany Antony to the war. Had he done so, the course of the campaign would almost certainly have been very different. But Cleopatra would not have it. Her hatred of Herod, and her jealousy of the influence which he had over Antony prevented it. Instead, she suggested that Herod should go and fight Malik, the king of the Arabs. Herod, it is true, had good cause to dislike him. He had never forgotten how Malik had denied him refuge in Petra when he was a fugitive, in order to please the Parthians. And now Malik was refusing to pay the rent for his ceded territories which Herod had guaranteed. In the past five years, Herod had assembled an efficient army, which he had trained and equipped as auxiliaries for Antony. He now, perforce, led them across the Jordan, though he managed to send a detachment, together with supplies, and a large sum of money, to Antony. The first battle with the Arabs, near the town of Dion in the Hauran, ended in victory. The youthful army was naturally elated at this result of its first engagement. Herod warned them to be prudent, but they merely clamoured to be once more led against the foe, so Herod put himself at their head and moved south. When they arrived at the basalt "lava-country", where

75

horses cannot manœuvre, the Arabs gave way. The Jews, disregarding Herod's advice, rushed headlong after them. At this juncture, Athenion, a general whom Cleopatra had sent up for the purpose, suddenly fell upon Herod's troops. They were at his mercy, he routed them and overran their camp. Only a very few escaped.

This was a grave disaster. Client kings of Rome were maintained by Rome to guard the frontiers of Rome. Unless they could do that, they had no right to exist. It was vital for Herod to redeem his failure. For the present, until he could enlist and train a new army, he had to be content with ignominious guerrillas; "he could only act like a private robber" as Josephus puts it. To crown his tribulations, in the spring of 31 B.C., Judaea was ravaged by one of the earthquakes which visit it from time to time, and have done more to lay the country waste even than the hand of man. Thirty thousand persons were killed, and countless cattle. Herod was encamped with the army in the Jordan valley, and so they escaped harm. But the disaster naturally still further depressed the Jews; and then came the news that the Arabs, who of course had heard wildly exaggerated accounts of the damage, had slaughtered the Jewish ambassadors.

Herod roused his troops with a stirring address. The earthquake, he said, was a natural phenomenon, and was not to be regarded as a judgment from God. If it had been, it showed that God was on their side really, "for had he been willing to afflict us still more thereby, he had not changed his mind so soon". The Arabs had never beaten them, only Athenion, by a trick. Let them go and avenge the ambassadors. After offering a sacrifice, Herod led his troops across the Jordan, and up the long defile to Philadelphia. In the smooth rolling plain to the south of the city, he completely outgeneralled the Arabs, captured the fort which protected their camp, killed 5,000 of their men, and forced the remainder to seek refuge in entrenchments, where they were tortured by thirst. Several thousands were killed in sorties. The rest surrendered, and hailed Herod as the Protector of their Nation. His prestige was restored. And in the nick of time. Octavian was on his way.

Antony made a last appeal to Herod. He sent one of his trusted friends, Alexas of Laodicea, to try to rally him to his aid. All that happened was that Herod succeeded in winning Alexas over to the cause of Octavian, which, however, was not to save him from the death sentence. Herod went further. He regarded Antony as already being to all intents and purposes, dead. Having himself repulsed the ruinous advances of Cleopatra Herod found it hard to forgive the criminal mania of a man who allowed himself to be destroyed by her. For more than a quarter of a century, Antony and he had been intimate friends; between them there existed a romantic bond first forged by the affinity of the dashing master of the horse for the fascinating Eastern boy. It was Herod who had been faithful. It was Antony who had broken the chain that bound them. To Herod's wisdom and friendship he had preferred the poison of the "serpent of old Nile". He was committing suicide: and he bid fair, utterly besotted as he now was, to drag his friends to death with him. It was a sorry end to a life that should have been fine.

The governor of Syria, Quintus Didius, saw Antony's behaviour in the same light. Acting in concert with Herod, he succeeded in arresting a detachment of gladiators who were on the way from Cyzicus to help Antony.

Even so, Herod was in a dangerous position. What would Octavian do? Would he still be Herod's friend? Herod's enemies were naturally jubilant—in secret. If Herod were out of favour—and how could he possibly explain away his ostentatious friendship with Antony and the help he had given him?—there was hope for them. Alexandra and her clique set to their evil work once more, and once more they were to involve a member of their own family in ruin and death. For the only possible rival to Herod, the only Hasmonean prince left, was poor old Hyrcanus. He was now 72 years old; he had seen many vicissitudes of fortune, but they had not taught him wisdom. He allowed himself to be inveigled by his scheming daughter into treasonable correspondence with Malik. The go-between took the letter to Herod, who read it, sealed it up again, and told the man to deliver it, and to bring him the answer. Malik's reply made it clear that he would do all in his power to support Hyrcanus and the Hasmoneans in a *coup d'état*. Hyrcanus was questioned. He denied having taken part in any plot. Herod thereupon summoned the Sanhedrin, produced the damning letters, and handed Hyrcanus over to the executioner to be strangled. This is the version of the affair that Herod gave in his memoirs. At the time, and later, there was doubt as to how guilty Hyrcanus had been. It is out of keeping with the poor man's character that he should have taken any initiative in anything. But, as on a former occasion, he may have thought that a little "insurance" would not be imprudent, and thus have become a puppet in the fatal schemes of Alexandra, whose hatred of Herod coupled with her corroding ambition had now brought to their deaths her father, her brother and her brother-in-law. Nor were they to be the last victims.

Even with Hyrcanus out of the way, Herod, before setting out on what he knew must be one of the most critical journeys of his career, decided to make assurance doubly sure. He therefore sent his mother, and his sister Salome and the whole of his own family down to Masada under the care of Pheroras, his only surviving brother, who was instructed that "if he heard any sad news about Herod; he should take charge of the government. Mariamme and Alexandra were confined in the Alexandrium under two trusted friends, who were told that if Herod came to grief, they were to kill the two women, and do their best to secure the succession for Herod's sons, and for Pheroras".

Chapter XII

HEROD AND OCTAVIAN

IN the early winter of 31 B.C., Octavian arrived at Samos, to undertake the redrawing of the map of the east. Discontent among his veterans and freedmen called him to Brindisi, but within a month he was back, at Rhodes this time. It was here, in the island that held such memories for Herod, and where he had prudently made so many good friends, that Herod came to seek audience of the man who was now at the age of thirty-two, the sole arbiter of the whole Roman world.

Herod had carefully thought out his approach. Two other client kings, Amyntas of Galatia, and Archelaus of Cappadocia (whose daughter Herod's son was later to marry) had managed to retain their thrones by espousing the winning side. Herod's case was different. With him, it was not a question of just trimming: he had been an active and convinced friend of Antony. He had done all he could to help him, with men, money and supplies; had it not been for Cleopatra, he would have fought by his side. It was only when he realized that Antony was obstinately bent on his own destruction at the hands of Cleopatra, that he had abandoned him to his fate.

He therefore went to Rhodes with all his usual panache; only, he did not wear the diadem, the circlet of gold encircling forehead and temples which, rather than the crown, was the official symbol of royalty. When he was granted an audience by Octavian, Herod neither offered excuses, nor sought pardon. He simply told the plain truth. He had been a close friend to Antony, and had done all in his power to help him attain the supreme power. Had he not been diverted to the Arabian war, he would have been in Antony's army. He had sent him money and corn—less, indeed, than a friend should have done, since true friendship demands loyalty to the full and to the end.

After his defeat he had not deserted Antony, but had advised him earnestly to get rid of Cleopatra, and to make it up with Octavian. But Antony would not listen, and had gone obstinately to his doom. Herod, too, had shared the defeat of his friend, and that was why he had not presumed to wear his diadem in the presents of the victor. But he had nothing to be ashamed of.

79

"What I ask of you," he concluded, "is to consider not whose friend, but what a good friend, I was."

Once again, the incantation of Herod's charm wove its spell. Octavian, the cold calculator, the careerist whose single-minded ambition had brought him so young to the zenith of power, was, for the second time, captivated by this strange Arab, ten years his senior, who had been, as he boasted, the "inseparable companion" of Octavian's most deadly rival. He bade him replace his diadem; he should be a king again, and with a throne more firmly founded than ever. Antony had done well to prefer Cleopatra, for as a result her madness had given Herod to Rome. Quintus Didius had written to him of Herod's help in the matter of the gladiators, which showed that he had been Caesar's friend before Caesar had become his. His kingdom would be confirmed by an official decree of the Senate, and as soon as possible, enlarged. "You shall find no loss in the want of Antony."

Antony and Cleopatra still lived. To close that account, and to take possession of the immense treasure of Egypt was Octavian's next task. Instead of sailing direct to Alexandria, Octavian agreed to visit Herod's kingdom, and to march down the coast in state. He had none of his great-uncle's feeling for the Jews, to whom he was, rather, hostile, possibly because one of his tutors, Atheno-dorus, had been born and brought up in Petra. He declined to visit Jerusalem, and was later to commend one of his grand-children for the same decision. So from Acre to the Egyptian frontier, down the most famous road in the world, the sumptuous progress moved. Octavian (he did not receive the title Augustus until three years later) and Herod rode together as friends, before the eyes of all men. A bodyguard of 150 soldiers surrounded the two rulers. The feasting was continual. For the passage of the desert—it was July—Herod had made all necessary preparations. Abundant supplies of water, plentiful magazines of food had been established at each stage, just as Antipater had furnished them for Julius Caesar. Herod was determined to make the best possible impression, not only on Octavian, but on his staff and army as well. For at the other end of the desert journey was Alexandria, and in Alexandria was Cleopatra. Who could tell, perhaps she might win over Octavian, as she had won his great-uncle, as she had won Antony? It was a terrible risk. Herod did all he could to guard against it. Then, bidding farewell to Octavian at the frontier, he waited, on tenterhooks.

First came the news of Antony's death. Then, that Octavian had killed off Caesarion, now sixteen, (his own cousin) and Antyllus, Antony's son by his first wife, that Cleopatra was dead,

The great fortress which dominated Jericho, from the west (p. 106).
The line of the mountains of Moab, beyond Jordan, with a glimpse of the
Dead Sea below, appears at the extreme left.

HYRCANIA

Herod's Bastille, in the wilderness of Judaea, seen from the east (p. 106).
Its Aramaic name was *Marda*, fortress, which survives in its modern
name of *Khirbet Mird*.

This remarkable air photograph, kindly supplied by Professor Mayer,
shows the great fortress of Masada (pp. 56, 106). Its roughly lozenge-
shaped *enceinte* crowns a precipitous hill-top, surrounded, except at one
point on the west, by deep *wadis*. (The diamond-shaped enclosures
outside the fortress are the remains of Roman works erected during the
Judaean war, A.D. 66-70.)

and that Octavian was on his way back. Herod breathed again. Later, the details of Cleopatra's last bid for life and power became known.

"In one of the finest rooms in the palace (says Dio Cassius) she placed a magnificent sofa. She then put on an artfully simple frock; she was in mourning, and looked wonderful in it, too. She arranged herself on the sofa, and put near her the various pictures and statues she had of Julius Caesar. All his letters to her, she had ready in her bosom.

"When young Caesar came in, she jumped up, graceful as ever, and greeted him with 'My Master! For heaven has given you the mastery now, and taken it away from me. See, that is how your father (i.e. Julius Caesar) used to look when he came to see me. Oh! so often! And of course you have heard how good he was to me, and made me queen of Egypt. But I want you to know something about him from me, personally: here are his letters, read them for yourself.' She then read out some of the most impassioned bits, and broke down, and cried, and kissed the letters, and fell on her knees at the foot of the statues. Then, in her most melting strain, she looked up at Octavian. 'Oh dear!' she said, 'what good are all these poor letters to me now? Still, in this young man, dear Caesar, you live again. . . . I wish I had died before you . . . but if I have him, I shall have you!'

"Words, movements, looks—the performance was beautifully subtle. Young Caesar was by no means unmoved by her ardour and the appeal to his passions. But he pretended to be. He avoided her eye and only said: 'Do not worry, woman: you shall come to no harm.' Cleopatra was much upset—not so much as a glance would he give her, not a word of love, nothing about the kingdom. She threw herself at his feet, and in a torrent of tears said: 'Caesar, I neither can live any longer nor do I want to. The only favour I ask of you in memory of your father is that since Heaven gave me Antony after him, I may also die with Antony.' Still no answer from Caesar: he wanted to keep her alive for his triumph."

She defeated him, and died, famously, by her own hand. She was thirty-nine. As Dio puts it: "She captivated the two greatest Romans of her day, and because of the third she destroyed herself."

Chapter XIII

HEROD AND MARIAMME

A S soon as Herod heard the good news of Cleopatra's death, he hastened to rejoin Octavian in Egypt. They met in the capital of the very woman who had tried to ruin him, whose spite, by ensuring his absence from Actium, had made possible his present elevation. Not only was he a king, but he was Caesar's friend. For the more Octavian saw of Herod, the more he was charmed by him. And not only Caesar, but Caesar's great minister, and exact co-eval, Marcus Vipsanius Agrippa, "the supreme example in history" (to quote Buchan's appraisal) "of a man of the first order whom loyalty constrained to take the second place". As Agrippa was to have so large a share in the governance of the East, it was to his and Herod's mutual advantage that they became such fast friends. Such was the force of Herod's personality, of his competence and charm, so warm his devotion, that before long it was being said that he was beloved by Caesar next after Agrippa, and by Agrippa next after Caesar.

As soon as he arrived in Egypt, Herod set about demonstrating his friendship in the most practical way possible. He gave Octavian a present of 800 talents, the equivalent of almost half a million sterling to-day. It came just when Octavian needed it most, though it was more than Herod's little realm could afford. Clearly, such an excellent king deserved a larger kingdom.

The precious groves and gardens in the Jordan valley, which Cleopatra had filched from him, were now restored. In addition he was given the towns of Gadara, Hippos, near the eastern shore of the Sea of Galilee, Samaria (the territory of the same name was already part of his kingdom), and, on the coast, Gaza, Anthedon (just north of it), Joppa, and a little place called Strato's tower, 25 miles south of Mt. Carmel. Zenodorus, the heir of Lysanias, was allowed to farm Chalcis. Tripoli, Damascus and Ascalon recovered their autonomy: Berytus (Beirut), which already before Actium had broken with Antony, received notable accessions of land. It was soon to become a Roman colony.

In addition to his new territories, Herod was also given Cleopatra's personal bodyguard of 400 Galatians. His final acquisition proved to be among the most valuable: it was the tutor of Cleopatra's children, a Greek called Nicolaus, of Damascus. Nicolaus was a man of wide learning and subtle talents. He was an historian of note, and an able orator. Herod had received little formal education, though we know that he attended a primary school as a child; now that he was an international figure, a wider culture would be seemly. So Nicolaus undertook to instruct the king in philosophy and rhetoric and gave him some history lessons. He soon made himself the indispensable confidant of that king, and on more than one occasion was to act successfully as his ambassador in the most delicate and critical negotiations. Herod urged him to take up historical writing; and no doubt it was Nicolaus who helped Herod to compose the *Memoirs* (now lost) which Josephus used in writing his history.

On the eastern frontier of Herod's kingdom, Octavian was content, for the time being, to leave things as they were. It happened that in this very year, 30 B.C., Malik died, and was succeeded by Obodas ('Aboud) III. Perhaps he would turn out to be more satisfactory. Octavian was soon to find out. So was Herod. Throughout his reign, this frontier, and the Arab king who ruled it, gave him constant anxiety, and in the end nearly proved his undoing. But in 30 B.C., all was calm.

Thus established, Herod should have been able to look forward to a long and prosperous reign. Had not old Menahem, the Essene, told him as a child that he would one day be king of the Jews, and that he would reign for—how long was it? Had he said? Menahem was sent for. The old man recalled his former prophecy, which had now been fulfilled. He recalled also, with the freedom to which his sanctity entitled him, that when he had made his original forecast, he had smacked Herod on the bottom, and had told him to remember the blow, as a sign of the change of fortune that would come upon him later. Herod pressed him now to say how long he was to reign: Menahem was silent. "Ten years?" asked Herod. "Yes," said the old man, "twenty years, nay thirty" but he would not give the exact limit. Already, in Herod's family, the change of fortune had began. It was now to reach its first awful crisis.

When Herod came back from Rhodes, the royal women had returned to the capital from their respective fortresses, and at once their venomous rivalries broke out again. The Hasmoneans, were, beyond doubt, a stuck-up lot. Their ancestry, after all, was not so ancient as all that—it went back less than 200 years, and then only to an obscure country priest. Most of the intervening representatives, though they called themselves "patriots" and "kings", had been by no means models of virtue. Cypros and Salome, proud of their long Arab pedigrees, felt, with reason, that they were "just as good" as Alexandra and Mariamme. The rift between the two camps was complete: in fact the only thing they could agree about was that Doris, Herod's first wife, was utterly common.

Since the execution of Hyrcanus and Aristobulus, Alexandra and Mariamme, who well knew that it was they who by their selfish yet gauche intrigues had been ultimately responsible for their deaths, loathed Herod; for whatever they plotted, he always seemed to get the better of them. Mariamme's hatred of him was as deep as his love for her. She had borne Herod three sons and two daughters, but she now refused to share his bed. Far from showing joy at his advancement, she made it quite clear that she would have welcomed a different outcome. She was rough-spoken and, as Josephus says, "treated her husband imperiously enough because she saw he was so fond of her as to be enslaved by her. She did not also take into consideration that she lived under a monarchy, and that she was at another's disposal."

So matters went on for a year. Herod was still the doting husband, Mariamme the hating wife. Herod, in love as he was, bore with her, greeted her insults with a smile, and would hear no ill of her. Salome decided to act. She realized that the only possible way of alienating Herod was to impugn Mariamme's chastity: he had already shown his pathological tendency to jealousy. One day, when Mariamme had once again refused Herod's embraces, and had flung in his teeth the murder of her grandfather and brother, he lost his temper and would have seized her by force. This was Salome's cue. She sent to Herod his cup-bearer (in those days of crude poisons a man's most trusty servant) to play a part in which he had been long rehearsed. He was to say that Mariamme had asked his assistance in preparing a love-potion. What its composition was, or whom it was for, he could not say, because the queen had kept it; but being a faithful servant, he thought he ought to tell his master. Gerod was furious, and at once ordered Mariamme's favourite eunuch to be tortured, because he was sure that Mariamme would have done nothing without his knowledge. The poor creature of course could say nothing about the mythical love-potion, and could only suggest to his tormenters that Mariamme's hatred of Herod was due to "something that Sohaemus had said to her". Sohaemus! Herod was beside himself with rage and jealousy. Sohaemus, his friend, the man to whom he had committed Mariamme, when, before going off to meet Caesar at Rhodes, he had sent her to the Alexandrium. What nameless treacheries had those two committed on that high mountain? For if Sohaemus had told Mariamme of his command to kill her, rather than let her fall into another man's hands or arms, it could only mean, it must mean, that they had been lovers!

> "O curse of marriage,
> That we can call these delicate creatures ours,
> And not their appetites!"

He would kill them both. No, he could not kill Mariamme. Suppose the story was false? But it must be true. Had not Mariamme herself praised the manner in which Sohaemus had looked after her, had she not begged and obtained for him an honourable government post? The case was clear.

> "But O, what damned minutes tells he o'er,
> Who dotes, yet doubts, suspects, yet strongly loves!"

Sohaemus was sent to his doom, untried, unheard. For Mariamme a more horrible fate was in store. Herod, whom jealousy had inflamed to the point of madness, determined to subject her to the mockery of a faked trial. A little court of sycophants was assembled, before which Herod acted both as counsel for the prosecution and as presiding judge. The story of the love-potion was told again, and Salome raked up the old tale of the pictures, making out that it was Mariamme herself who had sent her portrait to Antony. It was quite evident what sentence the court was expected to pass—death, and to death they accordingly condemned her.

Once the verdict was given, Herod became a little calmer, and his friends were relieved to see that he was disposed not to kill Mariamme, whom he had loved above all other, but to commute her sentence to one of imprisonment. Salome was determined that her victim was to die. She therefore spoke against clemency: so long as Mariamme lived, she said, Herod's life would be in danger, and there would be riots and civil war on her account. Herod allowed himself to be persuaded, and pronounced sentence of death.

Even now, Mariamme's sorrows were not at an end. As she was being led away to the gallows, her vile mother Alexandra, realizing that she too could hardly escape the vengeance of Herod in his present wild and determined mood, and hoping to show him that she was innocent of any complicity in Mariamme's plots, leapt from her seat, and, as her daughter passed her, abused her in the most brutal terms. She was ungrateful, shouted Alexandra, tearing her hair, an evil woman; and her punishment was no more than a just retribution for the odious way in which she had treated their common benefactor. The members of the court were aghast at this hypocritical exhibition, and none more than Mariamme. She uttered no word of reproach. She paused, looked at her mother in disdain at her breach of dignity, and that was all. Unmoved, with her beauty undimmed, she walked calmly on to her death.

Salome's victory nearly killed her brother. He abandoned himself to grief. He staggered about from room to room of the palace crying out for Mariamme, he sent his servants to summon her, as though she were still alive. He tried to find forgetfulness in society, in feasting and entertainments. But Mariamme was always present to him, "for his love to her was not of a calm nature, nor such as we usually meet with among husbands". Then plague broke out in Jerusalem, and carried off a number of citizens, including some of Herod's closest friends. He was more dejected than ever. He went on long hunting expeditions, making his headquarters in the town of Samaria, where he and Mariamme had been married. But the memories of his happiness only aggravated his distemper. He became much worse, both in mind and body. He was suffering from terrible pains in his neck and his mental affliction gave him the aspect of a madman. He refused to be ruled by his physicians, particularly as regards diet. They gave him up. Let him eat what he liked, they said, he could not last long.

Alexandra, hearing this excellent news, attempted another *coup d'état*. She tried to subvert the captains of the two fortresses that dominated Jerusalem and the Temple. One of the captains was a first cousin of Herod's. He reported the plot to the king, who at long last gave orders for Alexandra's execution.

Slowly, Herod began to recover. He was now forty-four. He had another twenty-six years to live; but he was never completely restored. Never again was he to be the brilliant charmer, the athletic extrovert who had captivated men and women of East and West alike. He became moody, suspicious, and liable to sudden accesses of vindictive passion.

The strangest part of the whole story is Herod's attitude to his sister. He never seemed to realize that it was Salome who had invented the calumny which had brought Mariamme to her death, for whatever faults the poor woman had, her chastity was inviolate. On the contrary, Herod trusted Salome, as will be seen, to the very last hour of his life. Capable she may have been, and faithful to Herod in her fashion. But as a character she was almost as vile as Alexandra.

After the execution of her first husband, Joseph, Salome had been married to an Edomite called Costobar. He was a prominent man, whose ancestors had been priests of the Edomite god Koze, before their enforced conversion to Judaism. Herod made him governor of Idumaea, a favour he rewarded by plotting with Cleopatra, whose vassal he offered to become. Herod would have executed Costobar, but Salome and Cypros interceded for him, and he was spared. Salome was now tired of him. She decided to divorce him, and sent him a formal deed dissolving their marriage. This was against Jewish law as it then was, which allowed the relief of divorce to husbands only. Salome met this objection by telling Herod that Costobar together with three others had formed a conspiracy to dethrone him, and that they were harbouring the sons of a certain Babas, a relation of the Hasmoneans, who had sided with Antigonus. It is true that in 37, when Herod took Jerusalem, Costobar had helped them to escape, and had hidden them in various farms on his estates. But for nearly ten years now they had lived in grateful obscurity. Nevertheless, they were rounded up and executed. So were the three friends, and so was Costobar. Salome had her divorce.

Such was the family life of Caesar's friend. Now surely, there would be peace? Yes, there would be, for a time. Later on, Mariamme's spirit would return in the persons of her children, to haunt and to torture Herod's last years.

Meanwhile, it is a relief to turn to the brighter side of Herod's life, for it was very bright.

Chapter XIV

THE CLIENT KING

WHEN Octavian returned to Rome, after settling the affairs of Egypt and Syria, he celebrated his victory by a triumph which lasted three days. That was in August, 29 B.C. Even before this, at the beginning of the year, the Senate had closed the Temple of Janus, thereby signifying that the Roman world was at peace. This had happened only twice since the foundation of the city. Everybody, everywhere, was sick of war. It seemed, as Virgil sang, that this tranquillity was the boon of some god.

"The nations" (to translate Abel's words) "were congratulating themselves on the longed-for return of peace; and as this return coincided with the moment when Caesar found himself sole master of the Roman State, it was bound to facilitate, to a singular degree, the establishment of the imperial régime. If, in the words of Tacitus, 'he won over the soldiers by his gifts, and the people by his distribution of corn', Caesar charmed the whole world by the sweets of peace."

It must be borne in mind, also, as Buchan points out, that the whole idea of representative government was completely alien to the ancient world. When, therefore, on the 13th January, 27 B.C., Octavian resigned all his offices, it surprised no one, and shocked few, when the Senate implored him to resume them. Three days later, the Senate hallowed Octavian's authority, by conferring on him the title *Augustus*, by which he was henceforth to be known. The word Augustus, *Sebastos* in Greek, had a religious significance, which raised the emperor above humanity and gave him a sacred character. The title "worshipful" (which is a general equivalent of Augustus) does not imply that its holder is to be an object of worship. Augustus always discouraged any ceremonial that might suggest that he was a god. But his "father" Julius Caesar had been formally deified after his death; and though in the west, Caesar-worship might be slow to catch on, in the more ardent east, where since time immemorial divinity had hedged a king, the cult of the emperors spread far and early. This aspect of Rome and its ruler was to be of vital importance in her dealings with the staunchly theocratic Jews.

Thus the empire came into being. Not that it was called that.

The word *imperium* means "command"; but just as "the Northern Command" may mean not only the office of the commander, but also the area in which he exercises it, so, gradually, "imperium" came to mean "empire". But that was much later.

The area ruled by Rome was not, by modern standards large: the whole of the Empire could fit comfortably into the United States or Brazil. But it contained almost the whole of the then known world, and the fountains of western religion and culture. As Samuel Johnson put it: "All our religion, almost all our law, almost all our art, almost all that sets us above savages, has come to us from the shores of the Mediterranean." It is for this reason that we still venerate the Roman Empire. But the Romans did not see it in that light at all. To them, the empire was a system of government and organization which had gradually been forced upon them by a double necessity: the need for security and the need for money. It was in repulsing her enemies, Gauls, Carthaginians, Greeks, that Rome had originally expanded her dominions. The further her legions were from Rome, the more expensive they became, and the more necessary it was to have sources of wealth to call upon. Italy was a poor country. And it had become further impoverished by war and the growth of Rome. It could no longer even feed itself, far less find the money to pay the legions, or to buy the luxuries which were in increasing demand. There were from time to time currency crises in Rome, which only imports of bullion could overcome, and, as may have been apparent from this narrative, every Roman of any standing seemed to be permanently short of cash. That is where the provinces came in. Their function was to provide money. They paid tribute, and the more flourishing they were the more they paid. That was why good government was so important. Sometimes, whole kingdoms had been "bequeathed" to Rome. Cyrene had been acquired in that way, so had Pergamum. The "bequest" of Cyprus had been barefaced robbery; but the sale of the last king's property had brought in the equivalent of three and a half million sterling. However they were acquired, once within the Roman orbit, the provinces had to be made to pay.

For us, living in the twentieth century, in the sunset radiance of the nineteenth, it is natural to suppose that the western provinces of the Roman Empire, the European provinces, were the most valuable. They were not. Spain, it is true, which was the oldest province in the West, seemed to the Romans to be their richest single possession. It was extremely fertile, but so were other regions. What the Romans valued in Spain were its mines. The silver and lead of Spain were the best to be had anywhere, and it also produced alluvial gold, tin, iron, copper, mercury, cinnabar, and the only known vein of mica. This wealth soon became a monopoly of the royal house. Augustus' grandfather had been a banker, so the family understood the value of money. Livia, Augustus' wife, owned Spanish mines. To this day, the depth of their shafts, and the relics of the machines by which, in the absence of suitable pumps, which were unknown in antiquity, they kept them free of water, excite admiration. Southern Gaul, too, was a productive land. But, taken as a whole, the Western portion of the Empire was poorer, less extensive, less populous and less alive than the Eastern. In the fourth century, the capital would be moved to Byzantium. That was a long time off; but even in the days of Augustus, the possibility of such a change was being discussed, and Horace thought it advisable to write a poem condemning the idea.

The East was gorgeous, and Rome held it in fee. The retaining wall, the bulwark of the East, was the Levant—the land which lies between the two former capitals of the Seleucids and Ptolemies, between Antioch and Alexandria. In the eyes of Augustus and Agrippa, the Levant had a triple importance which no other area had. First, it was very rich, second it was the threshold of even richer lands, third it was the frontier against Parthia, the dread enemy which Rome had never yet succeeded in conquering.

This area fell into two main divisions, Syria and Egypt. Egypt was a world in itself. Although it fronts the Mediterranean, Egypt is not a Mediterranean country. Not in Egypt grow the olive and the carob, the pine, the cypress and the myrtle, not in Egypt rise the hills and terraces of limestone that everywhere but here girdle the Inland Sea. Egypt is neither of Asia, nor yet of Europe, it is the gateway of Africa. Amid its burning sands the river Nile nourished crops of fabulous abundance. Porphyry, serpentine and granite were carved from its quarries. Glass, paper, linen came from its manufactories. Above all, there was the Arabian, Indian and Chinese luxury trade. Spices, precious stones, ivory and silks—all these came from the east, and many of the cargoes passed through Egypt. Now that Rome was rich and peaceful, the demand for such luxuries grew by leaps and bounds. "For these of old the trader unpearl'd the Indian seas, The nations of the nadir were diamondless for these." To satisfy them millions a year went east.

Augustus at once realized the importance of Egypt, not least because Rome's corn supply came now chiefly from there: it fed Rome for a third of the year. To be master of Egypt was to be master of Rome. So the master must be himself. Besides, in Egypt Augustus was the successor of the "heaven-born" Ptolemies. For the Egyptians he possessed a divine authority, which, in order to maintain the vital economy of this ancient and prosperous land, it was important to perpetuate. Into the Roman scheme, this anomaly could only fit by being kept out of it. So Egypt became the personal domain of the *Princeps*, or First Citizen, as he now liked to be known. His representative there was a prefect, of equestrian rank but with proconsular authority. Neither senators nor knights might enter Egypt without a special visa from Augustus himself.

Apart from Egypt, the empire at the beginning of Augustus' administration contained twenty-six provinces. Of these, the eleven less vulnerable and less lucrative were entrusted to the Senate. Their governors were called *proconsuls*, and must have held the office of *praetor*, or, in the case of "Asia" and "Africa" of *consul*.

The remaining fifteen provinces, were administered by Augustus. The five least important were governed by officers called *procurators*, the remainder by *legates*, who (as in the senatorial provinces) must have been either *consuls* or *praetors*.

Syria was the most important of the "imperial" provinces, and its governor was officially known as *legatus Augusti pro praetore*, even if the governor was an ex-consul as he was after the year B.C. 13. Syria was enormously wealthy. On the coast were those famous "cities of Lebanon, dream-shadow-dim", Tyre, Sidon, Byblos, the rising Berytus (Beirut), with Ptolemais (Acre) to the south, Laodicea (Lattaqia) and Seleucia, in the north. Seleucia was the port of Antioch, that lovely and opulent city on the Orontes, with its famous park of Daphne nearby. Antioch was second only to Alexandria as a centre of learning and culture. Inland were other towns, flourishing and famous. There was Damascus, then as now one of man's most beautiful habitations. There was Emesa (Homs), there was Hierapolis (Baalbek), there was Palmyra, remote, rich and cosmopolitan.

Syria produced corn, oil, wine and fruit. It produced the famous textiles and dyes of Tyre. It produced the exquisite jewellery and glass of which the surviving relics move the beholder to wonder in the museums of Beirut and Damascus. The Syrians were enterprising folk, and established themselves all over the Roman world, including Rome itself. A hundred years later, Juvenal would utter his famous complaint that "long since the Orontes has flowed into the Tiber". In Syria the three centuries of Seleucid rule had accentuated a process that was as old as Homer himself, the fusion of Greek and Semite. The country was bi-lingual, speaking Aramaic and Greek, and now in Berytus a specifically Roman culture was beginning to flower. It is easy to see why the Romans chose Beirut as their centre, why Agrippa elevated it into a Roman colony. It is the most Italian site in the whole of the Levant. Only in Beirut is found the combination of sea, plain and snow-capped mountain that could almost persuade the Italian expatriate that he was at home again.

No wonder that Syria was Rome's most prized possession in the East, that, with Egypt, it formed a zone vital to the prosperity, indeed to the existence, of the Empire. For this reason alone, Palestine, as the link between the two regions, the two continents, would have been important in the imperial scheme. But it had two other claims to consideration, the second and third which above have been attributed to the whole Levant: the first, riches, it did not possess, but it was the gateway to riches, and it was on the frontier.

Mention has already been made of Rome's expanding commerce with Arabia Felix, India and the Far East. Much of that trade reached the Mediterranean through Palmyra and Damascus. Some also, as we have seen, went via Alexandria. But at this period, before Hippalus had discovered the monsoon, most of the trade came overland, and the most frequented overland route was that which led from what is now the Aden Protectorate to Petra. From Petra roads led to Damascus and the North, to Alexandria, and to Gaza. The cosmopolitan opulence of Petra has already been mentioned. Under 'Aboud III, and even more under Harith IV who succeeded him in 9 B.C., Petra rose to the height of wealth and influence of which the sculptured memorials are world-famous. Augustus had heard all about Petra from his tutor, Athenodorus, and his banker ancestry told him its value. Indeed, so highly did Augustus regard Petra and its riches, that it was to lure him, as we shall shortly see, into almost the only blunder of his career. Palestine is the gateway to Petra. Moreover, Herod had already shown that he was capable of controlling that gateway and even Petra itself, with which through his mother, backed by the success of his arms, he had firm and lucrative ties.

Then there was the frontier. Beyond Syria lay the desert, beyond the desert the Euphrates, and beyond the Euphrates the Parthians. The memory of Carrhae held for the Romans a shameful terror which Antony's failure to redeem it had only deepened. The Roman legion had shown itself invincible everywhere except in the East. The Parthians relied on two sorts of cavalry: the heavy armour-plated horseman and the light, swiftly manoeuvring, squadrons, who could swoop down, fire a volley of arrows as they advanced and then another as they rode off—the famous "Parthian shot". Relays of camels, brought up fresh supplies of arrows. Thus, against the slow-moving foot soldiers of Rome, however brave, however well drilled they might be, the Parthians had a superiority analogous to that of the tank and the aeroplane over modern infantry. Only ten years earlier, these same Parthians had invaded Palestine, and had occupied the very capital itself. Worse, the people of Judaea, or many of them, had shown themselves willing collaborators. Were there not many Jews in Babylon, had not Hyrcanus himself been a refugee with the Parthians?

How was the menace to be held in check? Obviously, by the one man who had shown himself, even to his own cost, and against all apparent odds, their implacable enemy, and the steadfast champion of Rome.

Everything pointed to Herod. He alone could rule Palestine as Rome wanted it to be ruled, as the secure arterial road between Egypt and Syria, as the gateway to the Farther East, and as the bulwark against Parthia.

The idea of a client kingdom was by no means new. It had already lasted for two centuries. At this period, client kings governed Armenia, Cappadocia, Galatia and Commagene. As Tacitus put it, Rome made even kings the instruments of servitude. For the rôle of the client king was precarious. There is no analogy whatever between the client kingdoms of Rome, and the protectorates or trustee territories of our own day. The theory that authority is a trust, that the aim of government is autonomy, that dependent territories are to be trained for independence would have been incomprehensible to a Roman, even to the best Roman. Virgil himself, in a famous passage, warns his countrymen to leave the arts and sciences to others, and to concentrate on their own appointed task which was to "rule the nations". Kings might sometimes be the means of rule, that was all: it was always Rome that ruled.

A client king therefore held his kingdom merely on a "grace and favour" tenure. He could be dethroned at will. He could not bequeath his kingdom, except by Rome's permission, and then only to an heir approved by Rome. Frequently it happened that Rome, having used a king for a time, took over the kingdom and turned it into a province. That had happened in North Africa, it had happened in Asia, and it would happen again. Nor might a client king strike his own silver coins, only copper ones. The silver coinage was imperial. He must, too, be ready at all times to furnish contingents of troops for distant wars. The king, nevertheless, was supreme within his frontiers. He had full legisla-tive, judicial, fiscal and administrative authority. He was entitled to the diadem, the sceptre, the crown and the purple. He enjoyed two important privileges: he and his kingdom were exempt from the tribute, and from the garrisoning of Roman troops on his people and at their expense.

Within such cramping limits, with such slender prerogatives and prospects, it was not to be expected that many a king could achieve eminence. They were not meant to. But, as Buchan admits, Herod had that touch of genius which makes a man incalculable. He was determined to shine in the world, and shine he did. But before we describe his achievements it will be well to inquire into the condition of the land and the people over whom he had been called to be king.

Chapter XV

THE TWO JEWRIES

"AS for ourselves, therefore, we neither inhabit a maritime country, nor do we delight in merchandise, nor with such mixture with other men as arises from it; but the cities we dwell in are remote from the sea, and having a fruitful country for our habitation, we take pains in cultivating that only. Our principal care of all is this: to educate our children well; and we think it to be of the most necessary business of our whole life to observe the laws that have been given us, and to keep those rules of piety that have been delivered down to us."

Thus does Josephus, in his Apologia for his people known as *Against Apion*, describe the inhabitants of Palestine of his day. The description holds good *a fortiori* for the age of Herod. To those whose idea of the Jew in the Roman world is taken from pagan writers, particularly Josephus' contemporaries, Tacitus and Juvenal, this presentation of the Jew may seem strange. Was he not a trader, a commercial traveller, a banker perhaps, sometimes a musician or an actor, but always a townee, a dependant on an urban community? The answer is that the Jew was both a peasant and a townee, but in different places, just as to-day the Italian in Chicago is a townee, and not always a laudable one, while in Umbria and Tuscany he has remained a peasant. In each case the same national name is applied, and correctly applied, to two quite different societies. There was the Jewry of Palestine, and the Jewry of the Dispersion.

In Herod's day, the population of Palestine (according to Klausner, *From Jesus to Paul*, Ch. 3) was three and a half million, of whom three million were Jews. This number was about the same as that of all the Jews in the Dispersion added together. Despite the wide area over which the Jews were scattered, therefore, and the manifold occupations which they followed, Judaea and the Jews who lived in it were far more important than those who lived outside it, if only because three million concentrated in one region must be more powerful than, say, the one million who lived in Egypt as a minority among seven and a half million Egyptians. This simple fact is cardinal to any estimate of "The Jews" in Herod's day as compared with ours.

The Old Testament is a predominantly country book; so is the New Testament. How few of the scenes of the Bible are presented to us under a roof, how many of its persons as shepherds and herdsmen and fishermen. The imagery of the Bible is that of the village and the field. Corn, wine and olive, fruits, flocks and herds, these were the wealth of the land. The Judaean farmer was a skilful husbandman. He produced enough to feed himself and his family, and in good years the land produced a surplus of grain for export. The olive oil of Palestine was exported to Tyre and Sidon, Syria and Egypt. The dates and balsam of Jericho have already been mentioned, and the bitumen of the Dead Sea, "Judaean pitch", Pliny tells us, was world famous. The fish of the Sea of Galilee was plentiful and choice, so plentiful that it was salted for export, and a town on the shores of the lake was called Tarichaea, from the Greek word *tarichos*, meaning salted fish.

With the farm and the flocks, there went, as usual, the simple handicrafts of mankind, from smiths, tailors, masons, bakers, millers, dyers, carpenters, coopers, potters, butchers and barbers—crafts so universal that in our own tongue, as in others, they have all become family names—to engravers, copyists and glassmakers. But the artisans were few compared with the bulk of the people, who were small-holders. They worked their land with the help of their wives and children, just as their successors do to-day. They hoped to produce a little more than they needed for themselves, and this surplus they took to the market town for sale or barter.

There was also then, as now, a class of more wealthy proprietors, middle-class landowners, who traded in produce, lent money on loan, and laid the foundations of Hebrew trade. Really rich men were few, mostly connected with the court or the hierarchy. Nor were there many extensive estates: the country is too small, too fragmented to admit of them. But that such did exist, we know from the mention in the Gospels of the steward who administered a large property for an absentee landlord.

Judaean economy also included the artisan and the hireling, who might hire himself by the day, as in the parable of the labourers in the vineyard, or for a longer period, which might not exceed six years.

There was, too, a body of casual labourers, many of them landless peasants, the human price that humanity has always had to pay for the maintenance of the idyllic-seeming peasant economy. Small holdings go ill with large families. Pestilence or drought may at any time depress the nice balance between competence and want.

At the bottom of the social structure were the slaves, some

foreign but some also children of Israel. The Hebrew slaves were better fed than the "Canaanitish" slaves, but all of them were treated like cattle—in theory. In practice, the individual often triumphed over the institution, and there are many recorded cases of affection between master and slave. It is well to remember, too, that slavery was universally accepted in antiquity, and that neither Plato nor the Stoics nor St. Paul condemned slavery as such.

Josephus' emphasis on the rural basis of Palestine economy was just; nevertheless, during the past 300 years the Jews had been increasingly interested in commerce. They learnt it from the Greeks, as is shown by the large number of Hebrew commercial terms which are taken from the Greek, just as in the sixteenth century Italian commercial terms were taken into French and English. The anchor, symbol of sea-borne trade, appears on Jewish coins from Alexander Jannaeus till Herod and his successors; and the monument put up at Modin to Judas the Maccabee and his brothers was adorned with ships.

It was the merchants who formed one of the most important links with Overseas Jewry. This second Jewry is generally known as the Dispersion, a name which in its Greek form *Diaspora*, or Hebrew original *Galuth*, was used by the Jews of Palestine to denote those who lived outside the country. The word suggests compulsory exile, and may therefore be misleading. It is true that the kings of Babylonia and Assyria uprooted a certain number of Israelites and Judaeans from Palestine; but it is also true that a large number of others had left the country of their own accord in search of trade or occupation. "Seas unite, they do not divide." From the earliest eras of human history, the inhabitants of the countries bordering on the Mediterranean, Greeks, Phoenicians, Syrians and Egyptians, had sailed its waters, and had settled here and there. So had Jews. In many lands, they had gradually built up busy and influential communities. These had been reinforced by refugees, during the troubles which were endemic in Palestine during the struggles of the Ptolemies and the Seleucids, the Maccabean upheaval, and, finally the clashes with Rome and Parthia.

The Jews in Egypt penetrated to Elephantine, near Aswan. They made good soldiers, and were so employed by the Persians when they ruled Egypt in the sixth and fifth centuries B.C. They were also to be found in other provinces of the Persian empire. Artaxerxes III settled Jews in Hyrcania, by the Caspian Sea; whence the name Hyrcanus. There were Jews in Arabia, and a large community in Babylonia from the time of the Captivity. The Egyptian community was naturally greatly augmented during the period in which Palestine was a province of the Ptolemaic kingdom, that is from 320 to 198 B.C.

Jews had also settled in Asia Minor; Aristotle, who was there between the years 348 and 345 met a Jew who was, so Josephus tells us, quoting Clearchus, a pupil of Aristotle, "a Grecian not only in his language, but in his soul also". From Egypt and Greece, Jews spread all along northern Africa, and into Italy. As already related, they became an important community in Rome after the Pompeian conquest. Many of these settlers became prosperous citizens of their adopted countries, some rose to be high officers of state or generals.

So far, these Jewish communities do not differ from those of, say, Greeks, or Italians or Phoenicians settled outside their own countries.

But there were in fact two fundamental differences which made the Jewish settlements utterly unlike those of any other people. The first was their religion, the second their attachment to Jerusalem.

The Levant has a genius for religion. Because it has given us our three great monotheistic religions, it is easy to overlook the others. There were large numbers of them, and they all had enthusiastic adherents.

Egypt's gift to the religion of the Hellenistic world had been Serapis. The first Ptolemy, with his quick intelligence, realized that the old religion of Egypt would not do: the Greeks were not going to accept as gods animal deities with the heads of dogs, crocodiles and cats. Yet the august and compelling mystery of Egypt might be exploited, and a religion produced in which both Egyptians and Greeks could find comfort. So Serapis of Alexandria replaced Ammon of Thebes. The new religion was directed from the great Serapeum in Alexandria, rather as Judaism radiated from the Temple of Jerusalem. Serapis represented the dead Apis, assimilated to Osiris. He thus had an impeccable Egyptian pedigree. But the great statue of the new god in the Serapeum was purely Greek, the work of Bryaxis of Athens. Thus was the old Pharaonic faith mingled with the Greek mystery cults. The cult of Serapis became widely popular, and reached Rome, and established itself as one of the leading cults of the west. Not until A.D. 385, when the edict of Theodosius marked the end of paganism throughout the empire, was the Serapeum destroyed.

The Syrian cults never had the cohesion of those of Egypt or Asia Minor: they came in waves, from Phoenicia or the Lebanon, and each area kept its local god. But from very ancient times they had been deeply venerated, and they remained famous until the final eclipse of paganism. The builders of the Pyramids, Cheops and Khephren, thought it a privilege to send gifts to the temple of Byblos in Syria, that very temple which, as we shall see, was the prototype of temples in general. And the last two Roman emperors who tried to establish a state religion in opposition to Christianity Heliogabalus and Aurelian, each in his turn saw in the Syrian sun-god the only possible rival to Christ.

For religious variety, few areas in the world can ever have equalled the Levant. Even to-day, its narrow limits contain Jews (both Eastern and Western), Moslems (Shia and Sunni), Christians (Roman Catholics, Greek Orthodox, Armenians, Syrians, Uniates, Protestants and Druses). As late as 1948, an Alaouite leader who announced himself as God, had the misfortune to be executed for treason by the Syrian government.

The Syrian goddess *par excellence* was Atargatis, of Bambyce (Membidj), often confused with the Phoenician Astarte. Her husband was Hadad the god of Baalbek. Through the great slave-entrepot of Delos, the worship of Atargatis spread to Athens and Rome and later on even to Britain. Among the other gods of Syria were Adonis; Baal of Damascus; Dusares of Arabia; Allath the Arabian goddess; Baltis, Notre Dame of Osrhoene; Aziz, the strong god of Edessa; Malakhbel, the messenger of the Lord from Palmyra. All of these deities had their adherents far and wide. One of the most remarkable proofs of the exuberance and popularity of Syrian religion is provided by a quite obscure god, a sort of Jupiter who was worshipped in Doliche, a small town in Commagene. There is no reference to him in any ancient author, and yet more than 100 votive inscriptions from all over the empire testify to the devotion in which he was held.

None of these religions and cults made any claim to exclusiveness. Religion was simply a matter of choice and convenience. A worshipper could choose one of the local favourites, or he could patronize one of the fashionable international gods. To worship a single god, even to claim that your god was the best, was permissible. But for the Jews any such latitude was blasphemy. They claimed that for them it was lawful to worship only one and the same God. They went further: they claimed that their God was the only god there was, that all the others simply did not exist. They were just so many deceiving phantoms.

Clearly, any such view of religion must set those who held it absolutely apart from their pagan fellow-beings. But the actual religion of Judaism, in its belief and its practice was radically different from the rest.

This unique faith had been imported into Palestine by the

Hebrews at their first coming. Moses had conceived it in that awful desert that lies to the south and east of the Dead Sea. Here, the limestone of the Mediterranean gives way to matter more ancient, a red and fiery relic of the convulsions of the world's birth. There is nothing gentle, nothing human about it. It is harsh, remote, lunar. In its utter rejection of the integuments of this green earth, it seems to command those who stray across its calcined ribs to confess the nothingness of everything terrestrial, and to fall down and worship unity. The land is instinct with monotheism, and only a very insensitive person can escape its compulsion. Even the mouth of the Arnon river, the great purple cleft through which its waters flow to the Dead Sea, a marine Petra, where in the perpetual twilight the cataracts boom between their towering, shadowed walls, even this romantic chasm which in Europe or even Syria would have been the home of some famous and frequented deity, is deserted and bereft of sanctity, save that which it shares with the rest of the one God's creation.

From the contacts with Persia which the Exile had brought about, Judaism had developed a more sublime, more spiritual creed. For from Persia had come the idea of the infinite, first deduced by the Persian astronomers from the endless revolutions of the heavenly bodies: if they were perpetual, must not the spirit that made them be infinite? It followed that the soul of man, his creation, must be infinite, too. This faith was maintained and protected by an elaborate law, by the rite of circumcision, by the observation of the Sabbath, by abstention from forbidden meats, by the prohibition of the making of any graven image.

The centre of Judaism was the Temple in Jerusalem. Wherever the Jew might establish himself, he would build a synagogue; but he would revere the Temple in Jerusalem as well. For a time, when the Temple in Jerusalem had been profaned by Antiochus Epiphanes, a sanctuary on the model of the Jerusalem Temple was built in Lower Egypt, near Heliopolis: but this was never conceived of as a rival to the true Temple, only as a substitute for it. For Jerusalem was the one hearth and centre of the Faith. The Temple revenues were derived in part from tithes, from dues, and from the freewill offerings of Palestinian worshippers. But they depended very largely on gifts from the more wealthy communities of the Dispersion. To the Temple, Jews from all over the Dispersion, including the Jews of Egypt, made pilgrimages, and to it every Jew would pay a half-shekel, two drachmae, worth about half a crown to-day, each year. In every major town in which Jews lived, there was a bank into which these offerings were

HERODIUM

Herod's fortress-tomb from the north-west, with the mountains of Moab, beyond the Dead Sea, in the distance (p. 121). The outskirts of Bethlehem appear in the right foreground.

CAESAREA

Caesarea, now Kaisarieh, from the south (p. 125).

SAMARIA

Samaria-Sebaste as the site appears to-day, from the south. The modern village of Sebastiyeh is on the right of the ancient acropolis. The minaret rises above the remains of the Crusader church, now a mosque (p. 125).

paid, and the money was periodically transferred to Jerusalem.
It was transferred in cash.

This Temple-offering was yet another cause of friction between
the Jews and their Gentile neighbours. At a time when, as we have
seen, there were periodical shortages of specie, the export of this
money to Palestine caused resentment. An illuminating instance
of this feeling is furnished by Cicero. The governor of Asia Minor,
Valerius Flaccus, like so many of his republican confrères, was a
greedy rogue. Among those, and they were many, whose complaints secured his prosecution, were the Jews of his province. The
trial took place in the year 59. Cicero defended him, with what
outcome we do not know.

The Jews claimed that Flaccus had confiscated over 120 pounds
weight of gold which had been collected for the Temple offerings
in the cities of Apamea, Laodicea, Pergamum and Adramyttium.
Cicero, in his defence, begins by saying that he will speak in a
half-whisper, so that only the judges can hear him, because there
would not be wanting spies to repeat what he said to the Jews of
Rome, who would combine to do him harm—a remark which,
although no doubt exaggerated in order to prejudice the court, is
in itself a tribute to the influence of Roman Jewry even at this
early date. He then admits that it was the custom of the Jews to
send gold to Jerusalem "both from Italy and from all our provinces"; but, to palliate Flaccus' peculation, he says that the
money is still lying in the public treasury; all that Flaccus had
done was to impose a salutary measure of currency control, which
applied to everyone equally. Had not the Senate imposed a
similar embargo on the export of gold from Italy more than once,
notably when Cicero himself was consul and at his suggestion?
This was a plausible argument. There is no doubt that these
regular remittances of gold to Jerusalem did bring odium upon
the Jewish communities of the Dispersion. Whenever they sought
from Rome a reaffirmation of their rights and privileges—for they
enjoyed many, and were to all intents and purposes internally
autonomous—this matter of the Temple tribute was always a
prominent demand.

The objects on which the Temple funds were disbursed may be
studied in the tractate of the Mishnah called *Shekalim*. They paid for
the whole-offerings, the display of the shewbread, the preparation
of the incense, the wages of the women who wove the Temple
curtains, the rich garments of the High Priest, the "red heifer",
sacrificed outside the walls (*Numbers* xix—see Note I), and the
more familiar scapegoat; it supported the Temple librarians and
attendants. But the money might also be applied to more secular

uses, such as fortifications, repair of walls and water conduits and other urban needs. Even so, a large surplus accumulated. Crassus had coveted the Temple riches, and a century later, even after Herod's lavish expenditure, Tacitus could speak of the "incalculable wealth of the Temple". Most of it came from abroad, where many rich Jews would contribute far more than the minimum half-shekel. To the ruler of Judaea, therefore, it was of the first importance that this revenue should reach Jerusalem uninterrupted and unmolested.

Such were the two Jewries which existed in Herod's day: the predominantly agricultural community of Palestine, and the widespread, complex Dispersion, the two bound together by their Faith, and by devotion to its centre, the Temple in Jerusalem.

Herod was king of Judaea, but with his usual flair, he realized that to succeed in that rôle, he must play a leading part in the affairs of the Dispersion as well; and, incompatible as that might seem with his status of client king, he would show that he possessed the genius to do it.

Chapter XVI

HEROD'S POLICY

TO please Rome, and to please the Jews: could it be done? That was the task that fate had laid on Herod. To please Rome would not be difficult for so sensitive, charming, vigorous and versatile a character. Already, he had shown that he knew how to do it. But to please the Jews without going against Rome's wishes would be far harder. For Jewish nationalism still smouldered, ready to burst into flame at the first puff of fanaticism.

With it, Herod could have absolutely nothing to do. In the first place, the nationalists had shown again and again that nothing would give them greater satisfaction than his own death; in the second, there was no place for nationalism within the *Pax Romana*, least of all for a nationalism that had so recently collaborated with the chief enemy of Rome.

Herod's policy, therefore, must be to try to induce the Jews to find their true destiny and fulfilment in their religion, while at the same time taking their secular colour from Greece and Rome.

Herod has often been represented as the enemy of religion. The charge is founded on two bases. The first is that he could treat those who, in the name of religion, rebelled against him with utter ruthlessness. He did as we have seen in the case of the Galilee zealot-brigands, and shall see again. But it is the common experience of those who govern in the Levant that rebels pose as martyrs. Herod like his successors punished them not for their religion but for their politics.

The second basis of the indictment has far more weight. It was not that Herod disregarded Judaism: he never really understood it. To him, it was the religion of the Jews, and, now, of his own Idumaean people. He would (and did) observe it scrupulously. But having been brought up largely in foreign circles, in Petra, in his father's camps and comings and goings, Herod had failed to grasp the uniqueness, the sublimity of Judaism, both in itself, and as compared with the surrounding paganism. To us, who are the heirs of a tradition which has for 2,000 years mingled all that is finest in both Judaism and Hellenism, it is hard to picture a world where the two dwelt apart.

The Hellenism of Herod's day had long ceased to be Greece. It spoke, wrote and read Greek. Greek was the language of government, culture and commerce. Even the Jews made use of Greek, particularly those of the Dispersion. There had been an Authorized Greek Version of their scriptures, published by Alexandria University, for nearly three centuries. But the creative tradition was dead; and in the moral and spiritual realm, a decline had long since set in. The atmosphere of Rome was lewd, its society, despite the efforts of Augustus to reform it, vicious. The Princeps' own grand-daughter, the younger Julia, was to become a byword for depravity. There is hardly one of the most admired poets of the Augustan age whose pages are not stained by revolting obscenity. In England the incompatibility between the standards of the classics and those of the Bible has for centuries been solved by the typically English device of admiring the classics on weekdays, and denouncing them by inference on Sundays. But for the Jews of Herod's day no such compromise was possible. Of all the religions that flourished then, Judaism is the only one that flourishes now. It is the guide of millions, and, through its contribution to Christianity, whose Founder was born into the Jewish Faith, of many millions more. Cynics may say that men do now very much what they did then, that their conduct has not changed for the better. That may be true: but the standards by which that conduct is judged have; and that change has not been due to Hellenism.

"A religion," says Cumont, "in addition to reasons for belief, must give motives for action, and subjects for hope." Judaism gave all three, in a degree that made its votaries tenacious and happy. It also, to the general discomfort, made them so contemptuous of the religions of other people, that they came to despise those peoples themselves, and to exalt into a virtue an exclusiveness that should at most have been no more than a necessity.

Herod realized this defect. He thought he could break it down by superficial adjustments and compromises. He failed, because he never grasped the vital essence of Judaism. That it was different he knew; but why it was different he never did understand.

With this reservation, which was to cause so much trouble to Herod while he lived and so much damage to his fame when he was dead, Herod must be accounted a man of active piety. For this estimate we have not only the inferential evidence of his works and acts both in Palestine and in the Dispersion, but the direct testimony of Josephus. Herod's favour to the fearless Pharisees, Shemaiah and Abtalyon, his veneration of the outspoken Essene, Menahem, have already been recorded. The saintly and famous

Rabbi Hillel—admittedly a quietist—lived unmolested through-out Herod's reign. Josephus tells us that Herod showed honour to all the Essenes, the most spiritual, the least worldly of the Jewish sects, the secrets of whose central "monastery" on the shores of the Dead Sea are only now being brought to light by the labours of the Dominican *Ecole Biblique*. Josephus tells us also that "the main part of Herod's magnanimity was extended to the promotion of piety".

This, be it remembered, is the testimony of a Jewish historian who was of priestly family, and related to the Hasmoneans.

The strictness of Herod's rule, and the ardour, amounting to subservience, with which he promoted secular westernization, have obscured his zeal for enhancing the prestige of Judaism.

That Herod's rule was strict cannot be denied. It had to be. Like his Hasmonean predecessors, he kept a standing army, and like theirs, it was composed largely of mercenaries. Besides Jews, there were Thracians, Celts, Galatians and Germans, as well as Idumaeans and men from the city of Samaria. The army, cavalry and infantry together, amounted to several thousand men. The ranks were denoted by Greek terms, but in the formation a Roman influence is traceable. As a reserve, the king could also call on ex-soldiers and veterans whom he had organized into military colonies. These settlements, placed on the northern and eastern frontiers, and subject to military discipline, were a partial and useful sub-stitute for permanent garrisons. There were many Greek and Roman officers in Herod's Court and Government. It is noticeable that when Josephus mentions any particular category, e.g. minis-ters, Masters of the Horse or tutors to the royal children, the holders of the office are named in pairs, one Greek and one Roman. Herod wanted, it seems, to keep the balance between Greek and Roman influence.

The internal security of the kingdom was reinforced not only by two castles in the capital, but by a remarkable chain of fortresses. Many of these have already been mentioned in the course of this narrative, but it may now be well to consider them systematically. Taking those on the west bank of the Jordan first, and moving from north to south we begin with Alexandrium, on Mt. Sartaba, above the mouth of the Wadi Far'a to the east of Nablus. It took its name from Alexander Jannaeus, its reputed founder. Then 15 miles to the south, comes Docus, on the summit of the "Mount of Temp-tation" above Old Jericho. It was here that Simon, the father of Hyrcanus I, was murdered. Next, dominating the site of Herod's New Jericho, on either side of the Wadi Qilt, were Threx (*The Thracian*) and Tauros (*The Bull*), and later Herod's own creation of Cypros, called after his mother, which seems to have been built on the site of Threx, after it, and Tauros, had been destroyed by Pompey. A relic of the name survives to-day in the Arabic appellation *Jabr*. Eleven miles to the south, in the heart of the Wilderness of Judaea there is a hill called *Khirbet Mird*, on the summit of which Hyrcanus had built a fortress-prison, called after himself Hyrcania. It is a bare, desolate place, shut in by higher hills on the west, with only the leaden waters of the Dead Sea to vary the view of the tawny desert scenery. An early Christian anchorite, who thought it would make a suitably remote and comfortless hermitage, found himself unable to stay there on account of the number of demons already in possession.

The Herodium, 4 miles south-east of Bethlehem, was Herod's own creation. Finally, in the south, in the barren hills above Engeddi, was Masada.

On the east side of the Dead Sea, just north of the impassable rift through which the Arnon flows into the Dead Sea, stands Machaerus (*The Sword*), also said to have been built by Alexander Jannaeus. The cleft and the castle together assured the frontier between Herod's dominions and those of the Nabataeans. There was, too, on the east of the Dead Sea a second Herodium, which Josephus says was 200 stades from Jerusalem "upon a mountain towards Arabia". The site that best answers the description is a small ruined fortress known to-day as *Al-Hubbeisa*, "the little prison", to the east of the remains of the agricultural settlement which Herod called Livias, in honour of Augustus' wife. It is below Mt. Nebo, not far from the north-eastern shore of the Dead Sea.

These ten fortresses—or perhaps we should say nine, if Cypros and Threx really occupy the same site—form a closely-knit system. They have certain features in common which stamp them as being recognizably the work of a single school of military architecture, as are the fortresses of Vauban and his imitators. First, they are all on the tops of hills or mountains. Second, the stone building on the summit is, wherever possible, protected by a glaçis so steep that it is barely possible to walk straight up it. Third, in the base of the final cone, at the foot of the glaçis, are vast cisterns, one or more, excavated in the hill, and lined with hydraulic cement, to store rain water. Taurus, with a perennial aqueduct at its base, had only one: Alexandrium twelve. Fourth, wherever possible an aqueduct has brought additional supplies of water, generally rain catchment from adjacent hills or *wadis*, but in the case of the great Herodium from springs, to be stored in a large open tank, thus reserving the inner cisterns for use in emergency and siege.

Fifth, the actual cone of the fort is severed from the *massif* from which it protrudes by an artificial fosse.

These five features are the marks of the "Herodian" fortress, and nearly all of them are found in all nine of which the sites are now known and accessible. Below Herodium, Alexandrium and Machaerus, faubourgs, of which traces remain, were attached to the actual forts, because they were dwelling-places, as well as citadels.

Every castle in the system could signal to at least one other, in most cases to more than one. Herodium, Machaerus, Docus and Cypros could signal direct to Jerusalem as well. Where a fort was not visible from its neighbour (as in the case of Alexandrium and Cypros, 16 miles to the south), detached signal-stations were constructed on the nearest vantage-point. Sometimes, as at Machaerus, a relay-station was necessary to surmount an intervening hill. The exact method of signalling is unknown to us. In the air of Palestine visibility is good. It is possible, for instance, on some days in winter, when the atmosphere has been washed by rain, to see the snowcap of Mt. Hermon from the north end of the Dead Sea, 100 miles away. That fire signals were used at night by the Nabataeans we know from Diodorus Siculus (XIX, 97), and by the Jews, from the Mishnah (Rosh ha-Shanah 24) which mentions Sartaba (Alexandrium) as one of the stations.

With probably only two real exceptions, (the two Herodiums), Herod inherited this system, he did not create it. To him may justly be attributed the credit for having brought it to the pitch of efficiency, but by no means the odium of its invention. The question arises, who did invent it? Josephus gives Hyrcania to Hyrcanus, and Alexandrium and Machaerus to Alexander Jannaeus. That they refurbished the castles, and "called them after their own names", "thinking that their houses should continue for ever, and that their dwelling-places should endure from one generation to another" may well be true. But that does not account for the existence of Docus *before* the reign of John Hyrcanus, nor for the fact that all these fortresses were built to command the Jordan valley, all but two, Machaerus and the second Herodium on the west bank.

That Josephus could be wrong in his dates we know. He was an excellent recorder of events of which he had personal knowledge, or of which he could learn from almost contemporary sources. But any period older than a century before his day, and for which he lacked written records was to him a muddled antiquity. This splendid chain of castles, of which the nucleus consists of seven forts, seems to the modern student to be a single creation. That

Greek defensive architecture had reached the country in the third century B.C., we know from the remains of the *douane ornée*, known to-day as 'Arak al Emir, which a certain Tobiah erected in the Wadi Sir, to the east of Jordan, on what was then the main road from Jerusalem to Philadelphia (Amman) in the third century B.C. The location of the "Herodian" fortresses suggests that they were constructed to repel a threat from the north, to counter an attack moving down the Jordan valley. Their form recalls the mountain strongholds that Alexander stormed during his Indian campaigns, above all, the famous "Aornos", at the capture of which Ptolemy signally distinguished himself. None of the sites has been excavated; but it seems at least possible that in this system of fortresses we can still descry part of the works by which the first Ptolemy succeeded in preserving his hard-won Palestine from the rapacity of his northern neighbours, the Seleucids.

To return to Herod. His policy was clear and simple. He decided to do three things: to suppress nationalism, which he knew to be a suicidal folly, to promote the honour and welfare of Judaism, both in Palestine and in the Dispersion, and to foster westernization. This last meant pleasing Rome and imitating Greece. He set about doing it by a series of magnificent buildings, and political progresses. They were spread over a number of years; but as they formed instalments of a single policy, it will be convenient to describe them together. But before doing so, it will be necessary to tell of three events that might have wrecked the whole programme had not Herod been the man he was.

Herod's new Palace (p. 118) was built on the site of the present citadel, seen here from the east. The base of the so-called "Tower of David" (right) is all that remains of the tower "Phasael".

JERUSALEM

Jerusalem from the south. Herod's great Temple-Acropolis (Chapter XX), now the Haram-al-Sherif, is in the middle, surmounted by the dome of the Al-Aqsa Mosque, with the larger dome of the Qubbet-al-Sakhra, "Dome of the Rock" to the left. To the east, beyond the Kedron valley, lie Silwan (Siloam) and the Mount of Olives; to the west, the Tyropean valley, now largely filled in, and the Upper City.

Chapter XVII

TRIAL AND SUCCESS

AS part of his thank-offering to Augustus, Herod decided to institute a periodical festival on the lines of the Olympic Games. They were called "The Actian Games", and they were to be held on September 2nd, the anniversary of Actium, every five years. The first celebration thus fell in 27 B.C., the year after the events recorded in Chapter XIII. As a setting for the Festival, Herod had constructed the three buildings normally used for such celebrations, namely a hippodrome, a theatre, and an amphitheatre, for the games fell into three divisions: chariot-races, musical competitions, and athletic contests, which included gladiatorial shows—the traditional recreations of Greece and Rome combined.

Chariot-racing was not regarded as offensive by the majority of Jews, for the use of "chariots of iron" in warfare had been common military practice for centuries. Herod therefore saw no objection to building his hippodrome within the city, on a site between Siloam and what was then the Temple mount. It lies to-day between the south wall of the Temple area and the Dung Gate. Here were to be contested races between chariots drawn by two, three or even four pair of horses. The hippodrome was shaped like a very narrow U; and the chief thrill was provided by the sharp turn between the two legs, where it was considered legitimate to upset rivals by "boring" or squeezing them either into the middle wall or right off the track. So hot did the axles of the racers become, that grooms stood by the turning-point ready to throw water on them as they thundered by. It was a dangerous, but decent, sport.

The same could not always be said of the musical performances, which often contained items offensive to orthodox moralists. Herod therefore built his theatre right outside the walls of the city. Like all ancient theatres, it was designed for morning performances, and so the half-circle of tiered seats faced north, and the stage south, so that the light fell upon the actors, not into the eyes of the spectators. Herod built his theatre on a ridge 7 furlongs south of Jerusalem, called to-day Er-Ras, the head, on the south side of the Wadi Yasoul. It commands a wonderful view of the city and the Temple area.

The amphitheatre, in which the athletic contests and the gladiatorial shows were to be held, was built further away still. The exact site is unknown. Josephus tells us only that it was built "in the plain", meaning what is now called the *Baq'a*, the fairly flat region to the west of the railway-line just before it reaches Jerusalem. The amphitheatre was a circular arena, in which lions and other powerful or rare beasts were to fight with each other and with condemned criminals. There were also to be wrestling contests, in which the competitors would appear naked. To the circumcised Jews, and indeed to the Arabs, the exposure of the human body was, and still largely is, regarded as impious and subversive of decent conduct. The deliberate destruction of a son of man by a beast was an outrage. It was well that the amphitheatre was so distant: better had it never been built at all. It was lavishly decorated with imported fabrics and precious stones and metals. Inscriptions praising Augustus' victories were affixed to its walls and between them were erected gold and silver "trophies", that is shields, breastplates, helmets, swords and lances arranged in artistic groups.

It was these trophies that caused the trouble.

The Games were a great success. The lavish prizes had attracted the first artists and athletes of the day; and the foreign spectators were charmed and thrilled by the décor and the danger. But their pleasure only aggravated the indignation of the godly. They made a formal protest against the trophies, which they said were graven images. Herod asked them to meet him in the amphitheatre, where he had the trophies taken apart bit by bit, till only the bare poles that held them were left. Were wooden poles graven images? he asked. The assembly dissolved in laughter, which only increased the anger of the objectors. Ten of their number now formed a plot to assassinate the king as he entered the theatre. Fortunately one of Herod's detectives got wind of the conspiracy, and was able to warn him just in time. He was already on his way, but at once returned to the palace, and ordered the immediate arrest of the conspirators. They were rounded up, with their daggers beneath their cloaks. They made no attempt to deny their intention, claimed that their proposed regicide was an act of piety, and faced their awful end with the bravery of fanaticism. The detective was shortly afterwards seized by the mob, killed, torn limb from limb and thrown piecemeal to the dogs. Herod made more arrests, until some women, under torture, disclosed the ringleaders. They, and their entire families, were executed. There were no more plots.

Two years later in 25 B.C. not only Herod but the whole kingdom was threatened with disaster. The rains wholly failed, and so there was no harvest. The drought must have been exceptionally severe, for not only Palestine, but Syria too, where the normal rainfall is much more abundant, was ruined by it. There was no food to be had anywhere, nor any seed corn, and so the famine continued into a second year. Such slender reserves as the inhabitants had by them were soon exhausted, and they were reduced to eating herbs. Debility and pestilence followed. As all the sheep and goats had died, the people lacked not only food, but clothing as well, because there was no wool to make it from.

As Josephus remarks of this catastrophe, "It is a constant rule, that misfortunes are laid to the account of those that govern." It is: but it was just the sort of crisis that showed Herod at his brilliant best. The treasury was empty. Herod had already begun his lavish building programme, and now no one could pay any taxes. He therefore stripped his palace of its gold and silver fittings, and melted down the whole of his plate. The resulting bullion he sent to the prefect of Egypt, Petronius, whose friendship he had, with his usual foresight, already cultivated. It was easy now for him to ask a favour of the Roman which was that he would sell him corn, from the imperial granaries. As in the days of Jacob, relief came from Egypt.

Herod opened government food centres, from which his subjects could draw either corn, or, if they were too poor or ill to grind it and make their own bread, loaves already baked. There was also a distribution of clothing. In this way, their immediate necessities were relieved, and the famine overcome. But Herod realized that to restore normal life, it was necessary to restore the ruined agriculture of the region. This could only be done by replanting the devastated areas. He started with Syria, because it is more fertile than Palestine. He provided the farmers with seed; and then when it came to the harvest, he sent a land army of 50,000 workers, for whom he found the rations, into the country to reap it. From the new stock, he replenished the granaries of the farmers of Syria and Palestine alike; and distributed corn for current needs to the inhabitants of both countries 150,000 bushels abroad and 1,200,000 to his own people. It was a princely recompense. The crisis was over. There have been droughts in Palestine since those days; but none has ever been dealt with so swiftly and efficaciously. Herod was able to do it partly because he was so energetic and far-seeing, and through his flair for organization. But had he not been on terms of friendship with the Roman rulers both of Egypt and Syria, his plans would have come to naught.

His people were grateful to him: they realized that even if he was ruthless to those who opposed him, he was a thoughtful and generous father to those who did not.

While Herod was still occupied with the famine, he was assailed by an external threat of far more subtle danger. He conducted his economy and that of his kingdom on a lavish scale. Already he had begun the great building programme which we shall examine in the next chapters, besides maintaining a court which became, as he intended it to be, known far and wide for its splendour. He was able to disburse enormous sums. We have already seen how he always had the appropriate fee ready in cash for his Roman patrons. In the year 30, besides loading Octavian's soldiers with presents, he had given the prince himself the equivalent of nearly half a million sterling. He could find a dowry of £150,000 for the intended wedding of his eldest daughter to his brother Pheroras. His son Antipater received the same sum as travelling expenses when he visited Rome. Pheroras, besides the revenues of Trans-Jordan, had an annual allowance of £50,000. At his death, Herod was to make further enormous bequests. And yet, during his life, despite this prodigious expenditure, he was twice able to remit a portion of the annual taxation. He was never in debt.

Where did the money come from?

The annual ordinary revenue of the kingdom, derived from taxes (says Abel), could not have exceeded £500,000. It follows, therefore, that Herod had considerable sources of private revenue. His ancestors had evidently amassed some capital, because, even before he became king, Herod was able to meet large expenses. The palm and balsam groves of Jericho were also extremely lucrative. Later on, Augustus entrusted Herod with the exploitation of the Cyprus copper mines, of which he was permitted to retain half of the revenues. There were, too, the sheep-runs of Trans-Jordan, and the interest on the loans which he made to the king of the Nabataeans and the like. Taking all these sources into account, Abel estimates that the total annual revenues of Herod amounted to 2,115 talents, or £1,057,500 in current (1956) purchasing power. This, Abel adds, is only a seventh of the revenues of Egypt in the days of Ptolemy Philadelphus, as worked out by St. Jerome.

Herod must have had more money than that, and he can have acquired it from only one source, the Arabian trade. His mother was the daughter of one of the leading men of Petra, and as such must have inherited large commercial interests. Herod no doubt exploited and increased them. His control of the last link in the golden chain that bound Arabia to the Mediterranean enabled

The Temple of Bel, the best surviving example of an oriental *temenos* with *naos* within (p. 130). The Temple of Herod was built on the same general lines, and descended from the same original model, probably Babylonian.

JERUSALEM

An air-view from the south-east, showing the Temple Area, now the Haram-al-Sherif. Its development is described in Chapter XX. The Golden Gate is seen three-quarters along the east wall, moving north. The Double Gate is in the

him to do this. Throughout his life, Herod's relations with Petra were directed to maintaining his paramount influence there. At times he did it by diplomacy, but if that failed, as we have seen and shall see again, he instantly resorted to force rather than lose such a vital source of wealth.

Great therefore must have been his dismay, when he learned in the year 25 B.C. that Augustus had decided to conquer Arabia, and thus possess for himself the vast riches of the East that had hitherto flowed through Petra and Herod's own hands. The coming of Rome to Egypt had greatly increased sea-traffic in the Red Sea; nevertheless, such was the demand for luxuries in Rome that the trade of Petra still expanded. Augustus was not a banker's grandson for nothing. He realized that the drain of currency must in the end prove fatal, for the Arabians bought nothing from Rome in return. He also had heard all about Petra from his old tutor Athenodorus, who had been born there. Athenodorus also told the geographer Strabo, who tells us, that Augustus "determined to take them over or subdue them; and it counted for something that they had the reputation from all time of being very wealthy, disposing of their spices and the most valuable marble for silver and gold, and spending nothing of what they received upon outsiders. He hoped to enjoy them as rich friends or to conquer them as rich enemies. A further inducement was the attitude of the Nabataeans who were friendly, and promised full co-operation."

It was quite true that the king of the Nabataeans, 'Aboud, promised co-operation. But he was the man to promise anything to anyone who was strong. He was feckless and indolent. He left the management of affairs to his minister. And here Syllaeus enters the story. He was a handsome, capable rogue, of equal resource in the closet or the field. He was no friend of Herod, nor of Rome. He wanted to keep the control of Petra and its rich hinterland in his own hands. He therefore decided that come what might, the Roman expedition should not succeed. Fortunately for him, the Roman commander was a man of quite exceptional folly and gullibility, Aelius Gallus. Ironically enough, Syllaeus' intrigues played right into Herod's hands. He had to pretend that he was actively supporting the campaign. He did send a contingent of Jewish soldiers, but it was very small, only 500 strong. No doubt he was able to plead that the famine had so reduced the strength of his forces that he could not send more. This one battalion was large enough to observe all that went on, and to keep Herod informed, but too small for Herod to be blamed if the expedition was a failure. Syllaeus brought a camel corps of 1,000 and offered to be guide and quartermaster. The main army consisted of 10,000 infantry from Egypt.

Aelius Gallus would have been well advised to transport the whole army by sea from Berenice, the most southerly Egyptian harbour in the Red Sea, to the South Arabian coast direct, using his warships to secure his communications. But Syllaeus induced him instead to concentrate at Leuke Kome (*White Village*) the most southerly Nabataean port, on the eastern side of the Sea, and then to undertake a march of 900 miles over the desert which lay between him and the Yemenite capital. Aelius had built eighty warships before he realized that the enemy had no navy. He then constructed 130 transports, but he lost many of them with all hands, on the reefs, owing to faulty navigation, before he reached Leuke Kome. It was summer. The survivors were struck down by scurvy. They had perforce to winter there. In the following spring of 24 B.C., they started the march. Had the army followed the beaten track, over which, as Strabo says, the camel convoys moved constantly like an army, the journey should have taken two months. Syllaeus saw to it that it took six. He led them through the lands of a relative of his where they had to live on millet, dates and ghi. They finally reached Nejran. Their first encounter with the Arabs was successful; but Syllaeus managed to lead the army away to the south-east, and to set it down to besiege a desert fortress, probably Beihan, midway between Marib and Shabwa, on the very fringe of the rich spicelands. For six days they vainly assaulted the city, and then were forced to retire by lack of water. Two months brought the remnant back to Egypt. The expedition had been a complete failure.

Syllaeus was to be called to account fifteen years later. But much was to intervene before then, including the golden prime of Herod's reign. For the failure of the campaign had saved him, without alienating Rome, or causing a breach with Syllaeus.

Once again, Herod had snatched success out of danger.

Chapter XVIII

HEROD'S BUILDINGS (i)

JERUSALEM, JERICHO AND HERODIUM

WITH the possible exception of the Emperor Hadrian, Herod the Great was the most passionate builder of antiquity. It is by his buildings, their contemporary fame and the vestiges that yet survive, that he is most worthily remembered to-day.

His constructions fall into four categories or zones: Jerusalem, the rest of his kingdom, foreign countries, and finally, his greatest work, the Temple. The work went on methodically for twenty years, having been begun as soon as he was established as king in 37 B.C. The most productive period was the decade between his forty-sixth and fifty-sixth years, 27 to 17 B.C., though the Temple was not completed at his death, nor for many years after it, as we learn from the Gospel of St. John ii. 20.

When Herod and Sosius captured Jerusalem, Herod's first care was, as related in Chapter XV, to protect the Temple of the Lord from profanation; in fact he exhausted his private fortune to preserve it inviolate. His next object was to restore its defences. It was vulnerable only on the north, where the oval hill on which it stood was joined to the *massif* of Bezetha by a narrow neck of rock, through which a deep fosse had been cut. This fosse was guarded by a Tower called *Bira* in Hebrew or *Baris* in its Greek form. This tower had been ruined during the siege, though as we have seen it was able to shelter Antigonus until the moment of his surrender. It was very old, at least as old as the time of Nehemiah, when it was called the Tower of Hananeel. Later it had served as the residence of the high priestly rulers, for the theocratic strictness of the post-exilic restoration would not allow any earthly ruler, even a priestly one, to live within the precincts of the Temple, as the old kings had done. At first the High Priest found an inconvenient lodging on Mount Ophel, to the south of the Temple, until Simon the Maccabee moved up to the Bira. In it, he kept the ceremonial garments of the High Priest, which were worn only four times a year, at the feasts of Passover, Pentecost and Tabernacles, and on the Day of Atonement. Antiochus Epiphanes pulled down the Bira, and supplanted it with his own citadel of the Akra, on the north side of the Tyropaean. Alexandra the Queen Mother, being a woman, could not assume the pontificate, so she lived in a palace built on the site of the rival citadel or *Akra*, leaving the reconstructed Bira to Hyrcanus II, the High Priest. Herod also lived here when he first became king; but it had two disadvantages: it was overlooked from the higher ground on the west, which made it stuffy and insecure, and it contained his wife Mariamme's relations.

With his habitual flair for exploiting a situation, Herod decided to provide himself with a new palace, while at the same time rebuilding the Bira, the bulwark of the Temple and the residence of the High Priest. Since the Bira was a priestly dwelling, and the Idumaean was no priest, he could not live in the Bira itself; but he found an ingenious method of overcoming the difficulty. He pulled down the old, ruinous Bira, and rebuilt it on a new site 60 yards to the north. It could thus still serve as the High Priests' dwelling, and the sacred garments would still be kept there; but the palace of the secular monarch, namely himself, whom it was also to house, would not be in impious contiguity to the Holy Places. It would be connected with it only by two underground passages (of which traces still remain) and by two grand stairways. Both stairways have long since vanished; but the steps which lead to the "Antonia" minaret in the north-west angle of the Haram al Sherif still recall the site and function of one of them. The new castle was called Antonia, after Mark Antony.

The Antonia has analogies with the Tower of London. Like the Tower, it was to be a fortress, a palace and a prison. As the crowns and coronation regalia are kept in the Tower, so were the high-priestly vestments kept in the Antonia. As the Tower was built by a foreign Conqueror to ensure control of London, so was the Antonia built by a king who was a foreigner in the eyes of many of his subjects to ensure control of Jerusalem, for as Josephus says, "the Temple dominated the City, and the Antonia the Temple". Finally, even the outward aspect of the Antonia was like that of the original Norman Keep, or White Tower, for it was roughly four-square with a tower at each corner, three of them 75 feet high, and the fourth, at the south-east corner nearest to the Temple, over 100, so as to command a view of the whole of the precincts.

It was much larger than the White Tower. Its southern front was 375 feet long, almost exactly the same as Buckingham Palace. Inside, says Josephus, it was "like a town", with courts and porticoes and baths. The base of the edifice was protected and adorned by a glaçis of polished stone. It was Herod's first new building, and it was to set the tone for all the rest. It was a palace worthy to bear the name of Herod's friend and patron, Mark Antony; for when it was built, Antony's star still shone bright.

The Antonia contained the Gabbatha, the Pavement which formed Pilate's Hall of judgment, from which Christ was led forth to crucifixion (John xix). From one of the stairways of the Antonia, St. Paul made his great speech and apologia (Acts xxii). It is only of recent years that the site and nature of the building have been accurately determined. Within its ancient bounds now stand two convents, a school, a hospice, several streets and a number of dwellings—a catalogue which may help to indicate its huge original extent.

For a dozen years the Antonia served as Herod's chief palace. But events decided him to build another, twice as big and even more sumptuous, on the summit of the western hill, above the city, where the Jaffa Gate and the Citadel now stand. For one thing, he did not think it prudent to leave this dominating elevation in any hands but his: he remembered how his mother-in-law, Alexandra, had tried to seize it in the abortive *coup d'état* that had led to her death and how after he and Sosius had taken both the city walls, this fortress and the Temple had prolonged Antigonus' resistance; there had been a fort there for many centuries back. Secondly, strong as the Antonia was, it was shut in on the north and west by hills, and even to the south its view was limited by the high ground beyond the valley of Hinnom. It was impossible therefore to signal from the Antonia direct to any other of the chain of fortresses, a cardinal defect in what should be the very centre of the intelligence web. The higher ground of the summit commands a panorama, and signals can be sent and received to and from all points of the compass including such fortresses as Cypros, Herodium and Machaerus. There were, too, the associations of Antonia; it was here that Mariamme had lived and had been condemned, here that Herod had ranged half-demented calling out for her after her death. Nor was it suitable that Caesar's friend should continue to live in a place which bore the name of Caesar's defeated rival.

In the year 23, therefore, the new palace was begun. While it was building, Herod married his third wife. Six years earlier, Mariamme had gone to her death; and now a second Mariamme became his queen. She was the daughter of a priestly citizen of Jerusalem called Simon, who was himself the son of a very distinguished priest of Alexandria. His daughter Mariamme was reputed to be the most lovely woman of her time. Her beauty was much talked of, and reports of it came to the ears of Herod. He contrived to see her, and fell in love at first sight. He had no thoughts, Josephus is careful to point out, of anything but an honourable union with her, and yet her father was hardly of a station to warrant his becoming the father-in-law of the king. Herod solved the problem by dismissing the officiating High Priest—ever since the days of Ananel he had made it clear that he regarded the high priesthood as being in his own absolute gift— and appointed Simon in his place. He then married the new High Priest's daughter. It is generally believed that the Boethus who was the grandfather of Mariamme II was the founder of the Sadducean sect of the Boethusians. In that case, by allying himself with the family, Herod identified himself with some of the most active enemies of his opponents the Pharisees. It is typical of him that he should thus have combined love and policy.

The new Palace consisted of two sections. On the north side, that is on the site of the old castle, three splendid towers were constructed, called (from west to east) Hippicus, after a friend of that name who had fallen in battle, Phasael, after his brother who had died in the hands of the Parthians, and Mariamme after his wife. Josephus says it was named after Mariamme I, but it must surely have commemorated his new bride, at least in her own eyes, or at least equally. These towers stood on a scarp 30 feet high, and were themselves 128, 135 and 72 feet high. They were square and the bases consisted of solid cubes, fashioned of great stones so perfectly joined together that they appeared to be one block. Hippicus was 45 feet square at the base, Phasael 60 and Mariamme only 35. The upper parts were of rather smaller dimensions. Immediately above the foundations of Hippicus was a reservoir 35 feet deep to store rain-water, and then a two-storey building, surmounted by turreted battlements. The design of Phasael was similar, the lower storey contained a cloister and the second a bath and other fine rooms. It was so splendid that it looked like the Pharos, the famous lighthouse of Alexandria, only larger, says Josephus. (That the Pharos was a square tower of several storeys we now know from the representations of it in the mosaics at Jerash.) Mariamme, being named after a woman, was smaller, but more sumptuously furnished, and with greater variety.

To the south of the towers was the main palace, in which there were two great chambers called after Augustus and Agrippa. There were besides many other rooms, some of them big enough for 100 guests to sleep in at a time. The walls were encrusted with rare and costly marbles, the beams were of exceptional width, imported probably from Lebanon, and richly adorned. Exquisite paintings and sculptures delighted the eye, and the domestic appointments were of silver and gold. Outside, a series of porticoes, embellished with curiously carved pillars, surrounded green lawns and groves which were watered by deep canals and pools into which brazen spouts discharged their refreshing cascades. Above the watercourses were pigeon-houses, stocked with tame pigeons. It has been conjectured that these birds were not merely ornamental, but were in fact carrier-pigeons, the use of which was widely known in antiquity. They are twice mentioned in the Mishnah, on each occasion in a context which proves that they were not cage-birds. They were called "Herodian", after their breeder. The Mishnah also twice reprobates "pigeon-fliers", together with usurers and dice-players, which suggests that pigeons were used in matches on which bets were laid.

Of all this glory, little now remains. The palace was burned during the siege of Jerusalem in A.D. 70. Its ashes lie beneath the Citadel, the police barracks and the convent and gardens of the Armenian Patriarchate. When Titus had subdued the city, he left nothing of its ruins but the three towers of the palace, and of them, only the solid base of Phasael has survived. It now forms the lower courses of the so-called "Tower of David" in the Citadel, and even in decay it still dominates Jerusalem. Vestiges of Mariamme came to light in the courtyard of the Anglican Christ Church in 1901, and of Hippicus during the excavations which Mr. C. N. Johns made for the Palestine Government at intervals between 1937 and 1948.

Opposite to the palace, on the other verge of the upper reach of the valley of Hinnom, in the place now called Nikophorieh, Herod prepared a royal mausoleum. It was a hypogeum of four chambers, facing each other at the four cardinal points of the compass across a central vestibule. The exterior was decorated with columns and capitals, the interior lined with beautifully finished masonry. The door-way was closed with a rolling stone. How many of Herod's family were buried in this monument it is impossible to say. The tomb like every other in the land was rifled long ago, and only two empty sarcophagi were found in it when the hypogeum was discovered in 1891. During the war of 1939-45 it was prepared for use as an air-raid shelter. The sarcophagi have found an incongruous resting-place in a chapel on the roof of the Church of the Holy Sepulchre. One is 6 feet long inside, evidence, perhaps, of the stature of the Herodian family.

Like other Arabs who were to rule Palestine 700 years later, Herod longed for the wilderness as a retreat from the city. The desert fringe of Trans-Jordan is dotted with the hunting-lodges of the Omayyads. The most magnificent of them is the recently uncovered palace of Khirbet Mifjar, at the north-eastern limit of

Old Jericho. Its pillared courtyards, its pools, its luxurious baths, its glowing mosaics help the visitor to imagine how magnificent Herod's own Jericho must have been. He built his city 2 miles to the south of the Biblical Jericho, where the Wadi Qilt (*vallis cultus*, or cultivated valley) debouches on to the wide plain from the awful and desolate chasm which is the traditional Valley of the Shadow of Death. This gloomy recess is the only valley in Judaea which is abundantly supplied with springs, and it was no doubt that fact that determined Herod's choice of the site for his new city. The Hasmoneans had already erected a palace in the vicinity on the north side of the Wadi. Herod restored that, and on the south side, beneath his great new citadel of Cypros high on its hill-top, 800 feet above the plain, he built another, calling the two after Augustus and Agrippa. The valley was spanned by bridges and aqueducts of which traces remain. There are three main springs in the Wadi Qilt, and these, together with two more below Docus, were led to the site by aqueducts. After furnishing a piped supply for the palaces, and replenishing the great pools which adorned the extensive gardens and villas, these streams flowed on to nourish the famous date and balsam plantations. These had been so extended that they now stretched for a whole day's journey from north to south. Some idea of the abundance of the water supply may be gained from the fact that of the three springs in the Wadi Qilt one alone, the most westerly, now supplies 22,000 gallons every 24 hours to the city of Jerusalem. On the north side of the palace on the south bank of the stream, a terrace, nearly 200 yards long, was constructed, to furnish a shady walk. Its wall surface is varied by a succession of niches, alternately round-and square-headed, divided by clustered pilasters, with a hemicyclical, tiered water-garden in the middle of the range. The work, which is wholly of brick, is in the finest style of *opus reticulatum*.

Jericho being a sandy plain with no stone in the vicinity, brick has from neolithic times been the general building material. But Herod's brick-work is far finer than anything attempted there before or since. So fine is it, with its *opus reticulatum*, its colonnettes, its niches, its brick-terraced gardens, its rills and mirror-like basins, that it suggests Babylonian work. In the whole of Mesopotamia there is no stone whatever, and in consequence some of the finest brickwork the world has seen is the product of Babylonian and Iraqi bricklayers. Given the strong bonds between the Jewry of Babylon and Jerusalem, it is quite probable that Herod brought brickmakers and builders from Babylon. (In the twentieth century the compliment is being returned: the new royal palace at Baghdad is being built of stone quarried near Bethlehem.) In the present state of archaeological knowledge of this magnificent work—one of the finest of its kind in Asia—it is not possible to be dogmatic as to the date. It is at least possible that the terrace in its surviving form was part of the reconstruction of Jericho by Archelaus.

Herod's Jericho was completed by an amphitheatre, and a hippodrome, to the east of the old palace, from which it was separated by spacious gardens, and by a theatre and amphitheatre of which the vestiges may be traced in the northern skirts of the mountain on which Cypros stands. Twelve miles to the north, below the Alexandrium, Herod founded an agricultural settlement in memory of his brother Phasael wherein he planted a superior variety of date-palm which he called *Nicolaitan* (as one would to-day name a new rose or sweet pea) after his Secretary, Nicolaus. Vestiges of it remain to this day. So does the name—*Fusayil*—almost the only surviving oral relic of Herod and his family.

But Jericho was not remote enough for the solitary moods of an Arab monarch.

Herod had restored and re-equipped the fortresses, Alexandrium, Hyrcania, Machaerus and Masada. At Machaerus he had added a town below the castle. At Masada, he rebuilt the old castle, surrounded the mountain-top with a wall nearly a mile long, 20 feet high and 12 feet broad, with thirty-eight towers, over 70 feet high. In it he added a palace, of the pattern he had adopted for the Antonia, a quadrilateral with towers at the corners, which like his other palaces was richly furnished. The colonnades were supported by monoliths, and even in this waterless region, Herod contrived cisterns of such capacity that they were enough to supply baths. The excellence of his catchment system was shown when, from a single thunderstorm, it was able to collect enough water to avert the surrender of the large garrison (Chapter IX). The enormous stores of food and weapons he laid up in Masada, at the time when he thought that Cleopatra might persuade Antony to compel him to hand over his whole kingdom, were still intact when the Jews made their last desperate stand there against the Romans nearly 100 years later.

But mere restoration could not satisfy Herod. He decided that he would build an entirely new fortress, and would give it his own name. It need not, now that he was securely king, be so remote as Masada or Machaeras.

Seven and a half miles south-east of Jerusalem, and half that distance from Bethlehem, was the spot on which Herod had won the most critical battle of his life—when, as a fugitive from the Hasmoneans, he had turned on his pursuers and routed them

(Chapter VIII). Here there are twin hills, standing on high ground, and here Herod decided to construct his fortress. It was on the traditional conical plan; but the top of the cone and the glaçis were artificially produced, by removing the top of the eastern hill, and using the material to raise the height of the western one. On top of this, Herod built the standard four-towered castle, only, as the site was round, the castle was round too. As usual, one of the towers was larger than the other three. The top was reached by an ascent of 200 steps. At the base of the castle, Herod laid out a town, and although the place is in waterless land, gardens were provided, and ornamental pools, one of which had a little kiosk in the middle, like that in Hadrian's villa at Tivoli. The ruined bulk of the Herodium, as the new fortress-palace was called, still dominates the view to the south of Jerusalem. It is just a little higher than the Citadel of Jerusalem. The steps can still be descried, though their marble treads have long since gone, the glaçis is still there and the plan of the castle and the city can still be traced. The Herodium still looks gigantic, and inescapably sinister.

The water for this new creation was brought from Solomon's pools, just south of Bethlehem. Since the days of the Kings of Judah, there had been a reservoir here, from which an aqueduct had wound its way, along the hillsides to Jerusalem, taking 15 miles to cover the distance of five and a half. Herod drew upon this spring for his Herodium. But he had no wish to deprive Jerusalem of water, especially at a time when his sumptuous buildings called for an ever larger supply, not to mention the expanded services of the Temple. In Jerusalem itself, there is only one spring, the Virgin's fountain, which through the famous tunnel feeds the Pool of Siloam. For the rest, the city depended on cisterns and on open pools, supplied, like the fortresses, by conduits which collected rain-water. The only spring in the vicinity of Jerusalem from which water could flow to it—for the pump was unknown even to Greek and Roman engineers—was this one at Solomon's pools. In order to increase the supply to meet his needs, Herod constructed a further aqueduct, 15 miles long, to bring water from a spring, Arrub, just over 5 miles to the south of the reservoir, to which at the same time, he added two more pools. The total length of the extended aqueduct, was thus just over 30 miles, and it descended nearly 240 feet in the journey. This aqueduct of which extensive vestiges are still visible remained in use, with interruptions, until the early years of the present century. It supplied only the Temple, and the lower part of the city. It was useless therefore, as a source of water for the new Palace. Just how the water for this was obtained, we cannot be sure. That there was an aqueduct leading to it, Josephus tells us, and remains of a distribution system, though of a later date than Herod, have recently come to light. Moreover there are massive remains of a high-level aqueduct from the Pools, which by using syphons took a much shorter route. This has been traced as far as the vicinity of Herod's amphitheatre, but from there to the Birket Mamillah, from which the water flowed by gravity to the citadel the link is missing. It can however be said that the levels would permit of the supply coming in from that source.

Chapter XIX

HEROD'S BUILDINGS (ii)

SEBASTE, CAESAREA AND THE REST OF PALESTINE, SYRIA AND ASIA

TO restore and embellish Jerusalem, the ancient capital of the kings of Judah, was not enough for the new king of Judaea: he would refound also the long-deserted capital of the northern kingdom of Israel, Samaria, the city of Omri and of Ahab.

Samaria had not been an Israelite city for 700 years. It had seen many vicissitudes; it had been governed by Assyrians, Babylonians, Persians and, since the days of Alexander, Greeks. In the year 108 B.C., Hyrcanus I, with his two sons, Antigonus and Aristobulus, had entirely destroyed the city and done his best to obliterate its site. He had sold its inhabitants as slaves. Samaria was one of the cities that Pompey had restored to its former owners (Chapter IV) and Gabinius had rebuilt it as a small town, surrounded with a wall. In 30 B.C. Octavian had given it to Herod.

Herod had already established personal links with Samaria. Being Greek it had willingly lent itself as a base against the hated Hasmoneans; it had sheltered Herod's family, helped him with munitions, and had been the setting for his marriage with Mariamme I. Herod never forgot his friends. In the year 27, that is after he had built Antonia and the buildings for the Actian Games in Jerusalem, but not yet the Upper Palace, Herod undertook the restoration of Samaria. The task had, it is true, more than a sentimental attraction for him. The site was superb, both from the scenic and military points of view. And since it was a Greek city, it would give him the opportunity he needed—and which Judaea could never supply—of raising a worthy memorial to his benefactor, Augustus. This was being done by one city after another throughout the Roman world, and it was a shame that he, Augustus' chief friend, should lag behind.

First of all, a completely new circuit of walls was provided, two and a half miles long, with round towers at intervals. The chief gateway, protected by two towers which still impress the beholder, faced west, for it was from the west that its traffic came. In this city, which had been for so many centuries a stranger to Judaism, Herod felt himself free to give open expression to his veneration of the Emperor. He called the new foundation *Sebaste*, the Greek for Augusta, a name that in the Arabized form *Sebastiyeh*, it holds to this day. On the Hellenistic acropolis, above the débris of the ivory-plated halls of Omri and Ahab, a glistening temple in the Corinthian style was raised to Augustus, and at the foot of the twenty-four steps which led up to it, there was an altar before the effigy of Augustus himself. Water for the new city was syphoned across the valley from the copious springs of Naqura, to the east; the very same source as now furnishes a piped supply to *Sebastiyeh*; and there is a tradition still in the village of a second aqueduct from a more elevated spring near Nablus which would have supplied the Acropolis itself.

For some reason which it is not possible to understand, the whole town was largely remodelled about A.D. 200, and the columns and walls that are still visible over a wide area of the hill nearly all date from that epoch; but they enable us to form an idea of the grandeur of the Herodian city, with its temples, its theatre, its forum, its hippodrome, its shops, porticoes and streets. The acropolis is bare. Of the great white marble statue of the Patron, only the limbless and headless torso survives. It lies forlorn in the back yard of the Palestine Archaeological Museum.

With Jerusalem and Sebaste complete, the West might feel at home in the New Judaea. But the western visitor received a sorry welcome from the wind-swept reefs and shoals of Joppa. The new kingdom must have a port worthy of it. Since it did not exist, it must be created. In the year 22, the great work was begun. Midway between Joppa and Ptolemais, 24 miles north-west of Sebaste, there was a little anchorage called Strato's Tower. As at Sebaste, Herod would be able here to indulge his Greek tastes. The new harbour was called Caesarea, and like Sebaste it still keeps the name in its local form *Kaisarieh*.

Considered simply as an engineering feat, Caesarea was, with the sole exception of the Temple, the greatest of Herod's achievements. It took twelve years to build. The harbour was to be circular, and larger than the then haven of Peiraeus. It seemed impossible to some, but if Herod's friend Agrippa had created an artificial harbour in Italy why should not Herod create one at Strato's Tower? Enormous blocks of limestone, some 50 feet by 10 by 9, some even larger, were lowered into twenty fathoms of water. These formed a breakwater and quay, the seawall being raised as at Dover to protect the wharf buildings. It was 200 feet wide, and furnished with towers, the tallest of which was called

Drusus, after Augustus' stepson. Warehouses and lodgings for seamen were built in alcoves at the landward end of the great wall, and the quay itself provided a pleasant promenade. The entrance of the harbour (as of its modern successor at Haifa) was from the north, because the wind blows gentlest from that quarter. It was flanked by colossal statues, three on each side, those to the seaward side on a plinth, those to the landward side on a tower.

Above the harbour, as at Malta, was a town laid out on the "grid" plan that had been used at Alexandria. The port was dominated by a temple of Caesar, inside which were a colossal statue of Augustus copied from the Zeus at Olympia, and one of Rome, modelled on the Hera of Argos. There were of course, a theatre, amphitheatre and hippodrome. Water was brought from the hills, and a scientific drainage-system was installed. The inauguration of the city took place in 10 B.C., the twenty-eighth year of Herod's reign, with Games in honour of the Emperor which were to be repeated every fifth year. The decorations for the event included a gift of furniture sent by the Empress Livia herself. There were contests by day, and magnificent entertainments by night. It was Herod's most sumptuous public celebration. It was also, as it turned out, his last.

In 1884 when Laurence Oliphant visited Caesarea, "The old Roman wall could still be traced for a mile and a half, enclosing an area strewn with the remains of a theatre, hippodrome, temple, aqueducts and mole" but to-day only a few fallen columns remain to tell the tale of so much pride.

Throughout the kingdom, even in Syria itself, Herod was determined to display his talent for building and improving. In the south, the little seaside town of Anthedon, a Hellenistic creation, was rebuilt in honour once again of his friend, as Agrippias. Ascalon, 10 miles to the north, was a flourishing free city, an autonomous enclave. As suggested in Chapter I, Herod's great grandfather had come from Ascalon, for which reason he always showed it particular favour. Perhaps, too, because it was one of the regions in which the sweet camphire, the herb after which his mother was named, grew most abundantly. (Another of its products were the famous onions, known as Ascalots, or the shallots of our own day.) This city was embellished by Herod with baths, fountains and colonnades. He also had a residence here. Continuing north, we come to the one perpetual stream that flows from the hills of Judaea into the Mediterranean, just north of Jaffa. Here Herod constructed a town in honour of his father, and called it Antipatris. This foundation, being in the very highway of the Levant, up and down which every army must march, has long since disappeared; it was in ruins even in the fifth century. The Crusaders built a castle on the same site, called Le Toron des Fontaines Sourdes, the ruins of which still identify it. In Galilee, the provincial capital of Sepphoris, the town Herod had captured in a snowstorm, became a royal residence.

Gaba, on the east side of Carmel, just where the Plain of Esdraelon debouches, by the Kishon Valley, into the Bay of Acre, became one of his military colonies. It was peopled by cavalry veterans.

We now come to Herod's gifts to foreign towns. Ptolemais (Akko or Acre) where Herod had entertained Augustus on his first visit to Syria after Actium, was the first big city to the north outside his frontier. He presented it with a gymnasium. Being the athlete he was, it was a natural amenity for Herod to bestow. He similarly endowed both Damascus and Tripoli. Damascus was given a theatre as well, and so was Sidon. The walls of Byblos were restored at Herod's expense. Beirut and Tyre were particularly fortunate: he gave them assembly-rooms, temples, cloisters and market-places. Lattaqia was presented with a new water-supply. Antioch was enriched with a useful improvement. Despite the luxury of the former Seleucid capital, its main street, two and a half miles long, was unpaved and became a sea of mud and filth in the winter. Herod transformed it into a beautiful boulevard, the road-way paved with marble, and the pavements shaded with cloisters, like the main street of Jerash. Sometimes, Herod would present a city with a park, sometimes he would endow an athletic founda-tion, as for instance in the island of Cos.

What was Herod's object in thus adorning foreign cities? It was threefold. Partly, beyond question, he wished to indulge his taste for magnificence, and to receive from others that recognition of his favours which he gave so unstintingly to Augustus, but which his own people never gave to him. In Judaea, Herod could not even put his effigy on his coins, far less erect any sort of memorial which should redound to his personal glory. Not an inscription, not a statue, nothing might be erected to a human being, not even to so bountiful a ruler as Herod. To God only might glory and honour be ascribed.

In Greek cities, the embargo did not apply: here he could give his taste free rein, and he adequately thanked and praised for so doing. It was a frank and human ambition.

Herod's second motion arose from one of his best characteristics: his loyalty to his friends. The people of Rhodes like those of Samaria had shown him kindness when he was down and out. Now, in his prosperity, he sought to repay them. They had

127

provided him with a ship: he would provide them with the money to build other ships. Their temple of Apollo had been burned down: he would rebuild it, more splendid than before.

But Herod had another, equally laudable, aim in this munificence to Gentile cities. As we have seen, the question of the Temple money perpetually caused friction between the prosperous Jewish communities of the Dispersion and the Gentile cities which were their hosts. Herod recognized his obligations towards the Dispersion, no less than towards the Palestine Jewry. He was determined to do all in his power to support them, to make them popular, and to secure their rights. The charge of sycophancy sometimes brought against Herod collapses in the face of his outspoken championship of Jewish rights in the Gentile world. Of this aspect of Herod's policy, which was to have such far-reaching results, more will be said in a later chapter: it is too important to be treated merely in parenthesis.

This catalogue of Herod's magnificence is by no means complete; but it must already have begun to weary the reader. Let us turn then to his greatest and most pious achievement, the rebuilding of the Temple.

The Acropolis. For a comparison with Herod's Temple, see p. 131.

HEBRON

Surviving Herodian masonry in the Haram. The exterior of the Temple
was treated in the same way (p. 134).

Herodian masonry (left centre) incorporated in later Muslim construction. Note the massive stones, laid in alternate "header" and "stretcher" courses, and the extremely delicate batter at the corner, identical with that at the south-east corner of the Temple Area (p. 134).

JERUSALEM

Detail of Triple Gate (p. 131) from the outside, as it appears to-day.

Chapter XX

THE TEMPLE (i)

SITE, WALLS AND ENCLAVE

TO rebuild the Temple would be the crown of Herod's piety and splendour. The Temple of Jerusalem was, for the Jews, not only the hearth of their very life as a nation, but the most sacred place in the world, the gateway of the next: for here only might sacrifices be offered to the One God. Of old, there had been places of sacrifice in other centres; but since the introduction of the Deuteronomic legislation by King Josiah (about 630 B.C.) the Temple of Jerusalem was the sole legitimate sanctuary.

Its history was almost as old as that of Jewish Jerusalem. To atone for his sin in numbering the people, and in gratitude for the staying of the ensuing pestilence, David was directed by the prophet, Gad, to erect an altar unto the Lord on the threshing floor of Araunah the Jebusite (II Samuel xxiv). The threshing-floor would naturally be sited on the hill-top nearest the Jebusite city, where the wind would carry away the chaff. It was this rock, with the cave beneath it for the storing of the grain, similar in kind and site to so many others up and down Palestine, that became the altar of the Lord, and so the nucleus of a temple. Later it was identified with Mt. Moriah, on which Abraham was prevented from sacrificing his son Isaac. It is the same rock as we behold to-day beneath the Dome of the Rock.

The building of the first temple was undertaken by Solomon. Of its nature and extent we know but little, because it was destroyed by Nebuchadnezzar in 586 B.C. Seventy years later, after the return from the Exile, a restored Temple was dedicated, under the governorship of Zerubbabel. Some of the original materials may have been used; but the structure as a whole was a poor affair compared with the original (Haggai ii. 3). Nevertheless it was this makeshift building which was to last as long, probably, as its predecessor, far longer than its successor. In 168 B.C. it was desecrated and looted by Antiochus Epiphanes. Judas the Maccabee restored it three years later; it was damaged during Pompey's siege in 63; ten years later Crassus pillaged it; it had suffered further damage during the siege by Herod and Sosius. It was high time it was repaired. Herod's new Jerusalem was a wonderful creation; but it would be of little account in the eyes of either Jews of Gentiles, he thought, were the House of the Holy One to be left in ruin.

But it was no mere question of restoring one shrine, like a church or a mosque. The temple of the Semites, as it had developed over the centuries, was not a single building; it consisted of three separate components. First, there was a sacred area. This was, properly speaking, the temple, the Latin word *templum* from which we get our English word meaning, like the Greek *temenos*, "cut off", i.e. from secular use, and made holy, whence the word *hieron* was used as a synonym. Within this area was an altar, whereon offerings were sacrificed to the god. Thirdly, there was some holy symbol or object, a stone or an obelisk. Later, when men themselves began to live in houses, there was a house for the god to dwell in, called *naos* in Greek, *cella* in latin. The three elements are found in embryo in the earliest semitic temples—Byblos is a good example—and fully developed in the later ones, of which one of the finest and grandest now surviving is at Palmyra. This shows admirably the layout of a temple, with the *cella* in the middle of its area. The base of the altar is there, too, to the north-west of the *cella*.

In the course of time, the primitive enclosure had developed not only in size and grandeur, but also in many cases in strength as well. Temples contained such riches, that they needed strong walls to protect them. In Jerusalem, Antipater had taken particular care of this.

The exact bounds of the Temple as it was when Herod undertook his great reconstruction, we do not know—but archaeology has provided us with a general indication of what the site must have looked like before he began work. In its original form, the mountain of which Araunah's threshing-floor formed the rocky summit was shaped like half of a pear, cut in two from the stalk downwards, and then laid on a plate with the cut surface underneath. The fruit represents the rounded, rather oblong hill, with its broadest part towards the south, nearest Ophel and the old Jebusite city, the stalk gives an idea of the narrow neck which attached the hill to the general massif, the neck by which alone the hill could be assaulted, and to guard which first the Baris and later the Antonia had been built.

When Solomon built his temple, he also built a palace for himself, which is believed by the best authorities to have stood on the southern slope of the hill, and in the middle of it, between the sites of the later Double and Triple Gates. Gradually, no doubt, other buildings arose on the hill, and more walls were built to extend the area of it. But of one thing we can be certain, because Josephus expressly says so, that by the time Herod had finished work, the total area of the *hieron* was double what it had been when he started. What he had in fact proposed to himself to do was this: first, to restore the *cella* to the dimensions which the traditional scriptures ascribed to the Temple of Solomon, and secondly to make the Enclosure the largest artificial *temenos* in existence. These two aims seem at first sight disproportionate: why did not Herod make the actual shrine larger, and content himself with a smaller enclosure? The answer is twofold: first, the dimensions of the shrine were held to be sacrosanct; they must be those of the first, Solomonic, *cella*, which had been scrupulously observed in the post-Exilic Temple in all but the height, which was less than that of Solomon's shrine by 90 feet. Herod might, and did, announce as his purpose in rebuilding the Temple the restoration of the original dimensions. But alter or enlarge them he dare not. The second reason was that Herod was not of priestly family—indeed, some of his subjects scarcely counted him as a Jew, though in fact upon the correct interpretation of Deuteronomy xxiii. 8, he undoubtedly was, technically if not racially. Not being priestly, Herod could neither enter the inner courts of the Temple, nor could he take any part in the Temple services as a celebrant. To understand what this deprivation meant, it is necessary to realize that the qualifications for the priesthood were conferred by heredity and heredity alone. If a man was born of the seed of "the sons of Aaron", he was a priest, and as such had only to undergo the ceremony of consecration to belong to the Temple hierarchy. If he was not so descended, not all his piety nor wit could make him a priest. "The Priesthood" in Schurer's words "was therefore a fraternity fenced round with irremovable barriers, for they had been fixed for ever by natural descent." That being so, it was but natural that Herod should wish to magnify those portions of the Temple into which he, and all those like him, could have access. That is why he decided to make the outer enclosure of the Temple twice the size it had been before, and to adorn it with unprecedented magnificence. The area which he finally produced was 35 acres in extent. The dimensions of its four sides are: north 351 yards, south 309, east 518 and west 536. It is larger than the Acropolis at Athens, double its width, and its eastern wall more than 100 yards longer than the Acropolis' longitudinal axis. An equivalent area in London would be that enclosed by Pall Mall, St. James' Street, Jermyn Street, and Lower Regent Street.

It was a colossal conception; but before it could be undertaken there was opposition to be overcome. This was but natural, just as to-day the idea of pulling down the Church of the Holy Sepulchre in order to rebuild it meets with opposition, despite its ruinous state; conservatism and religion are old allies. In Herod's case there was also a suspicion among some of the priests that what he really wanted to do was to pull down the Temple of God, and put one of some pagan deity, or of the emperor, in its place; or that once the old Temple was gone, the vast plan would be abandoned ostensibly on the ground of expense.

Herod overcame these objections. He promised not to touch the existing structure until everything was ready for building the new one. A thousand carts were made, to transport the stone from the famous quarries on the north side of the city, and 10,000 expert masons were recruited from far and wide. To ensure that no profane hand touched the holy place, and also no doubt to conciliate the priesthood, 1,000 from among their number were trained as skilled stonecutters, carpenters and decorators. Herod issued them with priestly garments, a long narrow-sleeved cassock, like that which the Palestine peasant still wears, a turbaned skull-cap, a long girdle whose ends could be secured over the shoulders when working, and sandals, for no shoes were permitted on the holy ground.

By January of the year 19 B.C. all was ready and the great work began. In a year and a half, the new *cella* was finished, the portion which, with the altar, was essential for the Temple services. Eight years more went to the building of the courts and the outer enclosure. The final touches were not given until nearly three-quarters of a century later. Owing to the failure of a part of the foundations, some of the work done by the priests, which Herod's architects could not personally direct, collapsed in the reign of Nero, and it was only in the year A.D. 64 that the building was really finished.

It is hard even with the aid of air photographs, to give an idea of the enormous labour that Herod's plan entailed. To double the area of the esplanade, it was necessary to push the northern boundary back over 100 yards, digging away the living rock on the north-west, and filling in the deep valley which ran obliquely from the Antonia to the Golden Gate on the north-east. This brought the line right up to the base of the glaçis of the Antonia, which now, like its predecessor the Baris, dominated the Temple from its very verge. With typical sagacity, Herod, being unable on religious grounds to make his Antonia adjoin the Temple, had brought his Temple up to the Antonia. Due east of the Antonia, to compensate for the loss of security involved by the filling in of the valley, he constructed the great fosse which is known to-day as the Birket Isra'il. At the north-eastern corner, over against the Antonia, he built a corner tower, of which the lower courses still exist.

At the other end of the "pear", the labour was no less imposing. Here, it was a question not of scooping the rock away, but of building the ground up. This could be done only by constructing great retaining walls on the sides of the Kedron and Tyropoeon valleys.

As already noticed, some building had gone on in the region in the old days of the kings, but now it was completed by the raising of the great wall of which we still see the remains at the south-east corner of the Temple area. Until recently fourteen courses were visible above ground rising to a height of over 40 feet. While this book was being written, another seven courses have been laid bare. Beneath the soil and débris are hidden another fourteen courses. This corner of the Enclosure was supported on the extensive arcaded substructure which, in later reconstruction, exists to-day as "Solomon's Stables". There was a tower at the corner, too, raised high above the portico to be described later. It was the Pinnacle of the Temple mentioned in the story of the Temptation of Christ (Matt. iv. 5) and it stood 450 feet above the Kedron. Josephus says that it was so high above it that it was not possible to see the bottom of the valley. He makes the same observation about the view from Machaerus and from Masada, from which the inference is that he was near-sighted.

The south-west corner was similarly built up. Thus, round three sides of the whole area, and along that part of the north side which was not occupied by the Antonia, a continuous wall now ran, 1,140 yards in length. How was its surface to be rescued from a glaring monotony? The architect had thought of that. In order to see how he achieved variation, without any sacrifice of strength, we must examine the Haram at Hebron. Josephus does not mention this work among the buildings of Herod, either because his notes were deficient—he was writing in Rome, be it remembered —or because he had never seen it, or even because, after the behaviour of the Idumaeans during the siege and sack of Jerusalem in A.D. 70, he had no wish to glorify their city. But archaeological evidence points conclusively to the Herodian origin of the wall of the Hebron sanctuary. Each of the great stones was finished with a drafted margin and a light central boss. This in itself, while stressing the enormous size of the stones, and so of the strength of building, gives an air of variety to the total surface. In addition, the wall was divided into a number of bays, by the use of plain pilasters, jutting from the wall, whose shadows animate the intervening spaces, which are connected with the lower courses of the building by a sloping sill. At the top was a cornice with the same alternations. At the angles, each corner-stone is set back a few inches from the one below it, thus producing a hardly perceptible and very graceful batter. The whole composition had an air of simple majesty in keeping with its sacred nature. At Jerusalem, only two vestiges of this upper wall remain; but the almost perfectly preserved outer wall of the Hebron Haram gives us an idea of how the exterior of Herod's Temple looked.

We now pass to the interior of the Enclosure.

The photograph of the Temple of Bel at Palmyra, which in its surviving form is only a little later than that of Herod, shows clearly that the periphery of the *temenos* was adorned with a continuous portico. So it was at Jerusalem, only on a far larger scale. Those of the north, east and west sides were alike. Each of them consisted, as at Palmyra, of a double colonnade, which formed twin aisles, covered with a roof or a terrace, closed on the outer side by the main wall, into which the roof was joined, and open on the inner side. The porticoes were 45 feet wide, and the supporting pillars, gleaming white monoliths, nearly 30 feet high. On the north, the Antonia broke the line, and was connected with the porticoes to the south and east of it by two separate stairways. The eastern portico, known as the portico or porch of Solomon (Acts v. 12), was, in its central range at any rate, an older structure. It seems on this occasion to have been reconstructed to harmonize with the remainder.

On the south side, between the valleys of the Tyropoeon and the Kedron, the Temple area presents its most sublime aspect, seeming to ride upon the hill high above the green gardens of Siloam. It was this side therefore that Herod chose for his masterpiece. Above the ruins of the palace of the kings of Judah he erected a Royal Portico. It had three aisles instead of two, and was two storeys high. The two side aisles were 30 feet wide and nearly 50 feet high; the middle one half as wide again and double the height, the extra elevation being obtained by a second range of columns engaged in walls which rested on the architraves of the two inner rows of the lower colonnade. The whole edifice comprised 162 columns surmounted by Corinthian capitals. The roofs were of wood adorned with deeply carved sculptures (for since this part of the Enclosure was outside the Temple proper, the ban on the representation of figures did not, in Herod's estimation, apply to it). The central gallery of this great portico ended on the east side in the Tower of the Pinnacle, and on the west in a viaduct which carried its pavement across the Tyropoeon valley, and of which "Robinson's Arch" to-day represents the remains.

The colossal aspect of this Royal Portico is best conveyed in the words of Sir Charles Wilson, who in the late sixties of the last century made the first scientific examination of the Temple Area. In the record of his investigations, *The Recovery of Jerusalem*, page 9, he writes: "It is almost impossible to realize the effect which would be produced by a building longer and higher than York Cathedral, standing on a solid mass of masonry almost equal in height to the tallest of our church spires; and to this we must add the dazzling whiteness of stone fresh from the mason's hands."

Chapter XXI

THE TEMPLE (ii)

GATES, SHRINE AND LITURGY

UNDERNEATH the Royal Portico, or Basilica as it was also called, the wall of the Enclosure was pierced by two gates which gave access from the lower city on Mount Ophel, ascending to the level of the pavement by gently graded underground ramps. The western gate to the east of the Hippodrome, was double. Its threshold lay just above the master course of the wall, which here, on the back-bone of the ridge, rests on the rock itself. Much of this double gate has survived, and may still be seen beneath the Aqsa Mosque. It consists of twin bays which originally accommodated the doors, and behind them a vestibule, in the middle of which stands a great monolithic column, topped by a capital on which is carved a *calathos*, or basket, from which project leaves of rose and acanthus. This pillar provides an interesting test of the accuracy of one of Josephus' measurements. He says that the pillars of the portico were of such a size that three men could just join hands around them. This is exactly the girth of the pillar of the Double Gate. The lintels are of one single stone, also, and the ceiling is formed of flattened cupolas decorated in stucco. The whole composition, which recalls the style of the early Roman epoch, is one of the most important remains of Herodian architecture that we possess. It gives an impression of grace, confidence and strength in repose.

Forty yards further to the east was a triple gate, of which little remains except the ramp. The gate itself was completely remodelled at a later period. Only a portion of an engaged column in the west wall of the passage identifies the original builder for us. These two gates, being underground, were called by the Rabbis *Huldah*, which means "mole". Both of them also gave access to the vaults beneath the Temple, which were no doubt used as storehouses.

On the west side of the Temple there were four gates. One of them, known nowadays as "Barclay's Gate", is buried up to the relieving arch of the lintel, which may be descried at ground level just to the south of the "Wailing Wall". From inside we can

136

see the lintel itself, nearly 25 feet broad, made of five great stones beautifully compacted. Above it is the barrel of the original vault. This gate led down a flight of steps to the bottom of the Tyropean valley, which was then 70 feet lower. (In fact, the real *thalweg* of the Tyropean is another 30 feet deeper still, but it lies to the east of the line of the wall of Herod's enclosure, and so he simply built his south-west corner over it.) A hundred yards to the north of it was the Gate called Kiponos or Coponius, a strange name of which the meaning is obscure. Coponius himself was the first Procurator of Judaea, A.D. 6-8, after the banishment of Herod's son and successor, Archelaus. His brief tenure of the office was marked by a successful Samaritan attempt to defile the Temple. He would be the last man to be commemorated by a Gate in that same Temple. It may be connected with the Greek work *kepos* meaning a garden, but the connection is hard to see; because this gate led over a viaduct spanning the Tyropean like that from the Basilica to the south, and then straight up through the city to the New Palace. If the name did denote the way to the gardens, it must date from before the building of the Second Wall, when the region on the north of this gate was outside the walls. The arches of the viaduct, known as Wilson's Arch, (though there are at least seven of them) are still standing and still support the street which leads from the Citadel to the Bab al-Silsileh, or Gate of the Chain, which is the modern representative of the Gate Coponius. Still surviving also, is the vaulted underground passage, built into the viaduct below street level, by which troops could be sent into the Enclosure from the palace without being seen en route.

There were two other gates on this western side of the Temple, leading into the "suburbs", that is the area newly enclosed by the Second Wall, which would not be yet fully built over. The exact site of these gates is unknown.

On the north, there was one gate "which was not used". It was called *Tadi*, which means darkness. Its function had formerly been to act as an emergency exit for priests who might incur defilement while within the shrine. The extension of the Enclosure towards the north had carried the northern boundary of the *temenos* far beyond the original position of this gate; and for security reasons Herod had no intention of allowing any entrance to the Temple except under the eyes of the sentinels in Antonia. One gate there must be, for the sheep to be brought in by, for the sacrifices. The Sheep Gate, therefore, which is mentioned in John v. 2, was close to the fortress. The old name, however, still survives in one of the northern gates of the Haram, *Bab al'Atm*, the Gate of Darkness.

The eastern wall was pierced by one gate only, called that of

Shushan, from a representation of the famous palace which was carved over the doorway. This gate partly survives in the so-called Golden Gate of to-day. Like the other principal gates it was double, to allow of the easy passage of traffic in opposite directions. The gate has been reconstructed, but the elongation of its porch, and the division of it into bays, were originally occasioned no doubt by the necessity for fitting the Gate into the general scheme of "Solomon's Porch". Thus we have in this gate, which, like the Double and Triple Gates, has been blocked up since the end of the twelfth century, another vestige of Herod's Temple.

The great open space between the walls and the *hieron* proper had no particular name, because it had no particular function. It was paved with many coloured stones and served, as it still does, for rest and recreation, and to give scale and setting to the central buildings. By modern scholars, the space is known as the Court of the Gentiles, because everyone, without restriction of race or sex was admitted to it; but it had no such name when it was built.

The Jews called it "the mountain of the House", a far more expressive name, for there in the midst of the mountain stood the House itself. Those who approached it were left in no doubt as to whose House it was. All round the building ran a beautifully carved marble balustrade, breast-high, called the *Soreg*. It was pierced by four gates on the north, four on the south, one on the east and none on the west. At each gate stood a notice, engraved on stone in Latin and Greek, which said "Let no stranger come within the barrier and the court which surrounds the Temple. Every trespasser who is caught will be himself responsible for his ensuing death." Of these notices, one complete version and one fragmentary have been recovered.

From the gates, stairways of fourteen steps each led up to a platform, called the *Chel*, 15 feet wide, which ran round three sides of the *hieron*.

At last, we have reached the veritable Temple, itself. It was orientated to the East and stood up like a big, square fortress, about 500 feet long from west to east, and somewhat under 400 in width. The surrounding wall was 60 feet high outside. From the *Chel*, or first platform, a second ascent of five more steps led through gates in the great wall to the inner court. Each gate had a porch which was almost as high as the wall itself, flanked by massive columns. The leaves of the doors were of wood, covered with sheets of gold and silver. The Eastern Gate was larger than the eight side gates. Its enormous double doors were embellished with plaques of Corinthian bronze, whence it was known as the

Corinthian Gate. It was most probably the "gate which is called Beautiful" of Acts iii. 2.

The inner court was divided in two by a plain wall. The eastern portion was called the Court of the Women, not because it was reserved for the women exclusively, but because, in accordance with the immemorial custom of the East, which ordains that women shall be segregated from men during worship, women might not have access to the more holy precincts. In this court were the money-chests, each duly labelled, which received the offerings of the devout. In the angles of the court were chambers in which wine and oil were stored, and in which lepers and Nazarites performed their prescribed rites.

From this court, fifteen steps, arranged in a half-circle, led up to the court of the Priests, through a magnificent gate called the Gate of Nicanor, after the Alexandrian Jew who made it. Its double doors shone with gold plates. So famous was this work of art that when Nicanor's son died and was buried on the Mount of Olives, he was described on his ossuary as "the son of Nicanor the Alexandrian who made the doors". It took twenty men to open and shut them.

Immediately inside this gate was the court of Israel, accessible to every male Jew, priest or layman. Beyond it, and before the *naos* itself stood the altar, on either side of which was the court of the Priests. Thus, laymen might stand within sight of the altar, and take part in the services; but only the priests might actually approach it and the holy shrine which lay beyond. The altar was a great pile of unhewn stones, between 50 and 60 feet square, and 23 high, with "horns" of 18 inches at each corner. The officiating priest reached the top by means of a ramp without steps. This altar, the successor of the primitive rock-altar of Araunah's threshing-floor, stood on the *Sakhra*, which the Dome of the Rock now covers.

North of the altar were the requisites for sacrifice: rings to which the animals were fastened, tables for the flesh, fat and entrails, hooks for hanging up the pieces, a marble table for laying them out, and a silver table for the gold and silver vessels of the service. On the south was the great ablution laver. Sacrificial water was brought from the Pool of Siloam; but water for ablution and cleansing was furnished by the low-level aqueduct and by the vast storage cisterns holding upwards of ten million gallons which perform the same office to-day.

Finally, on the west of the altar, stood the temple itself, properly so-called, the *Hekal* or *naos*. It stood on a still higher terrace or plinth, and so was reached by yet another flight of twelve steps.

The porch was much larger than the body of the house, which led proud Jews to compare their Temple to a lion, with a great head surmounting a small body. It was 150 feet high and of the same width, the actual *naos* being only three-fifths as wide. Within the porch was a vestibule of nearly the same height from which a glimpse could be caught of the entrance to the Holy Place, the chief element of the Sanctuary. The entrance itself, little more than half as high as that in the porch, and more than 20 feet wide, had doors of precious metals, before which hung a Babylonian tapestry, embroidered with different coloured wools and representing a sort of map of the heavens. Above this door, a magnificent golden vine spread its tendrils and hung its bunches of grapes, which, to be seen at such a height, were as tall as a man. The Holy Place was 28 feet broad, twice as long and three times as high. Being surrounded with three storeys of chambers, it was dark, and the obscurity was increased by the smoke of the seven-branched candle-stick and the clouds that rose from the altar of incense above the table where the Shewbread was renewed. The farthest recess of the sanctuary was a room 28 feet square, separated from the rest by a veil. This was the Holy of Holies. In the days before the Exile, it had contained the Ark of the Covenant and the Mercy Seat. Now, it was completely empty. No one entered it, except the High Priest, once a year, on the Day of Atonement.

Above the sanctuary, or perhaps above the porch only, there was a large chamber in which a number of people could assemble. On its roof gilded spikes prevented the birds from settling and soiling the shrine. From afar, the golden façade glittered like the sun; and the whole monument, its white stones unweathered, shone like a mountain of snow.

Such was the fabulous setting which Herod had contrived for the worship of God. All that the Hellenism of the day could furnish of rare beauty and massive strength was dedicated to the Holy One of Israel. The inauguration coincided with the accession of the king, who offered a sacrifice of 300 oxen. That was in the summer of 18 B.C. The whole fabric was not completed until eight years later, and as we have seen the last touches were not given to the grandiose creation for another seventy-four years.

The new Temple added immensely to the prestige of the Jews and of their king among the Gentiles. Jerusalem became famous for its beauty. Tacitus would write of the wonderful aspect of its towered walls. Pliny would call it "by far the most famous city, not only of Judaea, but of the whole East". The rabbinical authors of the Mishna, too, would praise the Temple, and devote pages to declaring its glories in detail. But never by so much as a hint do they mention the man who built it for them.

Of the liturgy of the Temple, this is hardly the place to write other than briefly. The thousands of priests were divided into twenty-four "courses", which took it in turns to serve in the Temple week by week, a family being chosen for each day in the week, and the actual celebrants chosen from the family by lot (*cf.* Luke i. 8-10). The cleanliness and order of the Temple were the task of the Levites, who also provided some of the elaborate music.

Every morning, before sunrise, a lamb was sacrificed, while the silver trumpets rang out over the city. Every evening likewise. During the day many private persons would come to make the offerings prescribed for the various contingencies of human life and frailty. Not all these would be blood-offerings, but a great many were. The Temple therefore must have presented a strange mixture of splendour and squalor—the elaborate and beautiful ritual, the vestments, the jewels, the incense and the chants contrasting strangely with the blood, guts, flies and stench that must have hung continually over the great altar, despite the elaborate arrangements made for drainage and ablution. The flesh of the sacrifices, public and private, was the perquisite of the priests, who were able to distribute it to their families or sell it. Add the profits of those who changed money and those who sold the victims, and it will be seen that, quite apart from its religious importance, the Temple was an economic asset of the first importance.

By a pathetic irony, this dazzling memorial to Herod's piety was to be among the shortest-lived of his creations. Already, in the minds of many devout Jews, especially of the Dispersion, a more spiritual conception of Deity than of a god who delighted in the flesh of bulls and sheep was developing; already the synagogue, where instruction was given, the Law read, and prayer offered, had become the religious centre for thousands. Already in Jerusalem there were numbers of synagogues, one even in the Temple Enclosure itself. Soon, within those very courts, would be seen a Master who would proclaim the end of the old order, and the worship of God as Spirit, in spirit and in truth.

Less than fifty years later, the whole Temple would be consumed with fire. Not one stone would be left upon another. Soon, even Jews had forgotten what it had looked like, as we learn from the representation of it as a small Greek temple in the synagogue at Dura-Europos.

The sacred vessels and emblems, the Table of the Shewbread, the seven branched Candlestick and the Trumpets were carried to Rome, where in effigy they may still be seen on the Triumphal

Arch of Titus, by the Colosseum. In A.D. 455, Genseric, King of the Vandals, took the Golden Candlestick to Carthage, whence, in 533, Belisarius recovered it. Justinian returned it to Jerusalem, but nothing more is known of it. Presumably the Persians looted it when they sacked Jerusalem in 614. Later still, the site of the Temple, after lying desolate for more than 500 years, was cleansed and restored to the worship of the One God, by the Children of Ishmael, the race from which Herod himself had sprung.

Chapter XXII

HEYDAY

THE sixth decade of Herod's life, between the years 23 and 13 B.C., may be taken as the period of his greatest felicity. His country was at peace and prospering. After the ravages of the Hasmonean and Roman wars, during which many Palestinians had sought refuge in other countries, particularly Egypt, the population was increasing. The king planted new colonies, not only, as we have seen, on his frontiers, but in Samaria too. Following the Roman custom, he gave land to veterans. Sebaste received 6,000 soldiers, retired mercenaries, and near by there was a model settlement called the Five Villages, of which the Greek name Pente Komai survives still in its Arabic guise of Fandaqumia. The building of the new cities gave plenty of employment; and Herod's relations with the Roman government, particularly with the governors of Syria and Egypt, facilitated trade. The Nabataeans chafed at Herod's overlordship, but had to acquiesce in it.

Above all, Herod was the friend of Augustus and of Agrippa.

As good fortune would have it, he was to see both of them within his own frontiers and elsewhere, especially Agrippa. Herod and Agrippa had much in common. Both had climbed from obscurity to eminence, both had exceptional political talents, and both had a passion for building. Augustus' boast that he had found Rome a city of brick and had left it of marble would have been truer as a tribute to his friend Agrippa. For it was Agrippa who had embellished the city with splendid amenities—aqueducts, baths, porticoes, gardens; and like Herod, Agrippa built a temple, only his was dedicated to all the gods, the Pantheon, and unlike Herod's it still stands there in Rome, to astound and charm. Whether or not Agrippa found it prudent to leave Rome in order to abate the jealousy of his father-in-law, Marcellus, Augustus' sister's husband, and the mischief-making on the part of the empress, Livia, who may have resented Agrippa's influence with Augustus, certain it is that he set out for the Levant in 22 B.C., ostensibly to take over the governorship of Syria. In fact, he settled in Lesbos, making the town of Mytilene his headquarters. Here Herod paid him a visit that winter, to renew his friendship and to discuss politics. They had not met for nine years, not since Octavian's first visit to the East after Actium.

Herod, of course, was not the only visitor who made for Mytilene. The people of Gadara sent a deputation, which Agrippa refused to hear. They were Herod's subjects, and must understand that it was their duty and interest to obey him. So the deputation was arrested and sent back to Herod in chains.

Meanwhile the Nabataeans were causing trouble again. They had a grievance. As part of Octavian's post-Actium settlement (Chapter XIII), Zenodorus, it will be remembered, had been allowed to farm the principality of Chalcis, east of the Sea of Galilee. He was the heir of Lysanias, who had been so foolish as to side with the Parthians and Antigonus. Zenodorus was only tolerated, therefore, as a tenant on sufferance, not as a ruler by right. He could not or would not even keep order. The rich territory round Damascus was overrun with brigands, who found convenient bases in the basalt fastnesses of what is now the Jebel Druse. Zenodorus thought that he would help to pay his rent by making common cause with the brigands and taking a commission on their earnings. Naturally the Damascenes complained to Varro, the governor of Syria, who reported the matter to Caesar. Caesar ordered punitive measures, and gave the disturbed regions to Herod, on whose northern frontier they lay. Herod at once made an expedition into the country, tracked the robbers down to their lairs, and put an end to their depredations. That was in the same year as Agrippa went to Lesbos. Zenodorus, seeing how things were going, had offered to sell the Hauran to the Nabataeans for £25,000, and they, advised no doubt by Syllaeus, who thought that a *point d'appui* on Herod's northern flank would be a useful counter, had been so foolish as to buy it. They now complained that what they had bought had been given away by Augustus to their envied neighbour. They did everything they could to cause trouble. They raided, they ambushed and tried to get a hearing in the courts. They even tried to stir up a mutiny in the army. But it came to nothing: Herod was more than a match for them. He refused to be drawn into a formal dispute, because he knew that a "frontier war" was the one thing most calculated to antagonize Augustus. He was fair and firm, and gradually his wise measures bore fruit.

Agrippa's sojourn in the Aegean was but short. Augustus found that he could not do without him, and called him back to Rome. Maecaenas, the emperor's other close friend, had suggested a way out of the domestic difficulty: Marcellus was now dead, let Agrippa divorce Marcella, Augustus' niece, and marry Julia, Augustus' daughter instead. It would be Agrippa's third wife, it would involve a cruel divorce, but such matters never worried Augustus, if there was a political advantage to be obtained. So it was done. Julia was sixteen, and already once a widow. Agrippa was forty-three. It was an unequal match. Julia was to acquire a reputation for profligacy second only to that of the daughter she bore to Agrippa, known as the younger Julia.

Although Herod was thus deprived of the society of his friend, the next year he was honoured by that of Augustus himself during his visit to Syria. In the ten years since their last meeting, both had prospered; and each had done well by the other. This journey was to enhance the fame both of the Princeps and of his Client. Augustus had decided that the time had come to avenge the terrible wound of Carrhae (Chapter IV), and to recover the eagles and the prisoners, which the Parthians still retained. He therefore contrived to make Armenia his vassal, thus striking a shrewd blow at Parthian security. He had kept the son of their king Phraates as a hostage in Rome. He now sent him back demanding, in exchange, the prisoners and standards, and keeping a pretender, Tiridates, in Rome for use if necessary. Phraates returned the prisoners and the standards. It was a diplomatic triumph which Augustus, rightly, regarded as the greatest of his whole career. It was a theme of Roman poets for a generation.

Augustus was in a good mood when he met Herod at Antioch. Zenodorus, the king soon found, was still out for trouble. He induced the people of Gadara once again to lay complaints against Herod, thinking perhaps that Augustus would pay more attention to the representatives of a Greek colony. The Gadarenes were a stand-offish, native-hating lot, as is clear from Matthew viii. Their attitude was curiously like that of some modern colonial "whites". They thought it humiliating to be ruled by a local king: they wanted to come under the direct rule of the Roman governor of Syria. Zenodorus swore an oath that he would arrange it for them. He said that Herod was evidently afraid of them because when Agrippa had sent back the former accusers in chains to him, he had released them and let them go home. It was just the sort of situation Herod enjoyed: he listened calmly to the complaints because he foresaw the outcome. Augustus, at the end of the first day's hearing, gave Herod his hand, and made it quite clear that he was not going to listen either to the Gadarenes or to Zenodorus. Whereupon the deputation panicked and, realizing that they would not escape so lightly as they had the first time, committed suicide by various means. Zenodorus had a haemorrhage and died in Antioch. Augustus at once gave Herod the remainder of his possessions, which included the lovely country at the foot of Mt. Hermon and the source of the Jordan. It was on this occasion also that he was made one of the procurators of Syria, and the Roman governors enjoined to act always with his advice. Finally, Herod succeeded in convincing Augustus that a strong man was needed permanently in Trans-Jordan, and induced him to make his brother Pheroras Tetrarch of it. He escorted Augustus down to the sea, on his way back to Samos. As soon as he himself reached his new dominions, he set about building a white marble temple to Augustus at Panium (Banias) the hill above the grotto from which the Jordan issues. It was so fine that Herod's son Philip, when he became Tetrarch of Galilee after his father's death, put it on his coins. From the temple of Sia' in the Hauran has been recovered the base of a statue the inscription on which refers to "King Herod Lord", a testimony of his authority in his new realm.

It was now time for Herod to pay a state visit to Rome. He had been there once before, as a refugee. That was in 40 B.C., twenty-two years ago. Things were very different now. He must have kept up fairly close relations with the Roman court, and with leading Romans, of whom he had met so many in his career. His three sons by Mariamme I had been sent to Rome to complete their education. Augustus showed them marked favours and they lived with Asinius Pollio, one of the leading critics and men of letters of the capital and the first to found a public library. Pollio, Josephus tells us, was a particular friend of Herod's. It was to Pollio that Virgil had dedicated his famous *Fourth Eclogue*, a poem which tells of the advent of a wonderful child whose birth would usher in a new age of felicity. When Christianity became the state religion of Rome, it was believed—and the view was supported by Constantine the Great and St. Jerome—that Virgil had in this Eclogue prophesied the birth of Christ, which led to Virgil's being ranked with the Jewish prophets by the medieval church. It is at least possible that the theme of this poem owes something to Jewish ideas. The poem had been written some twenty years before but Pollio's friendship with the king of Judaea and his kindness to his sons may not be irrelevant to the discussion of its origin. May not Virgil, impressed by the Jewish prophet, have dedicated the resultant poem to a friend whom he knew to be sympathetic to things Jewish? Virgil had died the year before Herod's second visit to Rome; but he may well have met Horace, who in an Epistle published shortly afterwards, makes a reference to Herod's Jericho plantations, though he seems to have confused the palms with the balsam groves.

Augustus now gave Herod a distinguished reception and allowed him to take back with him his two elder sons, Alexander and Aristobulus. The youngest had died in Rome. Later, many people must have counted him fortunate to have done so.

During this visit to Rome, Herod did not see Agrippa, who had been absent in Gaul and Spain; but three years later, to his great joy, his old friend was back in the East. Herod went to meet him in Asia Minor, and invited him to tour Palestine. He had no misgivings now about the reception that Agrippa would have. For one thing, Agrippa had always shown himself a friend of the Jews: his name was even inscribed on one of the doors of the new Temple, though not everyone approved of that. For another, Herod had now established internal security beyond question, and a great many did not like that, either. Augustus had given him the rare privilege of demanding the extradition of Palestinian criminals who sought asylum beyond his frontiers; and Herod from his side had enacted a law by which housebreakers could be sold into slavery abroad. This drastic innovation gave great offence to national sentiment, to which it was repugnant that any son of Israel, even a bad one, should be subject to foreigners. There were, too, secret arrests and investigations in Hyrcania. Public assemblies were banned, and informers flourished. The régime was harsh for those who wished to change it. Many did; for the old Hasmonean spirit was still alive; and a feeling was somehow growing among many of all classes that a Messiah would shortly appear, who would restore the temporal and secular Judaean monarchy. For such dreamers, as for less exalted intriguers, Herod's government was no blessing. For the ordinary peasant, the merchant and the citizenry in general, it was an unprecedented dispensation of peace, prosperity and honour at home and abroad.

With Augustus, Herod was on terms of friendship, but not of intimacy. Augustus was master of the world and of those who lived in it, including Herod himself. Besides, Augustus was by temperament cold, almost impersonal in his dealings with other men. To an Arab, to whom personal relations are the only relations which count, Augustus could never be close. Agrippa was far more congenial. He lacked Antony's raffish bonhomie; but Herod was now middle-aged, and sought in his friends more reputable attractions. These he found in the character of Agrippa. Agrippa, as his portraits and his acts have delineated him for us, was, in his day, "the noblest Roman of them all". He had great talents, great strength of character, great virtues. He was a brilliant commander, a wise and energetic civil administrator. He was now the son-in-law of the Princeps, his heir, in the eyes of men: when, in 23,

Augustus had seemed to be on his death-bed, was it not to Agrippa that he had handed his signet-ring? To these attractions, Agrippa added a receptive and comprehending sympathy, which enabled him to work in harmony with men of other races. He was the ideal vicegerent for Asia Minor and the Levant, and it was to that region that he was sent back by Augustus in 15.

Augustus had slighted Athens. Agrippa tactfully righted the mistake by making it his first goal. Then, by way of the Thracian Chersonese or Dardanelles which was now his property, he reached Asia Minor. Herod lost no time in going to him there, and inviting him to visit Judaea. Agrippa, quite apart from his liking for Herod, saw an opportunity for engaging the goodwill of the Jews, for whom Augustus had shown little love. Despite his gout, he went through all the rigours of a state visit. A round of banquets and receptions was organized, the new cities of Caesarea and Sebaste were inspected, and the itinerary included even the remote western castles, Alexandrium, Herodium, the grim Hyrcania itself. Finally, he made a triumphal entry into Jerusalem, whose inhabitants, not for the last time, turned out in all their best array to give a rapturous welcome to an influential newcomer.

Agrippa was lodged in the great chambers of the new Palace, one of which bore his own name.

To show his appreciation, he provided banquets for the citizens, and offered a sacrifice of 100 oxen in the new Temple. He stayed some time in Jerusalem, and would willingly have stayed longer; but the autumn was far spent and he had to return to Asia Minor, and knew that it was not safe to sail there in the winter. Herod loaded him and his staff with gifts, and bade him farewell.

The visit had been a complete success. Here, in the reputed stronghold of anti-Roman intransigeance, Caesar's son-in-law and Deputy had been royally received. Agrippa's tact and goodwill had no doubt played a large part in this triumph. But Herod's ability, and the charm which he could still exert must have contributed to it.

The two friends were not long parted.

Of Palestine Jewry, Agrippa could now be counted the firm and powerful friend. Herod intended that he should prove equally favourable to the Jews of the Dispersion, whose protector, as we have seen (Chapter XIII), Herod considered himself. During the winter, which Herod spent in Palestine, he heard that Agrippa intended to make an expedition in the spring into the Black Sea. Herod decided to join him. He set sail for Rhodes, pressed on up the coast, past Cos, to Lesbos, where he intended to meet Agrippa. Unfortunately before he could make the land a strong northerly wind sprang up, which blew him back to Chios. He was storm-bound here for a considerable period, and spent the time in arranging for the complete restoration of the principal colonnade of the island's chief town, which had been damaged in the Mithridatic wars and never rebuilt. Herod found the necessary funds, and more also.

When the storm was over, he sailed north again; but by the time he reached Mitylene, Agrippa had already left. Herod followed him to Byzantium, where he heard that the imperial fleet had entered the Black Sea. Herod finally came up with them at Sinope, (*Sinub*) on the north shore of what is now Turkey, the only safe harbour between the Bosphorus and Batum. The sailors were delighted at the sight of this wholly unexpected reinforcement in these remote and unknown waters. So was Agrippa. That Herod should have left his own country, and sailed more than 1,000 miles to come to help him, at a time when he needed just the kind of help that Herod could give, touched him, and made him fonder than ever of the king. Josephus says of this occasion "Herod was all in all to Agrippa, in the management of the war, and a great assistant in civil affairs, and in giving him counsel as to private matters. He was also a pleasant companion for him when he relaxed himself, and a joint partaker with him in all things; in troubles because of his kindness; and in prosperity, because of the respect Agrippa had for him."

The war concerned the throne of the Cimmerrian Bosphorus, or Crimea, on the shores of the Sea of Azov. It had been seized by a usurper, and the object of Agrippa's expedition was to expel him and to instal in his place Polemon I, the king of Cappadocia, a region of high strategic importance, because it was the only barrier between the Parthians and the Black Sea. The campaign was a success; and the Senate offered Agrippa a triumph. He declined it. He had work to do in Asia: he was an ailing man, and might not have long to do it in. Leaving the fleet, there-fore, to sail back through the Dardanelles and await them at Ephesus, Agrippa and Herod set out overland. At each city they visited, Herod ingratiated himself with the populace, both by his personal donations and by his intervention with Agrippa on behalf of those who had grievances to lay before him. At Ilium (Troy), Herod was able to reconcile the citizens to the Government, with whom they had been at loggerheads. The Chians, remembering the ill wind which had recently blown them so much good, sent a deputation to discuss the matter of their arrears of taxation. Herod found the money. By the time the progress reached Ephesus, the reputation of the two friends was at its zenith throughout the whole of Asia Minor. They crossed to Lesbos, and set up their headquarters once more at Mitylene.

The Jews of the country now called a congress, and decided to enlist Herod's support in obtaining from Agrippa the redress of their grievances. The chief among them were three. First, there was the question of the Temple tribute (Chapter XV). Secondly, the Jews complained that they were being conscripted into the army, which meant that they were bound to transgress their dietary laws, and to work on the Sabbath. Thirdly, they were liable to be summoned to appear in the law courts on the Sabbath. All these abuses were infringements of immunities which had long been guaranteed to them by the Romans. Herod was determined to see justice done. He asked Agrippa to hold an official investigation, and appointed Nicolaus of Damascus to represent the Jewish case. Agrippa thereupon summoned an influential committee of the leading Romans of the region, and other notables to go into the matter.

Nicolaus made a long speech, in which, after explaining the main tenets of the Jewish religion, he recalled the many occasions on which it had been recognized by senatorial decree, paid a flattering tribute to Herod, not forgetting his father Antipater and the loyalty of both of them to Rome, and ended with a graceful encomium of Agrippa, and the excellent impression he had made on the Jews of Palestine. The Greeks who had urged their governors to treat the Jews like the rest of the inhabitants could find little to say in reply, except that "the Jews by the mere fact of living in their country committed an injustice".

Agrippa, having heard both sides announced that he was satisfied that the Jews were asking no more than that they should enjoy rights which had been given to them in days gone by, and he accordingly confirmed them (written decrees followed in due course). If they asked any further favours, he would be ready to grant them, he said, so long as they did not infringe the Roman authority. He declared the proceedings closed. Herod made a speech of thanks, and Agrippa saluted and embraced him. The Christian Church, in its vigorous infancy, was the direct beneficiary of Herod's efforts on behalf of the Jews of Asia, as may be gathered, for example, from I Corinthians xvi. 3.

It had been a wonderful year for them both, crowned by unbroken success in both war and policy. Each well knew how much he owed to the other in its achievement. Agrippa left Lesbos early in the spring of 13 for Italy. Herod made a swift passage back to Caesarea.

When he returned to Jerusalem, he summoned a general

assembly of the people, and gave them a detailed account of his voyage, stressing the advantages he had been able to secure for the Jews of Asia. Then, that his own subjects should share in the general felicity, he announced that he had decided to remit a quarter of their taxes for the year.

It was a happy day for king and people, the result of Herod's happy association with Agrippa.

They met only once more. Agrippa died next spring and with him died Herod's fortune.

Chapter XXIII

LAST YEARS—THE NABATAEANS

IT had been well for Herod, his family and his reputation had he died ten years before he did; for the last decade of his life, from 14 B.C. to 4 B.C., from his sixtieth to his seventieth year, was darkened by failure, disease and crime.

No one is so lonely as a despot. Against the absolute corruption of absolute power, he has no defence: no friend to counsel him, no peers to restrain or warn. Herod's mother was dead—Josephus does not tell us when she died, but it is a reasonable assumption that the fortress above Jericho was, like Hippicus, Phasael and Mariamme, a posthumous memorial. Of his siblings, only Pheroras and Salome remained. Pheroras, despite Herod's generosity to him, was jealous of his more brilliant brother. Salome was ruinously faithful to him.

In marriage, Herod was consistently unfortunate. Doris, Mariamme the first, and Mariamme the second, each was to contribute to his undoing. He had seven other wives, as the law allowed him, but none of them seems to have been of outstanding character, certainly not strong enough to counter Salome, Doris or Mariamme II. His children, as we shall see, were no comfort to him. Herod was completely alone, except for his evil sister. Had Agrippa lived, the story would have been different.

Or if Herod had died; but he was physically extremely tough. Even in his sixties, he still hunted, still, even, led his army in the field. It was not until his terrible disease, arterio-sclerosis (see Note II), had almost dissolved his very flesh, and had quite undermined his reason, that he gave up the ghost.

However we look at them, Herod's last ten years were tragic; but Josephus has made them seem more repulsive than they were. He devotes a disproportionate amount of space to them, both in the *War* and in the *Histories*, more than a third of the total he gives to Herod, and that, as we have seen, (Introduction) was one-sixth of his whole history. What was Josephus' object in dwelling on Herod's decline? We must remember for whom he was writing. As he himself tells us, Titus, the future Emperor, took a personal interest in the *War*. He was to all intents and purposes, its censor. Josephus had to be most careful to write nothing that might offend Rome or its masters. At the same time, Josephus was writing for Titus' Jewish mistress, Berenice. Berenice was the granddaughter of Herod's second son by Mariamme I, Aristobulus. She was a Hasmonean, and longed for posthumous revenge on Herod, who had killed her grandfather, great-grandmother, great-greatuncle and great-great-grandfather. Josephus, too, was related to the Hasmoneans. Herod's public career, which had been devoted to the Roman interest, he dare not attack; instead, he would blacken his private life. The material was there, Josephus had only to exploit it. The general public, then as now, loved nothing more than scandal, the story of the follies and misfortunes of others. Josephus gave them what they wanted, page after page of it, detail after dirty detail. What had succeeded in the *War* was expanded in the later *Archaeology*. Herod's biographer would gladly omit the repulsive recital; but it was a part of Herod's life, and as such it must be told; only it will be less irksome for the reader of a tale that is already long, if the skein is untangled, and its volume compressed.

First, then let us deal with the external circumstances of Herod's decline.

Successful as he had been with Rome, and even with his own people, Herod had never achieved satisfactory relations with his Arab neighbours. They were of course jealous of him. The fact that his grandfather had been a Nabataean noble, that he himself controlled the outlets of so much of Petra's trade was enough to irk them. But Herod had encroached upon their territory, for not only the Hauran, but Pheroras' tetrarchy of Peraea, had formerly belonged to the Nabataeans: their attempt to recover the Hauran has been recorded in the last chapter. Moreover Herod had beaten the Arabs in battle, and had hung trophies of his campaign, together with those of former Jewish victories, on the wall of his new Temple.

It was after this victory, in the year 31, that Herod had been hailed by the defeated Arabs as their overlord. But in the very next year the feeble Malik had been succeeded by 'Aboud III, whose all-powerful vizir Syllaeus was so soon to show, in Gallus' Arabian campaign, the stuff he was made of.

In the year 20, Syllaeus came to Jerusalem, probably to negotiate a loan of £30,000 of which his king found himself in need. He improved the occasion to make advances to Salome, now twice widowed and in her hungry forties. Someone told the king. At the next dinner party, he watched them: it was only too true, Salome was evidently taken by the lusty young Arab. Syllaeus, not wishing to appear precipitate, went back to Petra; but came over again two or three months later, on the pretext of the loan, and formally asked Herod for leave to marry Salome. Salome urged him to agree; she even wrote to the Empress asking for her support. Her brother Pheroras, the Tetrarch of Peraea, was naturally opposed to a match which was bound to compromise his authority. On reflection, Herod decided against it. He was not deceived by Syllaeus' argument that it would be to his political advantage: on the contrary, he saw clearly that Syllaeus intended to exploit the union for his own dynastic ambition. But he must not offend the Empress. He therefore artfully said that he could agree only on condition that Syllaeus became a Jew, to which Syllaeus brusquely replied that his people would stone him if he did. He retired to Petra, rebuffed and revengeful.

He had to wait eight years to show his spite. In 12 B.C., in circumstances which will shortly be related, Herod made his third and last visit to Rome. While he was away, the brigands of Trachonitis decided to revolt. Herod had made them take to farming, which they detested, and he had planted among them a military colony of Babylonian Jews, skilled archers, to keep them in order. Altogether they felt oppressed. They now spread a rumour that Herod was dead, and took to robbery again. Herod's generals soon overcame them, but forty of the leaders made for Trans-Jordan, where Syllaeus welcomed them with open arms, and provided them with a base from which to raid Palestine. As soon as Herod came back, despite his sixty-two years, he took the field in person, marched into the Jebel Druse, where, being unable to catch the brigands themselves, he killed their families. The law of the desert demanded blood for blood, and Palestine was exposed to loot and pillage. Herod now formally demanded of 'Aboud the repayment of the loan and the extradition of the brigands, for Trachonitis was part of Herod's kingdom, and the brigands were his subjects. He was careful to obtain the support of Saturninus the Governor of Syria, and of Volumnius the Chief of Staff there in taking this action, because he did not intend that there should be any doubt as to what the consequences must be if 'Aboud refused to comply with his ultimatum.

At first Syllaeus, who was now in complete control at Petra, temporized. He denied that any of the brigands were within his frontiers, and deferred the payment of the loan. Herod appealed to Saturninus and Volumnius, who ordered Syllaeus to refund the money, and, to save his face, arranged a "mutual extradition of offenders", though there was not one Nabataean absconded offender in Herod's kingdom.

Syllaeus disregarded both Herod and the Roman governor, and made off to Rome.

On his way there (it was now the year 10) he called at Miletus, and in the shrine of Apollo of Delphi, dedicated a votive tablet, in Latin and Greek, to Jupiter Dusares "for the safety of King 'Aboud" describing himself as "Syllaeus the brother of the king" —a pleasant little irony from an intended usurper and regicide.

When the day for payment had come and gone, Herod obtained permission from Saturninus and Volumnius to execute what was after all Saturninus' own judgment. Once again, and for the last time, Herod placed himself at the head of his army. He showed no signs of age, nor of the awful disease that was to kill him. With all his old panache he covered a seven days' journey in three, swept up to Raepta, or *Qal'at al Rabad*, the great castle which in its Saracen form still commands 'Ajlun, north of Jerash, captured the brigands there and destroyed the castle. He attacked no one else. But a Nabataean commander called Naqib intervened in an attempt to rescue the robbers. In his own defence Herod was forced to give battle. It was soon over; Naqib and about a score of his men were killed and the rest ran away. Herod's casualties were even smaller. The whole affair was little more than a skirmish. Herod put a garrison of 3,000 Idumaeans in Trachonitis and went home to Jerusalem, whence he sent a full report of the expedition to Saturninus.

Messengers posted from Petra to Rome to let Syllaeus know what had happened. He decided to turn it to account. He had already insinuated himself into Augustus' good graces, and was often seen in the palace. He now appeared in black. With tears in his eyes he told Caesar that Arabia was ravaged with war, that poor King 'Aboud had been insulted, that 2,500 of the leading citizens had been slaughtered by Herod, including his dear friend and cousin Naqib, and that Herod had pillaged the treasury of Raepta. He ended by saying that the only reason he had left the kingdom was to secure from Caesar that they should all live at peace.

Augustus, who ought to have known better, fell for this story. Without making any further inquiry, he asked one question and one only, both of his own officers who had come from Syria, and of those whom Herod had sent: had Herod led an army into Arabia or had he not? They were of course bound to say that he had. Augustus was furious. Just when he was about to dedicate the great *Ara Pacis*, the Altar of Peace, to celebrate the unbroken tranquillity of the whole empire, his friend Herod must needs go and do this. He would show him who was master: he dashed off a boorish letter to Herod, telling him that whereas hitherto he had treated him as a friend, he would now treat him as a servant.

The results of this intemperate folly were soon visible. Syllaeus of course gleefully informed the Nabataeans of Herod's fall from favour. They were so elevated by the news that they refused to extradite the remaining robbers, or to refund the debt, or even to pay the rent of the pastures they hired from Herod's subjects. The brigands of Trachonitis rose against the Idumaean garrison, and took to pillaging as before. Herod tried to explain matters to Augustus, and sent two embassies to Rome for the purpose. Augustus refused to hear either of them. The disorders in the north and beyond the Jordan went on unchecked, while Syllaeus basked in the imperial favour. At this very time, 'Aboud III died, and his brother Aeneas assumed the diadem as Harith IV, without seeking Caesar's approval. Syllaeus was delighted: already he saw Harith deposed and himself as king of the Nabataeans, Caesar's favourite, able at last to get even with the discredited Herod. But things turned out otherwise. Harith was a man of very different stamp from his brother. He sent an embassy with a letter to Augustus, bearing presents, including a costly golden crown, announcing his accession, and denouncing Syllaeus as a thief and a debauchee, who had had his former master Aboud poisoned. Still the infatuated Princeps refused to listen. He sent back the embassy and the presents.

Herod bore the situation with the fortitude he had so often shown in adversity. That his own dominions remained loyal to him is the surest proof that the majority of his subjects recognized the benefits which he had given them. Nevertheless things could not drag on like this indefinitely. Had Agrippa been alive, he would no doubt have been able to convince Augustus of the truth. Failing him, Herod bethought him once again of Nicolaus of Damascus. This subtle and eloquent Greek was well known in Rome, and he was further to ingratiate himself with Augustus by writing his biography. When he reached Rome, he found that the Nabataeans had split into two factions, and that one group wanted to bring Syllaeus to trial before Caesar. Nicolaus undertook to be their counsel. When the case was called, Nicolaus said no word about Herod, which he knew would be a tactical mistake, but contrived to build up a damning chain of proof against Syllaeus, supported by letters and other testimony, showing that he was just what Harith had said he was. To crown his iniquities he had alienated Augustus from Herod. Here Augustus interrupted Nicolaus, and asked him to tell him the truth about the campaign beyond Jordan. This was exactly the opening that Nicolaus had been leading up to. He gave Augustus a detailed account of the whole affair, and exposed the complete falsity of Syllaeus' version.

Finally he contrived to show that he had offended Caesar's personal honour, because when he was at Beirut, before Saturninus, it was by Caesar's fortune that he had sworn to repay the money he owed. To have taken so solemn an oath and then broken it was an insult to Augustus himself.

Caesar turned on Syllaeus, and asked him how many Nabataeans had been killed in the Raepta campaign. Syllaeus hesitated, and said he had been misinformed. Nicolaus then read out the debt contracts, the letters of Saturninus and Volumnius, and petitions from the cities that had been pillaged. The case was plain. Augustus condemned Syllaeus to make restitution to Herod, to repay the debt and then to be executed. Syllaeus managed to evade the sentence for the time being by the payment of a heavy fine. Once back in Petra, he showed no sign of carrying out Caesar's orders. On the contrary, furious at seeing Herod reconciled to Augustus, and Harith confirmed as king, he renewed his intrigues.

Realizing that he was making no progress he formed the mad idea of returning to Rome to try once more to insinuate himself in the Emperor's favour. But there he found himself confronted with Antipater, Herod's eldest son, and by envoys from King Harith. Besides the crimes originally proved against him, he was shown to have committed several others: the murder of Sohaemus, the leading man in Petra, and an attempt against Fabatus, Caesar's commissioner at Herod's court. He had offered Fabatus a large sum of money to assist him. Herod, as usual, outbribed his rival, and so Syllaeus tried to denounce Fabatus to Caesar, whereupon Fabatus revealed to Herod Syllaeus' plot to murder him by the hand of one of his bodyguards, a Nabataean by birth called Corinthus. Then Pheroras, Herod's brother, who had retired to his tetrarchy beyond Jordan, was poisoned by a Nabataean woman, sent by Syllaeus. Finally, Syllaeus' part in the disastrous expedition of Aelius Gallus fifteen years before was recalled. He was arrested by order of the Emperor and beheaded.

Such was the end of Syllaeus. Augustus was reconciled to his old friend Herod. He was annoyed with Harith at assuming the diadem, for he now wished to make Herod King of Arabia, in addition to his other realms. He would have done so, but was dissuaded partly by consideration of his age—he was now sixty-three but chiefly by the terrible disorder into which Herod's family affairs had now declined.

Chapter XXIV

ALEXANDER AND ARISTOBULUS

BY eight of his ten wives, Herod had children, fifteen in all. Of these fifteen, one died in Rome, of the rest, eight were too young to take any part in affairs during their father's lifetime, which was lucky for them. The children who formed the epicentre of the devastating storm that ruined Herod and his house were: first, Antipater, his first-born, by Doris; secondly, the four surviving children of Mariamme I, namely Alexander and Aristobulus and, in a lesser degree, two girls, Salampsio and Cypros.

Antipater was the eldest son of the king; but he had not been born in the purple, his mother was a nobody, and both he and she had been banished from the court as long ago as the year 37. Mariamme's boys on the other hand were born when Herod was king, of a mother who was herself royal; they had been brought up in the court, and had been educated at Rome, where they had moved in the highest circles of the imperial capital, and were the intimates of Caesar himself. This alone was enough to provoke a clash between the two boys and their elder half-brother. But Herod had dynastic ambitions: he wanted to found a royal line, and it was on Mariamme's sons that he relied. The two boys, it will be remembered, came back from Rome with their father in the year 18. About two years later, they were married. Alexander, the elder, made a very good match; the bride chosen for him being Glaphyra, the daughter of Archelaus, king of Cappadocia, the client state between the Taurus and Anti-Taurus mountains, in what is now eastern Turkey. The Cappadocians had never submitted to Alexander and their rulers had been recognized as kings since about 225 B.C. The old line had been deposed by Pompey, for siding with the Parthians, and he had given the kingdom to an energetic prince called Archelaus, whose friendship for Rome was beyond question. The country was prosperous, and produced slaves, racehorses and silver. The association of this northern kingdom with Judaea by the union of Glaphyra and Alexander seemed an ideal arrangement, from the point of all concerned, including the Romans.

The younger son, Aristobulus, married one of Salome's

daughters by Costobar called Berenice. Salome no doubt insisted on it. Herod himself had already married one of her daughters, but had no issue by her. She was determined to have her share in the dynastic fabric. Herod consented, though he must have foreseen that as Aristobulus' mother-in-law, his sister would have even more opportunity to indulge her animosity towards the children of Mariamme, who had been her victim. She was determined to ruin them both.

The royal family were thus divided into two factions: Salome, with Doris and Antipater as potential allies, on the one side and the children of Mariamme on the other. Salome found a powerful supporter in her brother Pheroras. He had his own reasons for wanting to make trouble. Despite all that Herod had done for him, he was jealous of his brother and was accused of plotting against him even during the first Mariamme's life. To jealousy he soon added resentment. Pheroras' first wife had been a sister-in-law of the King. After her death he had been betrothed to Herod's elder daughter by Mariamme, Salampsio but had thrown her over for a servant girl. Herod was naturally annoyed at the slight; but thinking that Pheroras' unworthy passion would cool, married Salampsio to his nephew Phasael, son of his late brother of the same name. Some time later, Herod took Pheroras to task for his discourtesy, as he accounted it, and offered him a second daughter, Cypros. Herod's secretary Ptolemy urged Pheroras to yield this time, and so it was agreed that Pheroras should divorce his wife, although he had already one son by her, and marry Cypros one month later. He swore he would have no more to do with the servant girl (whose name we do not know) but when the month was over, he found he could not bring himself to part from the woman he loved, whatever her estate, and continued to live with her. This led to a breach between the brothers, and enlisted Pheroras' wife among Herod's most active enemies.

The young men, by their birth, education and looks were generally popular. They no doubt found their old father provincial, and could hardly be expected to overlook the fact that he had murdered their mother. They talked: too much and too freely. Their enemies were subtle: they neither said nor did anything openly. Salome knew her brother. She played on his worst passion, suspicion. She had contrived to get rid of Mariamme by that means, and she would do the same for the children. Herod's absence with Agrippa in the year 14 gave her plenty of scope for elaborating her design. As soon as he had come back and made his public report to his people, she started to insinuate that he was in great danger, that his sons were plotting his death, and that they intended to escape to Archelaus, and then go on to Rome.

To counter this imagined plot, Herod decided to recall Antipater to court, thinking that when Mariamme's sons realized that they were not the only possible heirs, they would abandon their hostility to him. The result was far different. The boys felt that they had one more grievance, and Antipater, making up for his twenty-three years of banishment, undertook with all the vigour of his low and malicious nature the welcome task of ruining his hated half-brothers. To increase his standing, his father married him to the daughter of Antigonus, the Hasmonean prince who had been executed after the taking of Jerusalem by Herod and Sosius in 37. Doris was soon back, too. Antipater was publicly proclaimed Herod's heir, and he felt that his triumph was at hand when he persuaded his father to send him to Rome. When Agrippa left Mitylene early in the spring of 13, Herod went to meet him, taking Antipater with him. He commended his son to his dear friend, and asked him to present Antipater, together with a number of gifts to Augustus. Antipater cut a considerable figure in Rome, his only regret being, says Josephus, that he had no proper opportunities for continually calumniating his brothers. Still, he did what he could by correspondence; and Salome, Doris and Pheroras did a great deal more. The king was so cozened by this wicked cabal, that he was convinced that his sons were trying to poison him, and that he must lay the case before Caesar in person.

For the third and last time Herod set out for Italy. He met Augustus at Aquileia, between Venice and Trieste. Herod made a long accusation, which contained no single proved act or fact, only a rigmarole of suspicions and inferences. Alexander undertook the defence of himself and his brother. He sat in tears, in which by his aspect as much as by his speech he soon had nearly everyone else as well. Caesar, who knew both father and sons personally, saw how the land lay. He told the young men that although they were innocent of the calumnies that had been brought against them they were nevertheless to blame in not showing more respect for their father. Herod thereupon embraced them. The reconciliation was very affecting. Herod gave Caesar a present of £150,000, to pay for bread and circuses for the Roman populace. Caesar in return gave Herod the concession for the exploitation of the copper-mines of Cyprus, of which each party was to have half the proceeds. That Augustus, with his keen financial sense, should have committed this rich asset to Herod at this particular time is a clear indication that whatever he might think of the domestic ineptitude of his old friend, he still had the highest opinion of his public capacity. He also authorized him to nominate an heir to his whole kingdom, or to divide it up as he liked. Herod was inclined to do so immediately—he was getting old now—but Augustus graciously said he would not allow him to deprive himself of his authority, either over his kingdom or over his sons, so long as he lived.

On the way home, Herod called at Elis, where he made arrangements for the reorganization of the Olympic games. When he had attended them on his way to Rome, he learned that they had fallen on evil days, and were badly in need of money. Herod found it, and was named a Director, an honour which must have given great pleasure to so hardy an athlete as the old king. Then they touched at the island-palace of Archelaus, off the coast of Cilicia, to receive the congratulations of Archelaus, who had naturally been anxious about the meeting at Aquileia. He had asked his friends to do all they could to help Alexander, and must have been relieved and delighted at Caesar's politic dispositions. On reaching Jerusalem Herod once again assembled the people before the Temple, and announced to them that he nominated his heirs in the following order: first Antipater, as being the eldest, and then the sons of Mariamme, on account of their birth. Meanwhile, he bade his subjects remember that he himself was still king.

All this happened in the year 12. The next three years were crowded with events which have already been related, the Trachonitis revolt, the dedication of the Temple, Syllaeus' intrigues and death, the inauguration of Caesarea, Herod's disgrace, and his restoration to favour. During this period the family quarrel had been eclipsed by more public affairs; but the cabal had done everything they could do to aggravate it. Much of the chatter on both sides was petty. Glaphyra, for instance, said that she outranked all the other palace ladies, because she was descended from the Greek hero Temenos on her father's side, and from Darius, son of Hystaspes, on her mother's. Herod's family were really nobody, she would say, and his wives had been chosen for their looks not their pedigree—a remark which she intended as an insult, and which the poor little snobs took as one. Alexander and his brother were pardonably irritated when they saw Herod's more recent wives wearing their own mother's clothes, and Alexander threatened that when he became king he would make them work at the loom, dressed in sack-cloth, and kept under lock and key; and that he would make his brothers country schoolmasters, which was all that their education had fitted them for.

Pheroras took a hand as well. Egged on by Salome, he sought to inflame Alexander into overt rashness by telling him that Herod was madly in love with his wife Glaphyra. Herod, when he heard it, was furious with Pheroras, and even with Salome, whom he was the less disposed either to trust or to please when, soon after, she wanted to marry Syllaeus. The king, indulgent as always to his own kin, soon made it up with both of them. He even agreed that since Pheroras did not want to marry his daughter, she should be given to Pheroras's son instead, together with a dowry of £50,000. Salome steadily exploited her authority with her daughter Berenice to the detriment of Aristobulus, whose secrets the girl dutifully repeated to her mother.

The second crisis was provoked by Alexander, and "from no decent occasion".

Herod had as his body-servants three handsome eunuchs of whom he was very fond on account of their beauty. Alexander by liberal bribes had prevailed upon them to let him debauch them. When Herod was told of it, he had them tortured, whereupon they confessed not only their criminal conversation with Alexander, but also when, at Antipater's instigation, they were racked to the last extremity that Alexander had told them that Herod would not live much longer and that they had better come over to his, Alexander's side, instead of serving a dotard who dyed his grey hair black. The eunuchs said also that Alexander was confident of the succession and had assured them that he could count on supporters both in the court and in the army.

Herod now abandoned all restraint. The Palace was given over to a delirium of espionage, delation, blackmail and torture. Trusted friends, such as Andromachus and Gemellus, who had served him faithfully, were dismissed merely because they had been the tutors and intimates to his sons. One of the victims under torture declared that Alexander knew how jealous his father was of his prowess as a marksman, and of his fine carriage, and that he had plotted to kill his father while hunting, give out that it was an accident, and then claim the crown from Caesar. Herod believed the story, and much more of the like fantastic invention, such as that the King of Parthia intended to kill him by poison, which he kept in readiness at Ascalon.

Herod ordered Alexander's arrest. The young prince determined to turn the tables on his accusers. He wrote a confession in four books, in which he admitted his guilt, but said that Pheroras was his partner, and that Salome came to him by night and compelled him to endure her adulterous embraces, and that there was a general desire to get rid of Herod as soon as possible, even on the part of his closest friends, such as Ptolemy and Sapinnius, who were his confidential ministers.

In this critical situation, Archelaus hurried down from Cappadocia. He must rank among the pioneer psychiatrists. He realized that Herod was insane, so did many people; only Archelaus understood how to counter and subdue his mania. A man who suffered as Herod did from the hallucination that his son Alexander was coming upon him with a drawn sword, was clearly the victim of a fixed idea: to attempt to deny it would only increase Herod's fury, and make him believe that Archelaus really was in the plot, as some of the informers had said. Archelaus decided to play upon another, strong trait in Herod's complex character—his love of his own kin. Instead of defending Alexander, therefore, Archelaus attacked him, "Where is this wretched son-in-law of mine?" he cried out, "Where can I see the head of him who has plotted to murder his father? I'll tear it in pieces with my own hands. And I'll do the same to my daughter, too, who, innocent though she may be, is polluted by being the wife of such a creature." He was amazed at Herod's patience, he said, in keeping Alexander alive— he had not expected to find him still living—and a great deal more in the same vein; with the result that Herod, almost before he knew it, found himself defending his son against the violent tirade. He gave Archelaus Alexander's "confessions" to read, on which the Cappadocian commented that it was clear that malicious persons had been busy "for by such persons, not only young men are sometimes imposed upon, but old men also". It could happen even in the most distinguished families, including his own.

Herod was mollified. Pheroras saw that the game was up, for the present at any rate, and on Archelaus' advice, went in mourning to the king, confessed his guilt and asked for pardon. Herod once more forgave him.

Everyone was relieved. Torture and blackmail gave way to feasting and smiles. Herod ordered all his court to make suitable presents to Archelaus and his suite, and he himself did the same. He gave him £35,000, a golden throne set with precious stones, some eunuchs, and a concubine with the challenging name of *Pannychis*, "Mistress All-Night". Herod, to whom no doubt a change of air was welcome, accompanied the returning monarch as far as Antioch.

This reconciliation, alas, lasted an even shorter time than the first. The third and final crisis in the lives of the unfortunate princes came two years later, in the year 7 B.C. It was provoked by a wretch called Eurycles, a sinister adventurer from Sparta. He traded on his nationality to gain the entrée of the court. (There was a long-standing friendship between the Jews and the Spartans, for the reason that the Spartans were the least Greek Greeks, and had opposed the descendants of Alexander and other missionaries of Hellenism.) Eurycles wormed his way into the confidence of Herod, and Antipater, and the sons of Mariamme, to the young princes' great detriment. Another pretended hunting-plot was sharked up, two former masters of the horse, Tyrannus and Jucundus, being involved. Then a letter from the governor of Alexandrium was produced offering money to the princes to murder the king, and asylum afterwards. It was no use for Alexander to show that this was a counterfeit of Diophantus, a government clerk, who was in fact later executed for forgery. Herod held a durbar at Jericho, at which those who had been tortured were to make public accusation of Alexander and Aristobulus. The frothy populace stoned the poor wretches to death, and but for the intervention of Ptolemy and Pheroras would have killed the two princes as well. Antipater took care that Tyrannus and Jucundus were killed in the mêlée. Archelaus sent down an ambassador called Melas, before whom Alexander confessed that they had intended to take refuge with Archelaus, but only for the good reason that life in Palestine had become unbearable, and that Archelaus had promised to send them to Rome. Herod was now convinced of Archelaus' hostility.

Aristobulus thought he might bring his mother-in-law, Salome, to a more reasonable frame of mind by a little blackmail. He reminded her that she had been under suspicion of betraying official secrets when she was in love with Syllaeus. This was a false move. Salome made an indignant complaint to Herod, who of course took her side, and ordered the young men to be arrested and confined in separate prisons. He then sent off two trusted emissaries, Volumnius and Olympus, to Caesar with a long indictment of his sons.

Augustus was in a difficult position. He knew from experience that on this question of his sons Herod was demented. At the same time, he did not want to set a precedent for becoming the arbiter of the domestic troubles of his client kings: he had quite enough of his own. Besides he had told Herod at Aquileia that he would not deprive him of his paternal authority so long as he lived. He therefore decided to allow Herod to settle the question himself. He did what he could to save the young men by ordering that the inquiry should take place not in Jerusalem, but in Beirut, before a court of which the principal judges would be Saturninus, the governor of Syria, and his legates. Altogether 150 persons were summoned to attend, but the trial was a travesty of justice. Archelaus was not invited, nor were the two accused allowed to appear, for Herod well knew how they would affect their judges. They were kept in custody in a village near Sidon. Herod's speech gave unmistakable signs of his malady: it was rambling and violent. Saturninus saw no justification for the death penalty, nor did any of his suite. Volumnius, of course, did; and the rest, from various motives, "some out of flattery, some out of hatred of Herod, but none out of indignation at their crimes", voted for it. Nicolaus of Damascus landed at this juncture, on his return from Rome, and advised Herod to be lenient: it was what their friends in Rome expected, including, no doubt, Caesar.

The forlorn convoy set off along the coast to Tyre, and there took ship for Caesarea. Herod had still not made up his mind. The whole kingdom was in suspense. No one dared speak of the matter, nor even be present when it was mentioned. At Caesarea, the silence was broken by an old soldier, called Tero, whose son was a friend of Alexander's. Using the blunt freedom of his kind, he told Herod some home truths about Antipater and the feeling in the army. For a time Herod bore with him, but the old man went too far, and so worked on Herod that he ordered the arrest of all the persons whom Tero had named, and of Tero himself. At this point, as though to clinch the doom of the two princes, the royal barber, called Trypho, came forward, and said that Tero had often tried to persuade him to cut Herod's throat as he shaved him.

That was the end. Tero, his son, and the barber were put to the torture. To save his father, the son "confessed", whereupon the Teros, Trypho and 300 army officers were dragged before a popular court and stoned to death.

Alexander and Aristobulus were taken to Sebaste, the city in which Herod had married their mother. There was no danger of any popular outcry there: Herod had rebuilt it as a predominantly Greek colony, in which Jewish national sentiment had no place. There the poor young men were strangled, and their bodies sent down by night to the Alexandrium, to be buried beside their maternal grandfather, and many other of their ancestors.

Such was the sad and sordid end of these two princes on whom Herod and his people had set such high hopes, cut off by the same hand as had brought their mother to her death more than twenty years before. They had been imprudent, ungracious and ungrateful. But that they had plotted their father's death is not to be believed. It was Salome, once again, who had caused their undoing. It was around Salome that the envy, hatred, malice and all uncharitableness of the court collected and revolved. It was she who knew most of her brother's state of mind and body. The disease from which he was suffering was a form of arterio-sclerosis.

The symptoms which Josephus gives are those which to this day are to be found in old men in Palestine villages. Loathsome physical decay is accompanied by mental disorder, which may express itself in uncontrolled outbursts of violence. Salome, with her vile skill, exploited her brother's weakness, for the ruin of her rivals and of Herod himself.

She succeeded too—up to a point. By the irony of history, it was through the youths to whose destruction she had dedicated herself that Herod's line was perpetuated. The story of the kings of Judaea, of Chalcis and even of Armenia who were to spring from their line is outside the limits of this book, but the genealogical table[1] will indicate it to the curious. Glaphyra maintained her royal connections. After Alexander's death, she married, as his second wife, Juba II, the learned historian-king of Numidia. He tired of her, and sent her home, where Herod's son Archelaus met her and fell so violently in love with her that he divorced his wife in order to marry her, thereby transgressing the law in just the same manner as his half-brother Herod Antipas, Tetrarch of Galilee, was later to transgress it by marrying Herodias, who divorced his brother in order to do so, even though there had been a daughter, Salome, by the union. Both these marriages were accounted incestuous. Incestuous, too, would be the relations of Aristobulus' grand-daughter Berenice with her brother, Agrippa II.

The issue of Herod and Mariamme must be accursed, it seemed, even to the third and fourth generation.

[1] See p. 187.

Chapter XXV

ANTIPATER AND HEROD: THE END

ONE of the least comprehensible aspects of Herod's character was the kindness he showed to the children of those whom he had executed. Just as after Mariamme's death he had done all he could for Alexander and Aristobulus, as regards both their education and their marriages, so now he devoted great care to the upbringing of their children, Alexander's two sons, and Aristobulus' three sons and two daughters. (The poor widows were soon disposed of: Glaphyra, as we have seen, was sent back to her father. Herod returned the dowry to Archelaus "that there might be no dispute between them about it". Antipater managed to get Berenice married to his mother Doris' brother, which cannot have been an attractive match.) Herod could hardly be expected to live long enough to see these children married; but he decided to betroth them while still infants, so that their future might be assured. Alexander's firstborn was to marry Pheroras' daughter, and Aristobulus' firstborn, Antipater's daughter. Aristobulus' daughters were to marry Antipater's son and Herod's own son by Mariamme II, Herod-Philip. He was already married to Herodias, but a second wife was perfectly legal.

These arrangements did not suit Antipater at all. He thought that his rivals' children would be altogether too important and uncontrolled. He persuaded his father to revoke the settlement in two respects: he himself, not his son, would marry Aristobulus' second daughter, and his son should marry Pheroras' daughter, and thus (as he thought) inherit the Trans-Jordan tetrarchy.

Antipater was now at the apogee of his power. He was king in everything but name, his father sharing the authority with him. Herod had made a second will, whereby Antipater was to succeed him as king, and then his son by Mariamme II, Herod-Philip. It was evident that Herod could not live much longer; but Antipater was disinclined to wait: he had waited so long already. He was grey-haired, he complained to his mother, and was like to die before Herod, without ever wearing the crown. Besides, he was hated by the whole nation, who were well aware how he had deceived his father, and calumniated his half-brothers to their death. Antipater therefore lavished money on the Governor of Syria,

Saturninus, and on other influential people both in Syria and in Rome. He tried to hoodwink Salome, but she was too much for him. She had got over the Syllaeus affair, and was now married, for the third time, to a friend of Herod's called Alexas. The empress herself, to whom Salome had once more appealed for help, had advised her to bow to her brother's wishes. So Salome and Herod were close friends once more.

Antipater could count on Pheroras' support, and on that of his wife, who now headed a disreputable coterie, consisting of Doris, Antipater, Pheroras and their friends. They avoided each other by day, but held night-long drinking parties, at which they would elaborate their plans for the coming reign. When he was informed of these clandestine orgies, Herod once again demanded that Pheroras should renounce his wife. Pheroras once again refused and went back to Trans-Jordan. To Antipater, the king gave £25,000, as a bribe to have nothing to do with Pheroras.

Antipater felt that Jerusalem was getting too hot for him, so he arranged for his friends in Italy to write to Herod asking that he might be sent to Rome. Herod sent him off, with a magnificent suite. He also carried handsome presents from Herod, and Herod's second will.

While in Rome, Antipater took part in the second trial of Syllaeus, as already related (Chapter XXIII), but he found time to hire people to write letters to Jerusalem, accusing his younger half-brothers, Archelaus and Philip, who were now being educated in Rome, of disloyalty, hoping to get rid of them as he had got rid of Alexander and Aristobulus. He was required to keep strict accounts; but managed to charge the letter-writing to such items as clothes, carpets and plate. His total expenses during this second stay in Rome were £100,000, of which the greater part he said had been spent on the case against Syllaeus.

When Pheroras was on his death bed in the year 5, Herod, ill as he was, crossed over Jordan to share his brother's last hours, even though Pheroras had disregarded a summons from Herod when he, shortly before, had seemed about to die. Herod's brotherly affection touched Pheroras, and he died reconciled to him. He was the last of Herod's three brothers, and in the old days had shown himself a stalwart ally and supporter. Herod brought his body to Jerusalem, proclaimed state mourning, and gave him a magnificent funeral in the family mausoleum.

Two of Pheroras' freedmen, who had been in his confidence, came to Herod and told him that Pheroras had been poisoned. Maidservants under torture disclosed not only Syllaeus' plot to poison Pheroras, but also Antipater's to poison his father. Doris, his mother, was disgraced, deprived of all her splendid jewellery "worth many talents", and dismissed from court. Pheroras' wife tried to kill herself, but failed, and, upon Herod's promise of immunity, confessed the whole plot. She even produced the poison. "Then", says Josephus "did the ghosts of Alexander and Aristobulus go round all the palace, and became the inquisitors and discoverers of what could not otherwise be found out", among other things that Mariamme II had been implicated in the plot. Herod divorced her, struck her son Herod-Philip out of the succession, and deprived her father of the High Priesthood.

Antipater heard of his mother's disgrace, but the censorship was so effective that he heard little else. Herod, now in the last stages of his malady, was determined to deal with Antipater before he died. He wrote to him, mentioning his disappointment at Doris' behaviour, and saying that he was sure everything could be amicably arranged if Antipater would come home. Antipater started, intending to take the overland route through Asia Minor. At Tarentum, in the toe of Italy, he heard of Pheroras' death. This made him vaguely uneasy, but he pretended it was grief for his uncle that upset him. In Cilicia, he received a kind letter from his father, but even that did not wholly allay his suspicion. He was in two minds whether to go on to Palestine, or to wait for further news. Finally, persuaded by those of his suite who wanted to be home again, he decided to go, and took ship for Caesarea.

He sailed into the great harbour. The quays were deserted. Nobody was there to meet him. No man saluted him. Dark looks and curses were all that he encountered. He set off up the road to Jerusalem, deciding to brazen things out. Without doffing his purple, he made for the palace with his suite. The gatekeepers let him in, alone: his friends were shut out. He went to find his father, and came on him sitting in conference with Varus, the new governor of Syria. Antipater saw what had happened; but it was too late now to escape. He walked towards his father to embrace him. Herod repulsed him, called him a fratricide and a would-be parricide, and said that Varus would be his judge the next day. Such was the homecoming of the man who only a few months before had been the most pampered prince in Asia.

The trial gave Antipater a last opportunity to deploy his wiles, which he did with effect. But Nicolaus of Damascus took up the tale, and produced crushing evidence of guilt, exposing Antipater as a drunken fornicator, a slanderer of his brothers, and, beyond question, the author of a plot to murder his father: the very poison which had been procured in Egypt was produced in court. Varus

ordered it to be administered to two condemned felons, who died
on the spot.

Varus closed the court: the case was proved. After a private talk
with Herod, he left for Antioch the next day. Antipater was
thrown into prison, and messengers were sent off to report the
whole affair to Caesar. After they left, another discovery was
made: Antipater's Egyptian accomplice, Antiphilus, who had sent
him the poison, before he could hear of the trial and its outcome,
sent him a letter by the hand of a slave. This was intercepted; it
referred to another letter, from a certain Acme, a Jewess in the
service of no less a person than the Empress. The slave denied that
he was carrying any other letter; but it was discovered sewn into
the lining of his coat. The gist of the second letter was that at Antipater's instigation, Acme had written to Herod pretending that
she had found a letter from Salome to the Empress, in which
Salome had calumniated her brother. Herod would have killed
Antipater at once, but that he had laid the case before Caesar.
He therefore sent further messengers to Rome, with copies of the
incriminating letters. Caesar had Acme executed, and informed
Herod that he could deal with Antipater as he thought fit, both as
a father and as a king, and either execute or banish him.

Meanwhile, Herod knowing now that he was beyond hope of
cure, made a third will, in which Antipas, Herod's son by the
Samaritan Malthake, was named heir, Archelaus and Philip,
whom Antipater had accused, being passed over, although they
were older. Augustus was to have half a million sterling, and the
Empress Livia a quarter. Salome's share was magnificent.

It was now the autumn of the year 5. Herod's illness was gaining
upon him so rapidly that it was clear that not even he, for all his
great physical strength, could live much longer. But he was not
to die in peace, nor even in the mere agony of corporal dissolution.
Once again, he was called on to deal with a political crisis,
provoked by the Pharisees.

The Pharisees had originally been drawn to Herod by their
fierce hatred of the Hasmoneans: Pollio and Sameas had openly
counselled submission to him, as the agent of the Divine Will; but
they soon grew tired of a régime which they found gave them
little opportunity for meddling in politics to their own advantage.
When, in the year 20, Herod demanded an oath of loyalty from his
people, the Pharisees refused to take it, although it was at that very
time that Herod was undertaking the rebuilding of the Temple.
Other recalcitrants were punished, but not the Pharisees, whom
Herod forgave out of respect for Pollio. (The Essenes he exempted
altogether, because he knew that their creed forbade them to take

any form of oath.) The growing splendour of the kingdom and the stability of the government exacerbated (as it habitually does) the jealousy of a clique of hierophants who saw their hold on the people weakening; in an effort to reinforce it, they resorted (as such persons habitually do) to their favourite and familiar weapon —fanaticism. When Herod's domestic troubles became acute, the Pharisees spread the rumour that it was a punishment for his having robbed the tomb of David, or having been willing to do so but for the miraculous fire which drove him back (the miraculous fire which was to recur at least twice more in the folk-history of Jerusalem). The proof was the monument which Herod had erected to expiate his sacrilege. Nicolaus of Damascus records the monument, but says nothing of the profanation, which was evidently a re-hash of the story of John Hyrcanus, another enemy of the Pharisees (Chapter I).

About the year 7, their intransigence showed itself in refusing to take an oath of loyalty to Caesar and Herod; 6,000 of them refused, but Herod, not wanting to precipitate an open breach, contented himself with imposing a fine, which was immediately paid by Pheroras' wife. To requite her for this spiteful generosity, the Pharisees, who were commonly credited with powers of divination, announced that God had decreed that Herod's government should cease, and the power pass to Pheroras and his wife. Salome, as usual, found out about it, and told the king. It was discovered that a number of people at court had been corrupted, including a poor eunuch, called Bagoas, whom these bogus thaumaturges had persuaded that the power of procreation would be restored to him, and "one Carus, who exceeded all men of that time in comeliness, and was Herod's catamite". The plotters and their dupes were executed.

With the approach of the king's death the Pharisees became bolder. Two of their most learned doctors of the Law, Judas son of Sariphaeus and Matthias son of Margalothos, had acquired an ascendancy over the younger generation. They inveighed against Herod's pagan innovations; how could good Jews, they asked, abide the sight of the golden eagle which the king had placed above the great door of the Temple, contrary to the precepts of Moses? What a noble act it would be to destroy the graven image, even at the price of life itself. To the incitements of the doctors was added a rumour that the king was dead. A band of youths went into the Temple in broad daylight and cut down the offending eagle with axes. They were caught in the act by the captain of the guard on duty in Antonia. He arrested forty of them, together with Judas and Matthias, on the spot. They were sent down to Jericho, where

the king, dying though he was, insisted on hearing the case himself. He could not stand now, but was carried into the amphitheatre, where he had assembled all the notables. Lying on a
couch, he recounted all the labour and expense he had gone to in
building the Temple, and convicted the rash youths not of *lèse
majesté* but, which was worse, of sacrilege. The ringleaders were to
be burned alive, the others executed by the axe or the bowstring.
He also dismissed the High Priest, appointing his brother-in-law
in his stead. "And that very night there was an eclipse of the
moon", says Josephus, thus fixing the day as the 13th March,
4 B.C.

That Herod, in the awful physical and mental decay into which
he had fallen, and in this atmosphere of fervid Messianism, should
have ordered the massacre of the Innocents of Bethlehem is wholly
in keeping with all that we know of him. Bethlehem was but a few
miles distant from his palace-fortress of Herodium: there least of all
could any subversive cell be tolerated. Such an act was by no
means unheard of. In pagan antiquity, the life of a new-born child
was at the mercy of its father or of the state. As Abel points out, a
few months before the birth of Augustus, a prodigy having pre-
saged the birth of a king for the Roman people, the affrighted
Senate decreed that none of the children born that year were to be
brought up. Later on Nero, fearing the consequences of the
appearance of a comet, ordered the execution of leading aristocrats of Rome. Their children were driven from the city and died
from hunger or poison.

Herod was now in the last throes of his disease. He was dropsical, gangrenous and racked with burning pains. He could hardly
breathe. In one last effort to alleviate his suffering, he had himself
taken down to the Dead Sea, and rowed across to the springs of
Callirrhoe, on the east shore, just below Machairus. Certain of
these springs are, like many others in the region, warm, but unlike
the rest, they are not sulphurous, but sweet to the taste. They are
not as hot, nor as copious, as the steaming cascades of Zerqa
Ma'in, a few miles to the north-east, which being in a precipitous
cleft would be inaccessible to anyone in Herod's condition. The
baths of Callirrhoe are soothing and invigorating. The source
bubbles up a few score paces only from the shore, from which a
patient could be safely conveyed to it in a litter. On a rock shelf,
just above the beach where the stream runs into the barren waters
of the Sea, are the remains of a little columned pavilion, which
may well have been constructed for Herod. Poor man, the springs
could do him no good: still less did he profit from a bath of hot oil
into which his physicians lowered him. He fainted away from the

pain. The convoy set out on the return journey. In the mild spring sunshine, Herod looked for the last time on so many scenes of his fortune and misfortune, of his piety and his cruelty, on Masada, Hyrcania, Herodium, where he had decided to be buried; the glittering palaces and Temple of Jerusalem, throned on the horizon, the city which he dare not re-enter even dead, for fear of insult; the great towers of Cypros, Taurus and Docus above Jericho and there, dimly seen in the northern haze, the peak of the Alexandrium, where his two sons lay buried. Across the plain below Jericho he was borne, that plain over which he had so often ridden, armed and triumphant, at the head of his troops, back to his palace in the park. The Jericho spring is full of peace and solace: the storks patrol the rich furrows of the water-gardens by day, the fireflies spangle the sapphire shadows by night. Over the fields that surround the crumbling ramparts of the oldest city in the world, life gently renews itself year by year.

But in the spring of the year 4 B.C., there was no peace in Jericho; only horror and death. When he reached the palace the mad king was cheered by letters from Rome announcing Caesar's decision about Acme and Antipater, but he was almost fainting for hunger. He called for an apple and a fruit-knife, it being his custom to peel the fruit himself. When they were brought, he looked about him, and thinking that he was alone, lifted the knife to stab himself. His cousin Achiab, who was on guard unseen, rushed forward, with a loud cry, and caught his hand just in time. The ensuing tumult echoed through the palace. Antipater heard it in the dungeons and thinking that the king was dead, urged his jailer to release him, so that he might assume authority. The jailer went and told the king, who "although he was at death's door, raised himself on his elbow" and ordered his guards to kill Antipater at once, and send his body for burial hugger-mugger at Hyrcania. In the long struggle for life and power Herod had won by four days. (When he heard of Antipater's death Augustus made his celebrated remark—a poor pun in Greek—that he would rather be Herod's swine than his son.)

Once again, Herod made a new will, his fourth and last. He appointed Archelaus, his son by the Samaritan Malthake, as king of Judaea; Antipas tetrarch of Galilee and Trans-Jordan, and Philip tetrarch of Gaulonitis, Trachonitis and Paneas. Jamnia Ashdod, and the rich groves of Phasaelis went to Salome, with £5,000 in cash. The rest of the family were liberally provided for. Caesar was to have half a million sterling, Julia some choice plate and expensive clothes, and other friends a quarter of a million between them. Later on Augustus gave Salome Herod's palace at

Ascalon. When she died, fourteen years afterwards, she left nearly all her estate to the Empress.

On the fifth day after Antipater's execution Herod was dead. He died in the month of Nisan, at the end of March or the beginning of April, in the 750th year of Rome, or 4 B.C. (the year from which the Christian Era should properly and accurately be dated). He was seventy years old, and had reigned thirty-seven years since his confirmation as king by the Romans, and thirty-four since his capture of Jerusalem.

As soon as the king was dead, Salome, for the last time, took charge. She kept the news from all except her husband Alexas. Their first task was to go over to the hippodrome, and dismiss a number of notables whom, in his final access of mania, it was said, Herod had had arrested, with the idea that they should die with him. More probably they had merely been summoned to a conference; the hippodrome was no prison. Salome now told them that Herod commanded them to go home to their estates. When they had dispersed, she announced the king's death, and assembled the garrison in the amphitheatre. Shortly before he died, Herod had distributed a liberal donation to every officer and man in the army, so that when they now heard read Herod's letter thanking them for their fidelity, and asking them to show the same good-will to Archelaus, his son, they readily came to their new king regiment by regiment, and assured him of their loyalty. Then Ptolemy, who had been entrusted by Herod with his seal, read the will, which was to come into effect only after confirmation by Caesar. In accordance with Jewish law, seven days mourning was to be observed.

On the morrow, the funeral convoy left Jericho. All the regalia had been brought out. The body lay on a golden bier, encrusted with gems, beneath a long purple pall. The dead king wore his diadem, and a gold crown above it. His sceptre was in his right hand. Immediately next to the bier were his sons and all his family. Then came the army, in the following order: The Royal Guard, the Thracian Regiment, the German Regiment, the Galatian Regiment, Regiments of the Line, all in full battle order. The army was followed by 500 of Herod's servants, carrying spices. Up the steep road they climbed, the road that runs beneath Cypros, on the south side of the Wadi Qilt, the traditional Valley of the Shadow of Death. Soon, the glittering procession turned aside from the grim cleft of the valley, and moved south across the barren tors and downs of the Wilderness of Judaea. At last they came in sight of the Herodium, the round castle on the hill, standing where the desert meets the town. They passed through the gardens that Herod had planted, by the pavilions he had built. Up the marble stairway they went, and into the strong, cold keep at the top. There, they laid Herod in the tomb he had chosen for himself, this strange, sad king, solitary for ever in death, as he had been lonely and alien in his life, "for there, by his own command he was to be buried; and thus did Herod end his life".

Chapter XXVI

A VERDICT

FOR 2,000 years, Herod has been called "Great", and detested as one of the most wicked of men.

Josephus calls him "great" only once, and in a context which suggests that he had used the word only to distinguish Herod from his sons and descendants. That his great-grandson Agrippa the second used the appellation "great king" of himself, even when restoring a building originally erected by his great-grandfather, we know from an inscription found at Beirut; but by general consent, only to the first Herod has posterity given the title. That Herod was great by comparison with his descendants, his sons the two Tetrarchs, and the two Agrippas, his grandson and great-grandson, named after his Roman friend, it would not be difficult to show, whether the criterion be extent of territory or range of achievement; but does Herod deserve the title "great" in his own right?

That Herod was not all monster will, it is hoped, have been evident from the foregoing narrative. In his younger years he was attractive; his charm could cast a spell over men and women alike. That is no argument of greatness; nevertheless, the man who could become the friend of Antony, and of Augustus and, perhaps most important, of Agrippa, cannot have been an empty or unmeritorious man. To say that Herod won the confidence of the rulers of the world by flattery is to disregard facts. Everyone flattered these men, particularly their clients; but only Herod won their friendship, only Herod became the confidant of Agrippa, only Herod was appointed by Augustus official adviser to the Roman governor of Syria.

All this argues ability, and outstanding ability. That Herod possessed it, was proved by his administrative vigour; his famine relief measures, for instance, to this day have never been equalled in the Levant.

Of Herod's loyalty to his own kith and kin, his life offers many instances. His love for his brothers, and of his sister, was unswerving. Even Pheroras, who had allowed himself to be seduced into plotting against his life, even he was forgiven. Herod stood by his death-bed, ill as he himself was, and bore him no malice, only

The Golden Gate (p. 138) from the outside, as it now appears. The filling of the archways and the superstructure are Muslim work of the post-Crusader era.

The substructure beneath the south-east corner of the Temple Area (p. 133); Herodian piers with Crusader vaulting, now known as "Solomons' Stables".

The Temple as reconstructed by De Vogüé in *Le Temple de Jérusalem*. This great folio was published in 1864, before the field-work of Warren and Wilson, the English pioneer archaeologists. Nearly a century later, it is still regarded by the most

affection and forgiveness. This loyalty Herod carried over into his relations with his Roman friends. They knew that they could rely upon him absolutely. This virtue of trustworthiness lay at the heart of his political success. No one had a subtler flair for political meteorology than Herod. It was by his political genius, combined with his vigour, and helped, admittedly, by his great wealth, that Herod rose from obscurity to fame and power. But it was his trustworthiness that kept him there. We have seen what Augustus could do to him when he suspected him, wrongly as it turned out, of disloyalty. Had the charge at any time been substantiated, Herod would not have lasted very long. This quality was naturally represented by his enemies as subservience, or treachery. It always is, in relationships between East and West.

The catalogue of Herod's crimes which the Jews presented to Caesar after his death as recorded by Josephus need not be taken seriously: it has an absolutely familiar ring to anyone who is acquainted with the manner in which any government in that part of the world is accused by those who for one reason or another wish to overthrow it. Indeed, the very same people who were clamouring to be governed by the Romans directly, would soon be crying out for a lightening of the Roman yoke, and not long afterwards rising in revolt against the very same power that they had hailed as a liberator. That, also, is no unknown pheno-menon to students of later Near Eastern history. In fact, Herod had done great things for Palestine. By his political address, he had kept the Romans at a distance. His people were exempt from military service, they paid no tribute to Rome. No Roman administrative officials, no Roman tax-collectors were to be seen in the realm. When, in A.D. 6, after Archelaus' banishment, Judaea did become a Roman province, how soon were the Romans and their tribute, even their coins and emblems of their authority to become obnoxious to the Jews!

From such humiliation and such extortion, Herod had pro-tected his people; and on two occasions, as we have seen, he had actually remitted a portion of the taxes which were due to him. Not so the Romans.

The country was at peace during his reign, trade flourished, cities were restored, and new ones built: Samaria-Sebaste, Caesarea, Antipatris, Phasaelis, Anthedon-Agrippias. Jerusalem had been transformed, and the Temple itself had been rebuilt on a scale that excited the admiration of the world. Palestine and its citizens commanded prestige and influence, in the Roman world at large, and in the very court and family of Caesar itself. The Jewry of the Dispersion reaped a rich harvest in respect and security. None of Herod's benefactions is more to his credit than his bold championship of the rights of overseas Jewry. That in some degree he profited from it is true: the unimpeded flow of treasure to the Temple was an economic asset. But Herod had many economic assets: he had his family wealth—and it must be remembered that Herod was a very rich man, and knew how to use his riches, before ever he was king, as is abundantly proved by his early contacts with the venal Romans—he had his famous date and balsam groves, unique in the world of the day, and he had his revenues from the Eastern Trade. The Temple shekels, therefore, were not an essential head in his budget, apart from the fact that the purposes to which they might be applied were rigidly circumscribed. It would have been easy for Herod to turn a deaf ear to the complaints of the Jews of Asia, on the ground that they were outside his jurisdiction as, of course, they were. Herod decided that it was his duty to protect them; and at the risk of antagonizing the powerful majority among whom they lived, he used all his influence with Agrippa, his wealth, and his tact to conciliate the gentile cities that were the hosts of his co-religionists, and to secure from his Roman patrons, in the teeth of an interested opposition, the unequivocal ratification of their privileges.

To secure for Jewry a peaceful and prosperous existence in a secular world—this was Herod's aim for Palestine too. It was his greatest political achievement, and if he is to be called great, it is this which must justify the appellation.

Herod saw that in a world dominated by Rome, nationalism could bring only ruin. The last feeble fanatics of the Hasmonean house had proved it. In a unified world, there was no room for separatism. Religion should be the unique, superior and sublime bond of union of the Jew. In their secular capacity, they should be as other men, received and respected not only in Palestine but throughout the world. Let them glory in their Temple, the most majestic religious centre of the terrestrial world, but let them be good citizens of the state, whereby alone they might become happy citizens.

Many of his subjects could not bring themselves to accept such a destiny. How wrong they were, and how right Herod was, the awful events of the next century were to prove. Nationalism rose again. It provoked the inevitable repression, which was, as usual, savage and unjust. In the final clash, Rome annihilated Palestine Jewry. Herod's conception of Jewry, its responsibilities, its privileges and its destiny, was farsighted to the verge of prophecy. It was to be the pattern of the happy and honoured Jewry of the future, in which the Jew enjoys civic equality and religious freedom in a secular frame. It is the conception of Jewry that is the rule of life of the majority of Jews to-day. (Even the minority that still pursues the nationalist phantom, sees it arrayed in a western, secular garb.)

Such was the bright side of Herod's character and achievement.

We must now look without favour and without rancour at the other.

Herod lived in a brutal and violent age. Human life was of little more account than that of cattle. When even the cultivated Greeks could regard as "a mathematical axiom" a king's murder of his brothers, when crucifixions were ordered by the score as a commonplace sentence of a court of justice, where torture was a recognized legal process, when the destruction of man by man in the arena was a popular amusement—in such a world might not the murder of a relation or two pass as a necessity of state?

Now that we have for the first time a scientific diagnosis of Herod's disease, and now that we know so much more about the disease itself, it is easy to realize that for the last ten years of his life, and at times before that period, Herod was not *compos mentis*. He committed actions that had he been in his right mind he might well have avoided.

All this is true; but it cannot absolve Herod. He was a Jew, and outwardly a pious, even ardent Jew. It was not enough for him to plead, in moral matters, that he was doing as the Romans did. He was not in Rome. Such an argument indeed, invalidated the whole of the contention that it was possible to be a good Jew and a good Roman citizen or subject. It was this aspect of Herod's life and works that antagonized the best of his fellow Jews. Much of the opposition to him was ungrateful and captious: that the man who built the Temple should be mentioned in the Mishna solely as the man who introduced a breed of pigeons is, perhaps, less than generous. Besides, to the truly religious, Herod was, as we have seen, notably gracious. Nevertheless, it must be confessed that Herod failed to win the hearts even of his best subjects despite all his efforts to do so.

His lack of "nationalism" may be partly responsible for this failure. In an age of yeasty Messianism, no king could come to terms with pretenders, open or covert; and Herod's insistence on being the undisputed ruler of his kingdom must have infuriated many in a region where government of any kind has never been popular.

But the real cause of Herod's failure must be sought in himself. With all his brilliance, all his energy, all his wealth, Herod was ignorant. He was ignorant because he was insensitive. He was blasted with the defect that the Greeks called *anaesthesia*, lack of perception. He did not realize the spiritual world in which he lived. Herod could hardly have been expected to recognize in the birth of Christ the beginning of a new era, because this, the most important event of his whole life and reign, occurred only a few months before his death. Nevertheless, he could have learned from the Jews themselves, had he wished to. Some centuries before Herod's day, the prophets had propounded a spiritual view of religion which had already, in reality, made the Temple obsolete. The whole trend of contemporary Jewish thought and practice, in its highest expression, was towards spirituality and universality. "My house shall be called a house of prayer for all nations", no longer the slaughter-house of a tribal god. All round Herod were the signs of the coming of the new dispensation: the synagogues in which the law was expounded, the scriptures read and prayer offered were increasing within the very shadow of the Temple. The Essenes, whom Herod so highly regarded, only a few miles from his favourite palace at Jericho were living lives of spiritual austerity which would become the model for many in after centuries. Hillel's ministry fell largely within his reign. Never, before or since, has there been an age of such spiritual promise, never so many signs of more holy times. In less than a generation after Herod's death, the new dispensation of the spirit, for which the prophets of Israel, her teachers and writers had prepared the world, was to be vouchsafed. "Believe me, the hour cometh when ye shall neither in this mountain, nor yet at Jerusalem, worship the Father. Ye worship ye know not what: we know what we worship: for salvation is of the Jews. . . . God is Spirit, and they that worship him must worship him in spirit and in truth." In Herod's own realm, and to Herod's own people was the truth proclaimed.

Herod perceived none of these things. He was bent solely on the affairs of this world. His great crime against Jewry, for which he had done so much, was not that he repressed nationalism, but that he never realized its spiritual destiny. Herod's tragedy was not that he saw the vanity of the dream, but that he never beheld the glory of the vision.

THE END

CHRONOLOGICAL TABLE

YEAR		PALESTINE	ROMAN WORLD
B.C.	HEROD'S AGE		
73		Birth of Herod	
70	3		Birth of Virgil
67	6	Death of Queen Alexandra, Civil War; Herod sent to Petra	
65	8		Birth of Horace
64	9		Pompey in Syria; end of Seleucid monarchy
63	10	Pompey captures Jerusalem	Cicero Consul; Birth of Octavian (Augustus) and Agrippa
62	11	Hyrcanus High Priest Antipater paramount	
59	14		Julius Caesar Consul
58	15		Rome annexes Cyprus
57	16	Antony's first service in the Levant	
55	18	Antipater helps Gabinius in Egypt	Caesar's first expedition to Britain
54	19	Crassus pillages the Temple	Caesar's second expedition to Britain
53	20		Crassus killed at Carrhae
49	24		Caesar crosses the Rubicon
48	25		Caesar victor at Pharsalus Pompey killed in Egypt Caesar in Egypt
47	26	Antipater Procurator of Judaea Herod governor of Galilee; Appears before Sanhedrin	
45	28	Herod helps Caesarians at Apamea	
44	29		Assassination of Julius Caesar (15th March)
43	30	Antipater poisoned by Malichus	Octavian Consul for the first time; Cicero murdered; birth of Ovid
42	31	Herod banishes Doris, is betrothed to Mariamme	Battle of Philippi; suicide of Brutus and Cassius; Julius Caesar included among state gods of Rome
41	32	Herod Tetrarch of Galilee	Antony in Asia, meets Cleopatra
40	33	Parthians invade Palestine Death of Phasael Herod flees to Rome, appointed King of Judaea by Senate	Virgil's Fourth Eclogue
39	34	Herod returns to Palestine; war with Antigonus	
37 Feb	36	Herod and Sosius besiege Jerusalem Herod marries Mariamme	Antony marries Cleopatra
July		Fall of Jerusalem; Herod purges Sanhedrin	

181

YEAR		PALESTINE	ROMAN WORLD
B.C.	HEROD'S AGE		
35	38	Aristobulus the High Priest murdered Antony acquits Herod; Antonia built	
34	39	Cleopatra visits Palestine	Antony invades Armenia; triumphs at Alexandria. "Donations"
32	41	Nabataean war	Antony and Cleopatra winter (33-32) at Ephesus
31	42	Earthquake in Palestine	Battle of Actium (2nd September)
30	43	Hyrcanus II executed	
29	44	Mariamme and Alexandra executed	Temple of Janus closed
28	45	Salome divorces Costobar; Costobar executed	
27	46	Building of Sebaste (Samaria) begun	Octavian called "Augustus" Agrippa builds Pantheon in Rome
25	48	Famine	Aelius Gallus' Expedition to Arabia
23	50	Upper Palace ("Citadel") built in Jerusalem Herodium built Herod marries Mariamme II	
22	51	Caesarea begun Sons of Mariamme I go to Rome	Augustus presents Trachonitis, Batanea and Hauran to Herod
22/1	52	Herod with Agrippa in Mytilene	
20	53	Augustus in Syria	Augustus presents Ulatha and Panias to Herod
19	54	Syllaeus' intrigue with Salome	Virgil's death
18	55	Temple begun Herod's second visit to Rome; brings back his sons	
16	57	Betrothal of Alexander and Aristobulus	
15	58	Agrippa in Palestine	
14	59	Herod's journey with Agrippa Antipater and Doris restored to favour	
13	60	Antipater goes to Rome Herod's first will names him heir	
12	61	Herod's third and last visit to Italy; meets Augustus at Aquileia Herod becomes President of the Olympic Games; Revolt in Trachonitis; Death of M. V. Agrippa	
10	63	Dedication of the Temple	
9	64	Herod's punitive expedition against Nabataeans; inauguration of Caesarea; he loses Augustus' favour	Dedication of Ara Pacis by Augustus in Rome

YEAR		PALESTINE	ROMAN WORLD
B.C.	HEROD'S AGE		
8	65	Nicolaus of Damascus reconciles Augustus to Herod	Ovid banished; death of Horace
7	66	Alexander and Aristobulus executed after trial at Beirut; Herod's second will names Antipater as heir with Herod-Philip son of Mariamme II to succeed him	
6	67	Antipater returns to Rome; fall of Syllaeus; death of Pheroras	
5	68	Antipater comes back to Jerusalem Herod's third will names Antipas as heir	

Birth of Jesus Christ

4 (13th March)	69	Pharisees' attempted *coup d'état* Herod attempts suicide. Antipater executed. Fourth and last will names Archelaus king, Philip and Antipas tetrarchs	

end of March or
beginning of April Death of Herod

AUTHOR'S NOTES

Note I. The Red Heifer (page 101)

The description of the Red Heifer given in Numbers xix, would suggest that it was sacrificed regularly every year. I am indebted to Professor Norman Bentwich for the following note on the subject.

"The Red Heifer was in actual fact very rarely offered. The Mishnah, *Parah*, III, 6, gives an enumeration of the various times when the ceremony took place. According to Rabbi Meir there were seven from the time of Moses until the end of Second Temple days, the first being prepared in the time of Moses and the second by Ezra. According to the Sages who differ with Rabbi Meir there were seven during Second Temple days, thus nine in all. Two Red Heifers each were prepared by Simon the Just and John Hyrcanus, while Elijah Eini ben Hakof, Hananel the Egyptian and Ishmael the son of Piani prepared one each.

"As the ashes for purification were needed only in minute quantities, these could last for long periods. Indeed, it is believed that the ashes were preserved for a time even after the destruction of the Temple, and that they were used for proper purification ceremonies for some time after other Temple ceremonies of necessity had ceased."

We may therefore see in the Red Heifer and its ashes the last operative relic of Herod's Temple.

Note II. Herod's disease

The symptoms of Herod's disease are given in the *War* (I, xxxiii, 5) as follows: "The distemper seized his whole body, and greatly disordered all its parts with various symptoms; for there was a gentle fever upon him, and an intolerable itching over all the surface of his body, and continual pains in his colon, and dropsical tumours about his feet, and an inflammation of the abdomen, and a putrefaction of his privy member, that produced worms. Besides which he had a difficulty in breathing upon him, and could not breathe but when he sat upright, and had a convulsion of all his members."

In the *History* (XVII, vi, 5) this is repeated in an expanded form: "Herod's distemper greatly increased upon him after a severe manner: a fire glowed in him slowly, which did not so much

AUTHOR'S NOTES

appear to the touch outwardly, as it augmented his pains inwardly; for it brought upon him a vehement appetite for eating which he could not avoid to supply with one sort of food or another. His entrails were also exulcerated, and the chief violence of his pain lay in his colon; an aqueous and transparent liquor also had settled itself about his feet, and a like matter afflicted him at the bottom of his belly. Nay, farther, his privy member was putrefied and produced worms; and except when he sat upright he had a difficulty of breathing, which was very loathsome, on account of the stench of his breath, and the quickness of its returns; he had also convulsions in all parts of his body, which increased his strength to an insufferable degree."

On the foregoing texts, Mr. Norman Manson, C.B.E., F.R.C.S., formerly Warden of the Ophthalmic Hospital of St. John in Jerusalem, after consulting Dr Vicken Kalbian, of the Augusta Victoria Hospital, on the Mount of Olives, comments as follows:

"Josephus paints a vivid picture of the dying Herod's physical condition, which is not an unusual one in the untreated peasant of to-day.

"It is that of an aged arterio-sclerotic—the one-time athlete and hard liver—becoming increasingly prone to mood changes, delusions of persecution, uncontrolled outbursts of hypertensive cerebral attacks, even attempted suicide.

"Coincidentally heart and kidney function deteriorates and dropsy develops, affecting at an early stage the lungs, and causing breathlessness. Poisons, no longer excreted, accumulate in the blood. The mouth becomes ulcerated with foul breath, there is a burning pain in the stomach ('*zai nar*', 'like fire', the villager expresses it), ulceration of the bowel wall and diarrhoea. A low grade fever is a normal accompaniment of such a condition and convulsions may occur at any time.

"The dropsy steadily increases, the liver becomes enlarged and painful and the abdomen fills with fluid. At this stage the scrotum may be enormously distended and any dependent part gangrenous. Such a lesion would quickly become infested with maggots."

Note. This table is not complete. Herod married ten wives, by eight of whom he had issue, fourteen children in all, nine sons and five daughters. The names given here are those which come into this story. Rulers recognized by Rome as Ethnarchs, Kings or Tetrarchs are in italics. The dates below each name are those of death where known. Herod-Philip, Herod's son by Mariamme II, first husband of Herodias and father of Salome, who is mentioned (though not by name) in the Gospels as having demanded the death of John the Baptist, is to be distinguished from Philip, Herod's son by Cleopatra of Jerusalem, who from 4 B.C. to A.D. 34 was Tetrarch of Ituraea, etc. It was their half-brother, Antipas, who was Tetrarch of Galilee in the days of Christ.

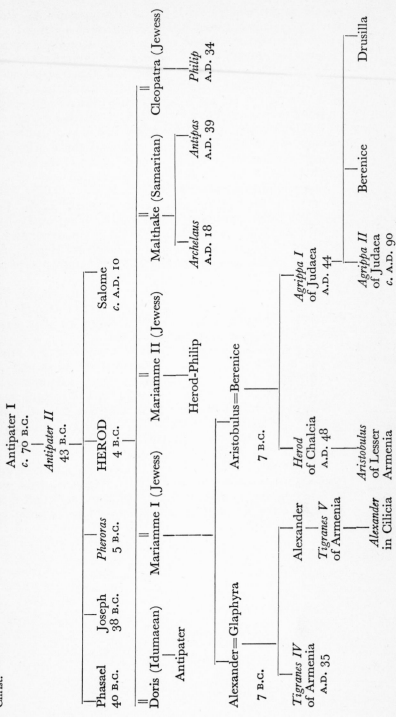

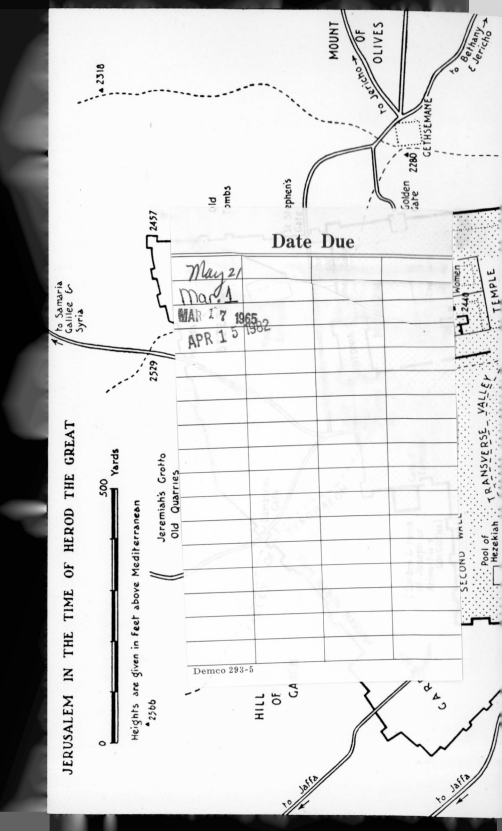

JERUSALEM IN THE TIME OF HEROD THE GREAT

0   500
Yards

Heights are given in feet above Mediterranean

▲2566

Jeremiah's Grotto
Old Quarries

▲2318

▲2457

to Samaria
Galilee &
Syria

2529

MOUNT

OF
OLIVES

to Jericho→

to Bethany
& Jericho→

GETHSEMANE

▲2280
Golden
Gate

St Stephen's
Gate

Old
Tombs

240   Women

TEMPLE

SECOND WALL

TRANSVERSE VALLEY

Pool of
Hezekiah

HILL
OF
GA

to Jaffa

to Jaffa

Date Due

May 21
Mar. 1
MAR 17 1965
APR 15 1982

Demco 293-5